Textual Practice

Contributions should be double spaced, and two copies should be sent. Address: Alan Sinfield, Textual Practice, Arts B, Sussex University, Brighton BN1 9QN, England.

Books for review should be addressed to Peter Nicholls, Arts B, Sussex University, Brighton BN1 9QN, England.

Advertisements. Enquiries to Routledge Journals, 2 Park Square, Milton Park, Abingdon, Oxon, OX14 4RN; jadvertising@routledge.com.

Subscription rates (calendar year only): UK full: £62.00; UK personal: £22.00; Rest of World full: £66.00; Rest of World personal: £24.00; USA full: $60.00; USA personal: $35.00. All rates include postage; airmail rates on application. Subscriptions to: Subscriptions Department, Routledge Journals, Cheriton House, North Way, Andover, Hants SP10 5BE. Sample copy requests: e-mail sample.journals@routledge.com

ISSN 0950–236X
Phototypeset by Intype, London.
© Routledge 1995

Transferred to Digital Printing 2004

Contents

Volume 9 Issue 2

Daphna Erdinast-Vulcan

Bakhtin's homesickness: a late reply to Julia Kristeva

Abstract

The article focuses on Bakhtin's early essays and fragments, written in 1919–24 and translated into English under the titles *Toward a Philosophy of the Act* and *Art and Answerability*. The belated English publication of these early writings opens up a different view of Bakhtin's subsequent work and calls for a re-evaluation of his position in the postmodern (post-Nietzschean) philosophical arena.

The article would take issue with some of Kristeva's (now widely current) views of Bakhtin, which celebrate the radically 'centrifugal' power of his work, and tend to dismiss, or even tactfully suppress his metaphysical outlook as an embarrassing rhetorical residue of the Russian cultural context. Following the 'centripetal' vectors in the early essays, I would argue that this outlook is, in fact, a fundamental enabling constituent of Bakhtin's work; that it is closely related to a 'theory', or rather, an 'anti-theory' of the subject; and that this theory deconstructs itself in a series of aporetic twists which I would attempt to outline and diagnose.

Finally, I would suggest that, rather than an unwitting precursor of our libertarian age, Bakhtin is all-too-aware of the stakes of the postmodern condition. His refusal of monologicity is not a purely emancipatory act: when the need for a *'point d'appui'* outside the subject, the most fundamental metaphysical need, remains unanswered, the problem of grounding emerges in full force both in the constitution of the subject and in the constitution of the ethics.

Situated on the borderline between a religious and an aggressively secularized culture, straddling both territories, Bakhtin –

Textual Practice 9(2) 1995, 223–242 © 1995 Routledge 0950–236X

T^P

like Dostoevsky, his hero – is not at home in either of them. It is precisely this liminal position and the symptomatic tensions it produces, which enables him to engage with the Mobius strip of ethics and subjectivity.

Keywords: Bakhtin's early works; Kristeva; subject (self); metaphysics; Dostoevsky; modernity; answerability

The sense of belatedness that runs through the following pages is neither accidental nor purely temporal. The very concept of belatedness, of an arrival after the event, presumes an enclosure of time and a being-out of that enclosure. It is therefore not only the trivial fact of chronocity and sequence, but a more radical displacement, better known, perhaps, under the name of Modernity. In what follows I will attempt to diagnose the symptoms of this sense of displacement, this incurable homesickness, in Bakhtin's work.

The essays which have yielded the concepts of dialogicity, polyphony, heteroglossia, and the carnivalesque, and turned Bakhtin into one of the canonized prophets of postmodernity, were written during a period of approximately twelve years between 1929 and 1941.[1] Ostensibly concerned with poetics but ranging far wider into a territory of their own, the thrust of these works is, to use Bakhtin's term, 'centrifugal' – radically anti-authoritarian, anti-theological, and anti-closural. The present discussion is concerned with another Bakhtinian voice, the 'centripetal' voice which emerges from the earlier papers, written between 1919 and 1924 and published in the Soviet Union only in the 1970s, following Bakhtin's rehabilitation and the publication of the later works.[2] The recent waning of the Bakhtinian vogue in the academic marketplace, the belated translation of these essays and the notorious slowness of academic publication mechanisms may have had something to do with the fact that these early writings have not received the attention they deserve. It seems, however, that there is more to this avoidance than these relatively trivial explanations would account for, as readers who have formed their view of Bakhtin on the basis of the later writings may well find the early works profoundly embarrassing. What emerges from these early essays, despite some attempts to homogenize and blend them into the later work, is a deep and unbridgeable rupture within Bakhtin's thought, a faultline which, I believe, is also symptomatic of the post-Nietzschean phase of Modernity.

The present discussion will engage at some length with Julia Kristeva's 'The ruin of a poetics', one of the earliest and still one of the very best expositions of what has become the current view of the

Bakhtinian breakthrough.[3] Obviously, much has come to light and still more has been written on Bakhtin since the publication of this pioneering essay, but it is precisely the generative nature of Kristeva's approach, its seminal status for a whole section of the Bakhtin industry, which has preserved its initial challenge. The concept of 'intertextuality', coined by Kristeva, is now 'one of the key formative concepts of poststructuralism' and the writings of the Bakhtin circle have come to be viewed as 'inaugural and constitutive' for postmodernist thought.[4] As the debate over the boundaries of postmodernist philosophy is far too complex for the scope of the present discussion, I would follow Rutland and reduce this cultural phenomenon to two key concepts which echo through Bakhtin's work as they do in the writings of Lacan, Foucault, and Lyotard: the focus on discursivity and the alleged collapse of master-narratives. I would argue, however, that the stakes involved in this debate are much higher than the title of Kristeva's exposition might lead us to think, for it is not only the 'ruin of a poetics' that lies at the heart of the Bakhtinian project, but a much further-reaching collapse, and perhaps also the beginning of some new construction work.

Setting off from the notion of discourse, 'the concept of a language which a speaker carries with him and/or of a speaker becoming himself within the language', Kristeva relates the Bakhtinian breakthrough to Freudian and Lacanian epistemology:

> 'Dialogic' is the term which indicates that the discourse belongs doubly to an 'I' and to the other, that *Spaltung* of the speaker which psychoanalysis was to establish with scientific caution, that topology of the speaker in relation to the 'treasure-house of meaning-signs' (Lacan) outside himself. The dialogic sees in every word a word about the word, addressed to the word; and it is only on condition that it belongs to this polyphony – to this 'intertextual' space – that the word is a 'full' word.[5]

Bakhtin's prophet of 'intertextuality' is Dostoevsky, whose polyphonic novels are 'built on that breach of the "I"', offering 'a plurality of languages, a confrontation of types of discourse and ideologies, with no conclusion and no synthesis – without monologic or any axial point'. 'Character' in Dostoevsky's novels is not the 'speaker–subject as an axis of representation'; it is 'nothing more than a discursive point of view of the "I" who writes through another "I"; a discourse (a "word") [which] maintains a dialogue with the discourse of the "I" who writes, and with itself. . . . We do not see him, but we do not hear him either; we listen to him dissolving his objectality in the discourse.' This unresolved confrontation of discourses, the fragmentation and pluralization of the speaking subject in the intertextual space, creates a 'contrapuntal, polyphonic ensemble', which 'lacks unity of speaker and of meaning' and which is 'plural, anti-totalitarian and anti-theological'.[6]

But, however passionate Bakhtin's celebration of Dostoevsky's dialogic revolution, it is not entirely untroubled as there are recurrent elements in the text which counteract its ostensible anti-theological thrust. Noting these elements with a distinctly apologetic note, Kristeva relegates them to the accidents of history, to the inevitable sociological and cultural 'theoretical limitations' of Bakhtin's text, which, though looking ahead of its time, is still fettered by the discursive framework of its historical context. Kristeva notes 'the lack of any theory of the language-user' and the 'unrecognized influence of Christianity in a humanist terminology' as evidenced by the 'continual mention of the heroes' "soul" and "conscience" '. Bakhtin's vocabulary, she concedes, is 'furtively influenced by theology: the term "conscience" may well occur more often than "discourse", and the word "voice" is not without some transcendental echoes'.[7] Against the embarrassment of these metaphysical echoes, Kristeva calls for a mining project which would extract from 'beneath the layers of traditional Russian culture which impose these language-habits', that 'new departure which Bakhtin's analysis introduces'; for a distillation of the 'advanced' contemporary 'kernel' of Bakhtin's ideas from 'worn-out ideological husk which surrounds them'. This salvage operation should, if we follow Kristeva's argument, turn Bakhtin into a 'hitherto unknown precursor [of our age], unaware of [his] role'.[8]

In another essay, Kristeva further elaborates the concept of dialogism which, she argues 'may well become the basis of our time's intellectual structure' as a 'logic of trangression'.[9] 'With Bakhtin', she argues, '[epic or "realist"] narrative is a prohibition, a monologism, a subordination of the code to 1, to God. Hence, the epic is religious and theological'; 'the narrator's absolute point of view ... coincides with the wholeness of a god or community. Within epic monologism we detect the presence of the "transcendental signified" and "self presence" as highlighted by Jacques Derrida.' The logic of dialogism, of the carnivalesque, and of the polyphonic novel, the arena where various 'texts meet, contradict and relativize each other', 'challenges God, authority, and social law; insofar as it is dialogical, it is rebellious'.[10]

Kristeva is right. Bakhtin, like the early, nostalgic Lukács, views the development of novelistic prose from the epic to the novel as a concomitant of 'centrifugal' ideological forces, challenging and decentralizing monolithic, unitary ideological systems: 'The novel begins by presuming a verbal and semantic decentering of the ideological world, a certain linguistic homelessness of literary consciousness, which no longer possesses a sacrosanct and unitary linguistic medium for containing ideological thought.'[11] And yet, even in this passage which hails the subversion of cultural hegemony, Bakhtin diagnoses the process of secularization as a kind of 'homelessness'. This use of the term is highly symptomatic. There is a deep-seated ambivalence in Bakhtin's work, an internal unresolved conflict which is most clearly visible in the early essays.

Following these early texts, with particular attention to 'Author and hero in aesthetic activity', I would argue that their author is incurably torn between the imperatives of 'intertextuality' and a deep sense of nostalgia for 'master-narrative' of authority; that rather than a worn-out rhetorical tic, the metaphysical outlook is a fundamental enabling constituent of Bakhtin's thought; that Bakhtin's metaphysics are closely related to a theory of the subject; and that this 'theory' deconstructs itself in a series of aporetic twists which I will attempt to outline. Finally, I would suggest that rather than an unwitting precursor of our age, Bakhtin is all-too-aware of the core unresolved questions of the postmodern condition.

Read on its own, with no reference to the early essays, *Problems in Dostoevsky's Poetics* (Kristeva's central source) is indeed a celebration of plurivocality, a poetic and cultural revolution. The divestment of the author's authority, the abdication of transgradience, the dismantling of axiological sovereignty *vis-à-vis* the hero, are all conceived in this monograph as the constituents of an emancipatory process. But this ostensibly liberating development appears to be far more complex and problematic when we read the Dostoevsky book against the context of the essay 'Author and hero in aesthetic activity', written only five years earlier.

The essay offers an oddly anachronistic prescription for the 'relationship' between the author and the fictional hero, a 'relationship' predicated on the author's 'transgradience', variously referred to 'outsideness', or 'exotopy', as translated by Todorov.[12] The position of the author (who is, as Bakhtin often and pointedly reminds his readers, not an historical being but a 'principle of seeing') in relation to the hero allows him an 'excess of knowledge':[13] he can contain the hero in his vision, he can know what the hero is in principle incapable of knowing. This 'excess of knowledge' enables the author to 'consummate' the hero, to see him in his wholeness, to gather the hero's moment of birth, the moment of his death, his background, the environment against which he acts (which is, for him, a mere 'horizon'), and the axiological 'rhythm' of his life which can only be perceived against its totality.

> The organizing power in all aesthetic forms is the axiological category of the other, the relationship to the other, enriched by an axiological excess of seeing for the purpose of achieving transgradient consummation.
>
> (AH, 188–9)

Whatever view one takes of the precise shade of Bakhtin's religiosity and the nuanced distinctions between the varieties of religious affiliation which could have influenced him, the intensely religious passion which runs through this early essay cannot be overlooked.[14] Entirely uninhibited in his use of devotional rhetoric, he models the 'aesthetic relationship' on a thoroughly religious paradigm: 'Aesthetic grace ... bestowed [upon an object] ... [is] a lovingly merciful justification of its being that is impossible from within the soul itself' (AH, 67). 'Aesthetic love', 'transgradient aesthetic form' is 'the relationship of a gift to a need; of an act of freely granted forgiveness to a transgression; of an act of grace to a sinner' (AH, 90). The aesthetic 'transgradience' of the artist is a projection of the divine otherness of God; his specific answerability 'can be founded only upon a deep trust in the highest level of authority that blesses a culture – upon *trust, that is, in the fact that there is another – the highest other – who answers for my own special answerability, and trust in the fact that I do not act in an axiological void*' (AH, 206, italics added). The human author derives his authority from the transcendental Auctor Mundi:

> The divinity of the artist consists in his partaking of the supreme outsideness. . . . Aesthetic activity collects the world scattered in meaning and condenses it into a finished and self-contained image . . . it finds an axiological position from which the transient in the world acquires the axiological weight of an event, acquires validity and stable determinateness.
>
> (AH, 191)

At the very point where Bakhtin does attempt a distinction between aesthetics and religion, it becomes clear that, whatever the differences of scale and gradation, it is, indeed, the same relational structure which dynamizes both:

> An aesthetic event can take place only when there are two participants present; it presupposes two noncoinciding consciousnesses. . . . When the other consciousness is the

encompassing consciousness of God, a religious event takes place (prayer, worship, ritual).

(AH, 22)

A whole, integral human being is the product of the aesthetic, creative point of view and of that point of view alone. . . . A whole, integral human being presupposes an aesthetically active subiectum situated outside him (we are abstracting from man's religious experience in the present context).

(AH, 82–3)

What emerges from the early essay appears to be diametrically opposed to the dialogic principles which Bakhtin was to celebrate only five years later. The world *zaviershit* – rightly translated as 'finalization', a violent act of closure, in the Dostoevsky book, is – just as rightly – rendered in the translation of the early essay as 'consummation', an operation of loving containment.[15]

The touchstone of this contradiction is the change in Bakhtin's attitude to Dostoevsky, who is perceived in the early essay as a maverick, a writer who has regrettably deviated from the prescriptive aesthetics of authorial transgradience. Viewed against this meta-physical postulate, Dostoevsky is named among other 'cases' of aes-thetic failure, when the author 'loses this valuational point of support *outside* the hero', when the hero 'takes possession of the author' who then becomes 'unable to find any convincing and stable axiological point of support *outside* the hero' (AH, 17), unable, in other words, to 'consummate' the hero. This type of aesthetic loss, writes Bakhtin, 'includes almost all of Dostoevsky's heroes' (AH, 20). Relating to the refusal of Dostoevsky's heroes 'to accept possible judgement by God or by man', Bakhtin postulates that these 'anthropomachic' and 'theo-machic' elements (i.e. the hostile positioning of the other) 'preclude aesthetic concord, preclude the concord intrinsic to prayer' (AH, 146).

But 'Author and hero', precisely like the Dostoevsky book or any of Bakhtin's other works, is not merely a theory of aesthetics. It is also – primarily, I would argue – an essay on the constitution of the subject. Throughout the discussion Bakhtin shifts his terms of reference back and forth, moving from 'author' and 'hero' to 'I-for-the-other' and 'I-for-myself' with no apparent concern about his blatant confusion of basic philosophical categories. Having discussed the deconstructive nature of this transgression elsewhere, I would like to focus here on its more troubling aspects.[16] The Bakhtinian 'architectonics' of the subject is predicated on the phenomenal situ-atedness of the subject, the 'inability in principle' of I-for-myself to yield a representation of the self.[17] I-for-myself cannot perceive the contours of my form, my own boundary-lines, which may be spatial (the back of my head, my own background), temporal (the moment of my birth and the moment of my death which can be conceptualized but never consciously experienced), or, according to Bakhtin, axiological. For Bakhtin, the axiological dimension is entirely analogous to the spatial and temporal dimensions of our reality as subjects. This is an analogy which must be reckoned with.

Strikingly similar to the Lacanian view of the mirror stage, Bakhtin's diagnosis of I-for-myself leads to the same need for a reflective consciousness. Bakhtin writes of the 'dark chaos of my inner sensation of myself'; of the 'boundless, "darkly stirring chaos" of needs and dissatisfactions, wherein the future dyad of the child's personality and the outside world confronting it is still submerged and dissolved' (AH, 50), and of the constitution/authoring of the subject by the transgradient other/author:

> I have to subsume myself under this category of the other in order to be able to see myself as a constituent in the unitary pictorial-plastic external world.
>
> (AH, 35)

> For self-consciousness, this integral image [of the self] is dispersed in life and enters the field of seeing the external world only in the form of fortuitous fragments. And what is lacking, moreover, is precisely external unity and continuity; a human being experiencing life in the category of his own I is incapable of gathering himself by himself into an outward whole that would be even relatively finished. . . . the point . . . is . . . the absence in principle of any unitary axiological approach from within a human being himself to his own outward expressedness in being. . . . In this sense one can speak of a human being's absolute need for the other, for the other's seeing, remembering, gathering, and unifying self-activity – the only self-activity capable of producing his outwardly finished personality. This outward personality could not exist, if the other did not create it.
>
> (AH, 35–6)

This inability of the subject to represent itself to itself as a whole, leads to its constitution by the containing, enveloping, transgradient gaze of the other, its 'author'. But whereas Lacan perceives the mirror stage as an inevitable delusion to be eventually displaced by the introduction (or, rather, fall) of the subject into the Symbolic Order, the early Bakhtin fully accepts the need for the constituting gaze of the other, and gives his unqualified blessing to the dyadic reflexive relationship it produces.

The position of the other/author outside and beyond the subject/ hero, referred to as a position of 'transgradience', entails an excess of knowledge. The other can contain the subject in his gaze, enclose him in space (against his background), enframe him in time (against and beyond the moment of his birth and his death), and ultimately – extrapolating to the axiological dimension – collect his moments of meaning and endow them with their ultimate significance.

An organism simply lives, without any justification *from within itself*, for the grace of justification can descend upon it only *from outside*. I myself cannot be the author of my own value, just as I cannot lift myself by my own hair. The biological life of an organism becomes a value only in *another's* sympathy and compassion with that life (motherhood). It is the *other's* sympathy and compassion that introduce biological life into a new value-context.

(AH, 55; see also p. 51)

There can be little doubt that at this point Bakhtin fully endorses an 'aestheticized' conception of the subject: 'It is only in a life perceived in the category of the other that my body can become aesthetically valid, and not in the context of my own life as lived for myself, that is, not in the context of my self-consciousness' (AH, 59, italics at source).

Here, precisely, is the point where the question of grounding becomes highly problematic. Assuming a relationship of Love, Grace and Consummation between the subject-hero and the other-author, Bakhtin seems to be oddly oblivious to the potentially dangerous role of the authoring other (oddly, because he himself was directly victimized by an institutionalized, political form of 'authoring'). This troubling aspect of the Bakhtinian theory of the subject has been lucidly articulated by Caryl Emerson who, quite rightly, I believe, attempts to correct the skewed image of the 'libertarian Baxtin' (based mainly on the essays from the 1930s) and presents him as 'an apostle of constraints' who privileges the 'outside perspective' as a source of value. Emerson argues that it is this very privilege, the 'deferment of one's self to the other for finalization [which] raises moral and ethical questions' concerning one's identity, the concept of responsibility and personal morality.[18] Ann Jefferson also notes Bakhtin's problematic assumption of the essential benevolence of the authoring other, and uses the work of Sartre (whose initial formulations regarding the constitutive function of the other's gaze are often strikingly close to those of Bakhtin), as a critique of Bakhtin's benign construction.[19]

Indeed, the assumption of a benign transgradience, of a loving 'consummation/finalization' by an authoritative other, is hard to reconcile with what we have come to think of as the Bakhtinian dialogic outlook. Such as assumption can only be enabled, or rather required, within a religious frame of reference, where God is the ultimate Other, 'the heavenly father who is *over me* and can be merciful to me and justify me where I, from within myself, cannot be merciful to myself and cannot justify myself in principle' (AH, 56, italics at source). The aesthetization of the subject, the gift of selfhood, is conceived as a form of Grace, 'the bestowal – from outside – of lovingly merciful acceptance and justification of the given. . . . In himself, a human being can only repent; and only the other can give absolution' (AH, 57). For Bakhtin, the aestheticized subject, the subject who is identical with himself, is not necessarily a fictitious construct, so long as the metaphysical analogy retains its validity, and the human act of authorship is a delegation of transcendental authority.

If this equation appears to be simple to the point of naïveté, it does not seem to trouble Bakhtin, who explicitly links this 'consummation' by the transgradient other to a state of blissful naïveté:

> I must become naïve in order to rejoice. From within myself, in my own self, in my own self-activity, I cannot become naïve, and, hence, I cannot rejoice. . . . Joy is possible for me only in God or in the world, that is only where I partake in being in a justified manner through the other and for the other, where I am passive and receive a bestowed gift. It is my otherness that rejoices in me not I for myself.
>
> (AH, 136–7)

> The more the moment of *trust* and the tones of faith and hope gain immediate actuality, the more certain aesthetic moments begin to penetrate into self-accounting. When the organizing role passes from repentance to trust, an aesthetic form, a *concord*, becomes possible. Anticipating through faith my justification in God, I change little by little from I-for-myself into the Other for God – I become naïve in God. It is at this stage of religious naïveté that psalms (as well as many Christian hymns and prayers) have their place; rhythm becomes possible, a rhythm that cherishes and elevates the image.
>
> (AH, 145; see also pp. 79, 82–3, 111)

Far from a residual stylistic tic, or a conceptual aberration, as Kristeva would have it, the echoes of transcendence of the essay and its religious tonality are, in fact, immanent to Bakhtin's aesthetic, narrative conceptualization of the subject which requires authoring from without:

> Ethical and aesthetic objectification requires a powerful *point d'appui* outside myself; it requires some genuine source of real strength out of which I would be capable of seeing myself as another.

> (AH, 31)

What we have here is nothing less than the naked need for a master-narrative and a master-narrator. This dangerously naïve formulation can only be deproblematized by the assumption of an Auctor Mundi, the Ultimate Other, who grants the subject an unconditional gift of selfhood. With this gesture of what I would call 'radical naïveté', the early Bakhtin throws the metaphysical blanket over the question of the subject.

What happens between the early essay and the Dostoevsky book? Is it a continuous, unbroken line of thought which would enable us to systematize Bakhtin's work, or a total shift of position? The first option should, I believe, be ruled out by our analysis so far, as any attempt to homogenize the Bakhtinian corpus, to square the circle, as it were, would require impossible philosophical contortions. The second option calls for the assumption that Bakhtin went through a process of secular conversion some time between 1924 and 1929.[20]

This view would get some support from the fact that Bakhtin's diagnosis of the Dostoevskean revolution does remain consistent through both phases: whether viewed as a maverick, an author who has failed to achieve transgradience in relation to his heroes, or as the prophet of a new era who has deliberately given up that authorial prerogative, Dostoevsky's work is placed at the far end of the secularization process which Bakhtin traces through the history of Western culture. In a rather sketchy overview of the evolution (or rather, devolution) of the authorial position through its various historical phases, Bakhtin marks Romanticism as a watershed, where 'the boundaries begin to be effaced, the center of value is transposed from the boundaries into the very life of the hero (into his cognitive-ethical directedness from within himself)'; 'there is an attempt to force an admission from within self-consciousness, which is possible only through the other; an attempt to do without God, without listeners, without an author' (AH, 180, 181).

The divestment of authorial transgradience is clearly a concomitant of the process of secularization, whose final stage is defined by Bakhtin as the 'crisis of authorship': 'the very position of the author's outsideness is shaken and is no longer considered essential: one contests the author's right to be situated outside lived life and to consummate it. All stable transgradient forms begin to disintegrate (first of all in prose – from Dostoevsky to Bely ...)' (AH, 203). A similar diagnosis, albeit with a different attitude, may be found in Bakhtin's notes for the revision of the Dostoevsky book, nearly forty years later, where Bakhtin engages once again with the historical crisis that has given birth to the Dostoevskean novel. Bakhtin now hails Dostoevsky as the spearhead of a new cultural era, and celebrates the 'radical change in the position of the author', which is clearly more than an aesthetic revolution as it announces the 'birth of a new form of novel (a new form of visualization and a new human being-personality; overcoming materialization)'.[21] Dostoevsky's replacement of the reified model of the world by a dialogic one ushers in a new, polyphonic, secular cultural era.[22]

But, neat as it is, the secularization theory is rendered problematic by the fact that Bakhtin himself gave the early manuscripts to his editors in 1970, well after the publication of his later writings. He had apparently felt no need to disown these early unpublished papers. The question is further complicated when we note the dynamics of what I would call 'aporetic moments' in both these phases. Even in his latest writings, Bakhtin's celebration of dialogicity and polyphony is never unequivocal. A distinct note of nostalgia creeps into the text as late as 1971, when Bakhtin writes of the lost 'earthly paradise' from which Dostoevsky's heroes were expelled, and the 'privilege of naïveté' which was denied them.[23] This late 'lapsarian' metaphor is identical to the conception of Dostoevsky's world half a century earlier: the author's loss of his transgradient position leaves the hero on his own 'in the light of to-be-attained meaning' where he 'begins to see his own nakedness and to be ashamed, and paradise is lost' (AH, 172).

If we can dismiss these references as a form of recidivism, mere twinges of nostalgia for a lost world, there is a far more poignant aporetic moment with which we must reckon on a more conceptual level. In 'The problem of the text', written towards the end of his career, Bakhtin introduces the *superaddressee* into the concept of the dialogue:

The author of the utterance, with a greater or lesser awareness, presupposes a higher superaddressee (third), whose absolutely just responsive understanding is presumed either in some metaphysical distance or in a distant historical time.... In various ages and with various understandings of the world, this superaddressee and his ideally true responsive understanding assume various ideological expressions (God, absolute truth, the course of dispassionate human conscience, the people, the court of history, science, and so forth).... Each dialogue takes place as if against the background of the responsive understanding of an invisibly present third party who stands above all the participants in the dialogue.

Bakhtin seems to be aware of the problematic implications of this new addition, for he hastily adds that this superaddressee, who is 'a constitutive aspect of the whole utterance', is not 'any mystical or metaphysical being (although, given a certain understanding of the world, he can be expressed as such)'.[24] This disclaimer notwithstanding, it is hard to conceive of this ultimate listener as anything but that '*tertium non datur*', the meta-discursive monologic voice, which, according to Kristeva, was expunged by the conception of dialogicity (Kristeva, 111). It does not take much philosophical acumen to realize that this late supplement actually hollows out the very notion of dialogicity and sterilizes its more radical implications. The superaddressee is probably, as I have written elsewhere, none other than that 'supreme-author' or 'ultimate Other' who stages his comeback through the back door.[25]

But Bakhtin's aporetics work both ways. Even in the early essays, where Bakhtin predicates both his 'poetics' and his theory of the subject on a narrative metaphysical conception, the subject of ethics is positioned outside, beyond the seductions of 'consummation' by the authorial other. Muted though they are at this stage, there are several references to the ethical modality as that which subverts the narrativization or the aesthetization of the subject. While Bakhtin identifies the position of I-for-the-other (a position of transgradience, surplus of knowledge, and containment by the other/author) with an aesthetic modality, the position of I-for-myself is identified with an ethical modality, a non-coincidence in principle of 'is' and 'ought'. Against that 'whole, integral human being' which is produced aesthetically by the transgradient other, Bakhtin positions the 'ethical subiectum' who is 'nonunitary in principle' (AH, 83).

> The *subiectum* of lived life and the *subiectum* of aesthetic activity which gives form to that life are in principle incapable of coinciding with one another.
>
> (AH, 86)

> The ethical *subiectum* is present to itself as a task, the task of actualizing himself as a value, and is in principle incapable of being given, of being present-on-hand, of being contemplated: it is I-for-myself.
>
> (AH, 100)

That 'rhythm' of a life, which can only be enabled in a state of religious naïveté, and perceived retrospectively from a position of transgradience, becomes 'a distortion and a lie' when 'I from within myself, participate in the unitary and unique event of being'.

> [The ethical moment] is a moment where that which *is* in me must overcome itself for the sake of that which *ought* to be; where being and obligation meet in conflict with me; where *is* and *ought* mutually exclude each other. It is a moment of fundamental and essential dissonance, inasmuch as what-is and what-ought-to-be, what-is-given and what-is-imposed-as-a-task, are incapable of being rhythmically bound within me myself from within me myself, i.e. they are incapable of being perceived on one and the same plane.
>
> (AH, 118, italics at source)

> Free will and self-activity are incompatible with rhythm. A life (lived experience, striving, performed action, thought) that is lived and experienced in the categories of moral freedom and of self-activity cannot be rhythmicized. In this sense, ethical freedom ('freedom of the will') is not only freedom from cognitive necessity (causal necessity), but also freedom from aesthetic necessity.
>
> (AH, 119)

A similar distinction is made in 'Toward a philosophy of the act', a fragment of what might have been the introduction to the monumental philosophical project Bakhtin had in mind in the 1920s. Bakhtin writes of the irreducible difference between aesthetic seeing (based on 'outsideness'), and the 'world that is correlated with me' (I-for-myself) which is 'fundamentally and essentially incapable of becoming part of an aesthetic architectonic'. Against the narrativized conception of the subject which emerges from 'Author and hero', Bakhtin writes of the need to resist this 'temptation of aestheticism', the inclination to act out a conception of oneself through the eyes of the other, which must be refused by the intensely situated, participative, and answerable subject.[26]

If we add up the points raised here, the meaning of the Dostoevskean/Bakhtinian revolution may be formulated as a shift from an aesthetic to an ethical modality. 'Aesthetic culture', according to Bakhtin,

> is a culture of boundaries and hence presupposes that life is enveloped by a warm atmosphere of deepest trust. A confident and founded act of constituting and shaping the boundaries of man and his world (outer as well as inner boundaries) presupposes the existence of a firm and secure position outside of him . . . presupposes an essential axiological consolidateness of the enveloping atmosphere.
>
> (AH, 203)

Dostoevsky is positioned, according to Bakhtin's conception, at the graveside of aesthetic culture, at the point where boundary lines are no longer recognized and all forms of transgradience are refused (AH, 203–4). He has discarded the aesthetic modality, as prescribed by the early Bakhtin, in favour of the ethical, and replaced the containing, 'finalizing' gaze of the other with the dialogic voice of the 'I'.

But this refusal is not a purely emancipatory act. When the need for a *point d'appui* outside the subject, the most fundamental metaphysical need, remains unanswered, the problem of grounding emerges in full force both in the constitution of the subject and in the constitution of ethics. What guarantees do we have for the ethical authority of that other/author? One tentative answer to the problem is provided by the communitarian outlook which Bakhtin seems to suggest at one point.

> The other who possesses me does not come into conflict with my I-for-myself, so long as I do not sever myself axiologically from the world of others, so long as I perceive myself within a collective (a family, a nation, civilized mankind). In this case, the axiological position of the other within me is authoritative for me; he can narrate the story of my life and I shall be in full inner agreement with him. So long as my life proceeds in indissoluble unity with the collective of others, it is interpreted, constructed, and organized . . . on the plane of another's possible consciousness of my life; my life is perceived and constructed as a possible story that might be told about it by the other to still others (to descendants). My consciousness of a possible narrator, the axiological context of a possible narrator, organizes my acts, thoughts, and feelings.
>
> (AH, 153)

It is only an intimate, organic axiological participation in the world of others that renders the biographical self-objectification of a life authoritative and productive; only such participation strengthens and renders nonfortuitous the position of the other in me – the possible author of my life.

(AH, 155)

A sense of communal solidarity, of organic participation in the life of others, bestows its own mode of authority and truth on the narrative of life. But that source of communal authority which operates, for example, in epic discourse is (at least according to Bakhtin's view in 'Discourse in the novel') no less 'monologic' or metaphysical than the overtly religious construction.[27] It is precisely this problem of grounding, this metaphysical vacuum which, I suggest, has enabled the return of the superaddressee, the ultimate other, into Bakhtin's last essays. He, too, like Dostoevsky, his hero, was amongst the disinherited.

In Bakhtin's 'Notes toward a reworking of the Dostoevksy book' there is an oblique note on Dostoevsky's conception of atheism as 'a lack of faith in this sense, as indifference toward an ultimate value which makes demands on the whole man, as a rejection of the ultimate position'. In the same paragraph, however, there is a comment on 'Dostoevsky's vacillations as regards the content of that ultimate value'.[28] This has been, of course, the core question of Western ethics throughout the process of secularization: how is one to choose that 'ultimate value' without recourse to the ultimate authoritative Other? It is the very same question which lies at the core of Dostoevsky's work, for even the most radically polyphonic of his novels still conclude on a note of, almost forced, but extreme, piety. On this issue, too, one would have to question Kristeva's position:

> The remark of old Karamazov, 'God is dead, everything is allowed', seems to have been decoded as what it becomes, if one goes just a step further towards what he refrains from saying, 'God is dead, everything is interdiction'.[29]

There is just one small word between that formulation and the Bakhtinian/Dostoevskean text. The ideological struggle amongst the Karamazovs revolves on a much more tentative formulation: 'If God is dead, everything is allowed'.[30] That 'if' is precisely what is at stake here. Living on the threshold of a secularized civilization, Dostoevsky himself was surely aware of the need for ethical grounding: the removal of the ultimate narrator, the unmooring of the subject, and the uncoupling of ethics from metaphysics has left an impossible legacy for the following century.

Bakhtin, too, is a latecomer. His nostalgia for a state of naïveté is symptomatic of the modernist homesickness and the quest for a name. Knowing only too well that there is no 'internal sovereign territory' where the subject can name itself, that 'self-nomination is imposture',[31] he looks back to that prelapsarian region where 'the organizing force of the I is replaced by the organizing force of God; my earthly determinateness, my earthly name, is surmounted, and I gain a clear understanding of the name written in heaven in the Book of Life – the memory of the future' (AH, 145). A lapsed meta-physician or a nostalgic radical, he is fully aware of that 'if', which many of the postmodernists have so casually suppressed. Straddling both territories, Bakhtin is not at home in either one of them: he is an exile/citizen in the a-topia of postmodernity, where there is no real recourse to a superaddressee, no ultimate listener and no primary author. It is that state of homelessness, he tells us, in which we have got to make our name.

University of Haifa

Notes

1 *Problems in Dostoevsky's Poetics* (1929; 2nd edn 1963), trans. and ed. Caryl Emerson, Introduction Wayne C. Booth (Minneapolis: University of Minnesota Press, 1984); 'Discourse in the novel' (1934–5), in *The Dialogic Imagination* ed. Michael Holquist, trans. Caryl Emerson and Michael Holquist (Austin: Texas University Press, 1981), pp. 259–422; 'Forms of time and of the chronotope in the novel' (1937–8), in *The Dialogic Imagination*, pp. 84–258; 'From the prehistory of novelistic discourse' (1940), in *The Dialogic Imagination*, pp. 41–83; *Rablais and His World* (1940), trans. Helene Iswolsky (Cambridge, Mass.: MIT Press, 1968); 'Epic and novel' (1941), in *The Dialogic Imagination*, pp. 3–40.
2 'Author and hero in aesthetic activity' (written c. 1922–4; first published in the Soviet Union in 1977–8), in *Art and Answerability: Early Philosophical Essays by M. M. Bakhtin*, trans. and notes by Vadim Liapunov, ed. Michael Holquist and Vadim Liapunov, Supplement translated by Kenneth Brostrom (Austin: Texas University Press, 1990); hereafter abbreviated AH. *Toward a Philosophy of the Act* (written c. 1919–21; first published in the Soviet Union in 1986), trans. and notes by Vadim Liapunov, eds Michael Holquist and Vadim Liapunov (Austin: Texas University Press), 1993.
3 Julia Kristeva, 'The ruin of a poetics' (1970), in *Russian Formalism*, ed. Stephen Bann and John E. Bowle (Paris: Seuil, 1970; Edinburgh: Scottish University Press, 1973), pp. 102–19.
4 Barry Rutland, 'Bakhtinian categories and the discourse of postmodernism', *Critical Studies*, vol. 2, no. 1/2 (1990), p. 127.
5 'The ruin of a poetics', pp. 108–9.

6 ibid., pp. 110–11.
7 Ibid, pp. 106, 110.
8 Ibid, pp. 107, 110.
9 Julia Kristeva, 'Word, dialogue and novel', in *Desire in Language: A Semiotic Approach to Literature and Art* (1969), ed. Leon S. Roudiez, trans. Thomas Gora, Alice Jardine and Leon S. Roudiez (New York: Columbia University Press, 1980), p. 89.
10 Ibid, pp. 70, 77–9.
11 'Discourse in the novel' (1934–5), in *The Dialogic Imagination*, p. 367.
12 Tzvetan Todorov, *Mikhail Bakhtin: The Dialogic Principle*, trans. Wlad Godzich, Theory and History of Literature, vol. 13 (Manchester: Manchester University Press, 1984).
13 One should note, at the very outset, that both 'author' and 'hero' are referred to as masculine throughout the essay. For the sake of authenticity, though not without some obvious misgivings, I have followed Bakhtin's discursive bias throughout this discussion.
14 The question of Bakhtin's religious affiliation has been one of the major bones of contention in Bakhtin scholarship. In their biography of Bakhtin, Clark and Holquist portray Bakhtin as a deeply religious man, and describe in detail a number of religious associations with which Bakhtin was probably involved. According to Holquist, the essays collected in *Art and Answerability* were to have been a magnum opus which would 'completely rethink West European metaphysics in the light of religious thought; [would] show, as it were, that philosophy had in a sense always been anticipated by religion'. This view came under heavy attack from I. R. Titunik, Gary Saul Morson and Caryl Emerson who object to the circumstantial nature of Holquist's evidence and to what they view as a reading of Bakhtin's works as 'a kind of theology in code'. However, Morson and Emerson also concede 'Bakhtin's prophetic tone verges on the theological.' See Katerina Clark and Michael Holquist, *Mikhail Bakhtin* (Cambridge, Mass.: Harvard University Press, 1984), ch. 5, pp. 120–45); Michael Holquist, 'The politics of representation' in *Allegory and Representation*, ed. Stephen Greenblatt, Selected papers from the English Institute, 1979–1980, n. s. no. 5 (Baltimore: Johns Hopkins University Press, 1981) p. 171; I. R. Titunik, 'The Baxtin problem', *Slavic and East European Journal*, vol. 30, no. 1 (Spring 1986), pp. 91–5; Katerina Clark and Michael Holquist, 'A continuing dialogue', ibid., 96–102; Gary Saul Morson and Caryl Emerson (eds), *Rethinking Bakhtin: Extensions and Challenges* (Evanston: Northwestern University Press, 1989), 'Introduction', pp. 1–60; Gary Saul Morson and Caryl Emerson, *Michael Bakhtin: Creation of a Prosaics* (Stanford, Ca.: Stanford University Press, 1990), pp. 60–1, 114.
15 *Art and Answerability*, p. 233, translator's note no. 6; See *Bakhtin and Cultural Theory*, ed. Ken Hirschkop and David Shepherd (Manchester: Manchester University Press, 1989), Glossary, pp. 193–4. It is noteworthy that in *The Formal Method in Literary Scholarship* which, according to Clark and Holquist, may have been authored, co-authored or influenced by Bakhtin, the word 'finalization' (*zavershenie*) is used in reference to the distinctive quality of aesthetics: 'except for art, no sphere of ideological activity knows finalization in the strict sense of the word; 'Every [artistic] genre represents a special way of constructing and finalizing a

whole, finalizing it essentially and thematically . . . and not just conditionally or compositionally.' M. M. Bakhtin/P. N. Medvedev, *The Formal Method in Literary Scholarship* (1928), foreword by Wlad Godzich, trans. by Albert Wehrle (1978; Cambridge, Mass.: Harvard University Press, 1985), pp. 129–30.

The conjunction of finalization and art may, of course, be perceived as evidence for diametrically opposing interpretations of Bakhtin's work, depending on one's view of the disputed texts. However, even with a strong measure of scepticism regarding the wholesale attribution of the book to Bakhtin, it is still highly probable that this aesthetic concept was common currency within the Bakhtin circle at the time.

16 'Borderlines and contraband: the deconstruction of the subject in Bakhtin's early works', forthcoming.

17 For a thorough discussion of this 'authored self' see Michael Holquist, *Dialogism: Bakhtin and his World* (London and New York: Routledge, 1990), ch. 2; Gary Saul Morson and Caryl Emerson, *Mikhael Bakhtin: Creation of a Prosaics* (Stanford, Ca.: Stanford University Press, 1990), ch. 5. These accounts of Bakhtin's theory of the subject are both extremely valuable, not least for their differences of approach, but it seems to me that both have not fully addressed the fundamental conflict between the aesthetic and the ethical vectors in the construction of the subject.

18 Caryl Emerson, 'Problems with Baxtin's poetics', *Slavic and East European Journal*, vol. 32, no. 4 (1988), pp. 507, 511, 512.

19 Ann Jefferson, 'Bodymatters: Self and Other in Bakhtin, Sartre and Barthes', in Ken Hirschkop and David Shepherd, (eds), *Bakhtin and Cultural Theory* (Manchester: Manchester University Press, 1989), pp. 152–77.

20 Bakhtin was arrested and sent to exile in 1926, presumably for engaging in religious activities. (See Clark and Holquist, *Mikhail Bakhtin*, p. 140.)

21 'Toward a reworking of the Dostoevsky book' (1961), in *Problems of Dostoevsky's Poetics*, Appendix II, p. 291.

22 ibid., pp. 292–3.

In his last Notes of 1970–1, Bakhtin refers once again to the 'process of expunging the sacred and authoritarian word . . . with its indisputability, unconditionality and unequivocality'. The monologic novel is no longer possible when 'the primary author . . . clothes himself in silence', and the 'quest for the authorial position' becomes at this point 'the most critical problem of contemporary literature'. 'From notes made in 1970–71', in *Speech Genres and Other Late Essays*, trans. Vern W. McGee, ed. Caryl Emerson and Michael Holquist (Austin: Texas University Press, Slavonic Series, no. 8, 1986), pp. 133, 149.

23 ibid., p. 139.

24 'The problem of the text', 1959–61, in *Speech Genres and Other Late Essays*, trans. Vern W. McGee, ed. Caryl Emerson and Michael Holquist (Austin: Texas University Press, Slavonic Series, no. 8, 1986), p. 126.

25 'Narrative, modernism, and the crisis of authority: a Bakhtinian perspective', *Science in Context*, vol. 7, no. 1 (1994), pp. 143–58. Morson and Emerson who view the superaddressee as a 'principle of hope' argue (rather cloudily, to my mind) that the superaddressee itself is 'not an ideological but a metalinguistic fact constitutive of all utterances' but then conclude that 'God may be dead, but in some form the superaddressee is always with us.' They, too, note that for Bakhtin there seems to be a

correlation between the need to be heard and the need for God (*Prosaics*, pp. 135–6). For an interesting view of the 'superaddressee', see Iris M. Zavala, 'Bakhtin and the Third: communication as response'. Zavala sees the position of the Third as an escape clause from the dyadic-monological conceptualization of most Western epistemologies, a triangulation of the dialogic communication model. Suggesting that the 'third' is, in fact, an 'emancipatory totality', an anticipation of discursive understanding or resistance, Zavala nonetheless (quite rightly, I believe) relates this construct to Saint Augustine's third 'I'. *Critical Studies*, vol. 1, no. 2 (1989), pp. 43–63.

26 *Toward a Philosophy of the Act*, pp. 74–5, 18.
27 A very similar view of the narrative of communality as a substitute for metaphysical narratives has been offered by Alasdair MacIntyre in *After Virtue* (1981; 2nd edn London: Duckworth, 1985).
28 'Toward a reworking of the Dostoevsky book', p. 294.
29 'The ruin of a poetics', p. 115.
30 Fyodor Dostoevsky, *The Brothers Karamazov* (1881; Harmondsworth, Middlesex: Penguin Books, 1958), pp. 77–8, 156, 273–5, 294–309; Bakhtin, *Problems in Dostoevsky's Poetics*, p. 89).
31 'Toward a reworking of the Dostoevsky book', pp. 287–8.

J. Hillis Miller

History, narrative and responsibility: speech acts
in Henry James's 'The Aspern Papers'

Abstract

Speech act theory, as inaugurated by J. L. Austin's *How to Do
Things with Words* (1962), has generated two distinct traditions
of such theorizing. One is associated with John Searle and analytic
philosophy. The other is represented by Paul de Man and Jacques
Derrida, both in their literary studies and in their reflections about
politics and society. A Searlean speech act is rational, predictable,
bound by rules and conventions. It leaves intact the rules and
conventions that enable and authorize it. For de Man and Derrida,
in somewhat different ways, each performative, even though it
may repeat forms of words used innumerable times before, is
singular and inaugural. It changes the rules and institutions themselves, indeed all the surrounding context, rather than simply
depending on them to get something efficiently done.

Henry James's 'The Aspern Papers' would seem to have little
to do with such distinctions. The story appears, as its preface
suggests, primarily to have to do with history and, more particularly, with literary history. The story itself, however, shifts from
the focus on the recovery through narrative of the recent historical
past to a focus on the responsibility towards Juliana Bordereau
and her niece, Tina, the narrator incurs when he tries to wrest
the Aspern papers from them. The narrator wants knowledge of
Aspern's liaison with Juliana the papers presumably contain. What
he never understands, though the reader is given the opportunity
by the story to understand it, is that history, at least history in
the sense of the life experience of a great writer, cannot be objectively known. It can only be known from the inside, to to speak,
in an act of doing and of taking responsibility for that doing, that
repeats the episode from the past that is to be understood.

Textual Practice **9**(2) 1995, 243–267   © 1995 J. Hillis Miller 0950–236X

Keywords: Henry James; 'The Aspern Papers'; speech acts; history; responsibility

I

No doubt people have long known that language can make something happen. Nevertheless, the publication in 1962 of J. L. Austin's *How to Do Things with Words* marked a watershed in speech act theory. Austin himself had developed his ideas as early as 1939. He had published one essay using these ideas in 1946, had lectured at Oxford in 1952 and thereafter on 'Words and Deeds', and had delivered the lectures on which the book is based at Harvard in 1955. Even so, *How to Do Things with Words* is the basic speech act (though Austin would not have called it that) from which speech act theory in all its contradictory complexity has sprung. I call the book a speech act because it was inaugural. It used words to make something happen, though not quite what Austin may have intended or foreseen. In any case, he was dead by the time the book was published, though that did not deprive the book of performative force, any more than does the death of someone who has made a will. I shall return to this point.

Since this present essay depends on a certain version of speech act theory, a word about this theory here may be helpful. I say 'a word' because a full account would be a long story indeed. Speech act theory, moreover, remains controversial. No account of it can be merely factual or, as Austin would say, 'constative'. A recent example of the continuing controversy is an essay in a book by Stanley Cavell in which Cavell takes it upon himself to defend Austin once more from Derrida's supposed misunderstanding of him.[1]

Austin's book has engendered two radically different forms of appropriation and development. One has remained within linguistics and analytical philosophy. This branch of speech act theory has minimized what is problematic or contradictory in Austin's work on speech acts, for example his shifts in terminology[2] and his gift, a gift he shares with every great philosopher, for choosing examples that put the greatest pressure on the conceptual formulations they are apparently meant simply to exemplify. This first way of thinking about speech acts has attempted to develop a coherent theory of speech acts, with clear and reasonable distinctions among different kinds of speech acts, a standard terminology, and a more or less infallible set of rules for distinguishing between speech acts and other uses of language, between one kind of speech act and another, as well as between 'felicitous' and 'infelicitous' speech acts. The work of John Searle[3] and the discussion of speech acts in a recent book by Jacob Mey[4] are salient points within this tradition. The title of one of Searle's essays, 'A classification of illocutionary acts',[5] indicates the bent of this sort of work. It assumes speech acts can be classified and analysed, that they can be dominated by philosophical or linguistic reasoning.

The other branch of thinking about speech acts is best represented by the work of Paul de Man, Jacques Derrida, Shoshana Felman, Werner Hamacher, and others, that is, by an important strand within so-called 'deconstruction'. Derrida's discussion of Austin in 'Signature event context' (original French version 1971) elicited a vigorous reply from Searle in 1977. That in turn led to Derrida's response in 'Limited Inc abc . . .' (1977).[6] Meanwhile, in *Allegories of Reading* (1979) and in other later essays, as well as in his teaching, Paul de Man was appropriating speech act theory for his own way of reading reading.

What's the difference between these two ways of taking up the legacy of Austin? For the first way, the different kinds of speech acts all in one way or another depend on the notion of the thinking, self-aware 'I'. This ego is in full possession of itself and of what it does with words. In a speech act it utters or writes with conscious intention a set of words meant to have a certain result. The predictable efficacy of such an utterance is controlled and delimited by a clear context of rules and regulations, conventions, laws, institutions. These ensure the felicity of a good speech act. The minister in the appropriate circumstances says, 'I pronounce you man and wife', and, behold!, the couple are married, before God and man and in the eyes of the law. On the other hand, no one thinks an actor and actress performing a marriage on the stage are married when another actor playing the minister utters the same words. (The example is Austin's.)

For de Man and Derrida, on the other hand, in slightly different ways in each case, all these assumptions are profoundly problematic. Rather than multiplying distinctions among different kinds of speech acts, they tend to use, as I have in this essay, the term 'performative' as an all-inclusive term naming the general power of words to do something. Moreover, as Derrida puts it in 'Signature event context', the context of a performative utterance can never be 'saturated'. The context cannot be identified and controlled enough to ensure the distinction between a felicitous and an infelicitous speech act. Derrida and de Man tend, as I do, to see a swarming of speech acts even in language that does not fit the delimited notion of speech acts as opposed to other uses of language in the work of Searle or others of that ilk. When a conservative politician in the United States says, 'The American people do not want universal health care run by the government', this looks like a statement of fact. It is actually a performative statement tending to bring about the situation it pretends only to describe. Soon such politicians and their hacks in the media will be saying: 'The American people do not want multiculturalism, queer theory, minority discourse, or cultural studies taught.' In fact they are already saying it. What we call ideology is generated by performative signs (including pictures, of course, as well as speech, written language, and music) masking as constative assertions.

No form of words, moreover, is ever wholly performative or wholly constative, though the cognitive and performative functions of a given piece of language can never be reconciled fully or made to jibe. In 'Psyche: Inventions of the Other', Derrida speaks of this as 'the infinitely rapid oscillation between the performative and constative'. He goes on to say:

> This instability constitutes that very event – let us say, the work – whose invention disturbs normally, as it were, the norms, the statutes, and the rules. It calls for a new theory and for the constitution of new statutes and conventions that, capable of recording the possibility of such events, would be able to account for them. I am not sure that speech act theory, in its present state and dominant form, is capable of this.[7]

This constant contamination of the performative by the constative and of the constative by the performative means that we are surrounded by language that is to some degree performative. It also means that it is not so certain, for example, that a marriage on the stage does not make *something* happen. Austin's attempt to exclude literature generally from the realm of speech acts fails to recognize, according to de Man and Derrida, the many ways in which literature makes something happen. A Searlean speech act, moreover, leaves intact the rules and conventions that enabled it, whereas for de Man and Derrida, in somewhat different ways, each performative, even though it may repeat forms of words used perhaps innumerable times before, is radically singular and inaugural. It changes the rules and institutions themselves, indeed all the surrounding context, rather than simply depending on them to get something efficiently done.

For both Derrida and de Man the efficacy of a performative does not depend on the conscious intention of the speaking or writing subject. The 'author' of the words does not even need to be still alive for his or her words to be effective. In a certain sense, the moment of performative efficacy is always the death of the author, as de Man implies in words I am about to cite. De Man is at his most radical in insisting that words in themselves have a performative effect that may go counter to the intention of the speaker or writer and do not depend on his or her continued existence as a conscious 'I' for their power. We intend to do one thing or intend to do nothing at all, and, behold!, something we had neither foreseen nor intended happens anyway, as a result of the words. As de Man says (in one of the essays on Rousseau in *Allegories of Reading* that makes explicit reference to Austin),

> writing always includes the moment of dispossession in favor of the arbitrary power play of the signifier and from the point of view of the subject, this can only be experienced as a dismemberment, a beheading, or a castration. . . . It is no longer certain that language, as excuse, exists because of a prior guilt but just as possible that since language, as a machine, performs anyway, we have to produce guilt (and all its train of psychic consequences) in order to make the excuse meaningful. . . . The narrative [of Rousseau's *Confessions*] begins to vacillate only when it appears that these (negative) cognitions fail to make the performative function of the discourse predictable and that, consequently, the linguistic model cannot be reduced to a mere system of tropes. Performative rhetoric and cognitive rhetoric, the rhetoric of tropes, fail to converge.[8]

This means that we are always likely to be doing things with words whenever we speak or write, but that full understanding of what we are doing is forbidden – before, during, and after. Human temporality may be another name for the impossibility of bringing together the cognitive and performative functions of language. We die with an unappeased desire to know.

Such language as that in my last sentence, however, would also, with a different twist, be characteristic of Derrida, for example in his recent book, *Aporias*.[9] Derrida's more recent work, in published essays and books as well as in spoken seminars – his work on gifts, on the force of law, on witnessing, on friendship, on sexual difference, on responsiveness and responsibility, on ghosts in Marx – could be said to be a long exploration of the performative efficacy of language and other signs. Derrida keeps returning in one way or another to an aporia whereby a form of words works performatively, on its own, to bring something singular and unheard of, something not amenable to any law, into the open, while at the same time, after the fact, seeming to be a response to something that was already there.

The United States 'Declaration of Independence' is paradigmatic of this aporia. The Declaration speaks in the name of the People of the United States that the document itself brings into existence. The people must pre-exist the declaration for it to be efficacious, but the people did not exist before the declaration called it into being.[10] Derrida, however, says something similar about a speech act in the form of an apostrophe that brings sexual difference into being. Here is his characteristically scrupulous formulation in 'Fourmis', by way of a discussion of Hélène Cixous's work:

> All of that *seems* to institute sexual difference in the most prag-
> matic, the most performative, *act* of reading/writing, here the
> experience of an originary apostrophe also recalling the origin of
> the apostrophe, the 'you' which, interrupting the silence of what
> is hidden and does not speak [le 'tu' qui, interrompant le silence
> de ce qui est tu], brings to birth, engenders, and provokes, calls
> but in truth *recalls* [appelle mais en vérité *rappelle*] the 'he' into
> being. For that act is not only an appearance that *seems to give
> rise to* [*semble se donner*] sexual difference, it is not simply active
> or decisive, creative or productive. Reading as much as it writes,
> deciphering or citing as much as it inscribes, this act is also an act
> of memory (the other is already there, irreducibly), this act enacts
> [cet acte prend acte]. In calling you back, it remembers. [En te
> rappelant, il se rappelle.][11]

It is a matter of great delicacy and intellectual tact to distinguish rightly between de Man and Derrida, since distinguishing between them involves getting right the deepest and most obscure bases of their thought, no easy task. Such a distinction, however, might focus on the way de Man's notion of performative language is associated with two central and difficult ideas in his work: his particular concept of irony and his concept (if that is the right word for it) of the non-phenomenal materiality of language. Because language is material, it has force. It can make things happen. Because this materiality is non-phenomenal, not open to sense perception, its effects are not open to verification or prediction, just as irony is a pervasive force in language that makes it potentially, or in fact inevitably, unreadable, unintelligible. Performativity, prosopopoeia, irony, and non-phenom-enal materiality – these in their intertwining form a knot or node in de Man's work, especially in his last essays.

For Derrida, on the other hand, the performative force of lan-guage is characteristically associated with what he calls the 'other' of language. He would not be likely to use the term 'materiality' to name this otherness. In an interview with Richard Kearney published in 1984 Derrida responded sharply to the charge that deconstruction sees language as referring only to itself: 'It is totally false to suggest that deconstruction is a suspension of reference. Deconstruction is always concerned with the "other" of language. I never cease to be surprised by critics who see my work as a declaration that there is nothing beyond language, that we are imprisoned in language; it is, in fact, saying the exact opposite.'[12] The other in question here is something radically other, not a social, psychological, or material, phenomenal other. As Derrida puts this in *Aporias*, 'Every other is wholly other. [Tout autre est tout autre.]'[13] A performative speech act, for Derrida, is a response to the call of this wholly other. A performative calls or invokes, while at the same time itself being called. It is a use of language 'to give a place to the other, to let the other come [donner lieu à l'autre, laisser venir l'autre]'.[14] Such a performative does not fit the paradigm of the lawful, rule-obeying speech act as defined by Austin or Searle. Passages at the end of 'Psyché: Invention de l'autre' (not included in Peggy Kamuf's selective translation) state succinctly the relation of the Derridean performative to the wholly other. Speaking of the repetition of the word 'par [by]' in Francis Ponge's little poem, 'Fable' (Par le mot *par* ...), Derrida says:

The very movement of this fabulous repetition can, according to a crossing of chance and necessity, produce the novelty of an event. Not just the singular invention of a performative, since every performative assumes conventions and institutional rules; but in twisting those rules through respect for those very rules [mais en tournant ces règles dans le respect de ces règles mêmes] in order to let the other come or announce itself in the opening of this dehiscence [dans l'ouverture de cette déhiscence].[15] This is perhaps what one calls deconstruction.... The deconstruction about which I speak does not invent and does not affirm, it does not let the other come, except to the degree in which, performative, it is not solely that but continues to perturb the conditions of the performative and of what distinguishes it peacefully from the constative.[16]

It may be, however, that what de Man calls the non-phenomenal materiality of language, the feature that gives it performative force, is another name for what Derrida calls 'the other of language', since both of these names are themselves performative catachreses, figurative names for what has no proper name and is, strictly speaking, unknown and unknowable. As Derrida says, the other always comes in 'multiple voices'.[17] De Man's and Derrida's 'calling', in the sense that they give names to this other of language, are themselves

examples of what they name. In any case, I hold (another performative there!) that the concept of performative language, more in the
Derridean or de Manian than in the Searlean sense, is an indispensable
tool in the right reading of literary works. The following tentative
and preliminary use of this tool, in a reading of 'The Aspern'Papers',
is drawn from a book in progress on 'Speech Acts in Henry James'.

II

The relation between history and narrative seems at first glance fairly
straightforward. History and narration have been inseparably associated in literary theory and in our everyday assumptions at least since
Aristotle. In the *Poetics* Aristotle prefers a probable fiction to an
improbable history as the plot for a tragedy. Though narration is not
the only way to represent history, it is certainly one of the major
ways. We tend to assume that historical events occurred as a concat-
enated sequence that can be retold now as a story of some kind: first
this happened and then that happened, and so on. Some form of
causal or rationalizable connection is presumed. This will explain
what happened and make it understandable. Narrative will tell the
truth about history. Both narrative and history belong to the regime
of truth. Narration is one of the chief ways to account for history,
to take account of it, to rationalize and explain it, to find out its
reason or ground. Fictional narrations, on the other hand, have 'historically', at least in the West, tended to present themselves in the
guise of histories, as in Fielding's title, *The History of Tom Jones*, or
in Thackeray's full title for *Henry Esmond: The History of Henry
Esmond, Esq., A Colonel in the Service of Her Majesty Q. Anne,
Written by Himself*, or in Henry James's remark in his essay on
Anthony Trollope that unless a fictional narration maintains the
illusion of its historicity, it has no ground to stand on: 'It is impossible
to imagine what a novelist takes himself to be unless he regards
himself as an historian and his narrative as history. It is only as an
historian that he has the smallest *locus standi*.'[18] That figure of the
locus standi returns in Henry James's story, 'The Aspern Papers'. The
motif appears there, as I shall show, in various figures arguing that
biographical knowledge forms an indispensable ground for measuring
literature's value. This intimate and unbreakable connection between
narrative and history in the Western tradition seems unproblematic
enough.

Raising questions about 'responsibility', however, adds a complication. This further wrinkle may upset the presumed symmetry

between narrative and history. If both narrative and history are of the order of truth, responsibility is of the order of doing, of ethics, of performative rather than of constative uses of language. Do narrative and history in any way involve questions of responsibility, of obligation, of ethical response to an imperative demand? I shall try to explore this question by considering Henry James's novella of 1888, 'The Aspern Papers'.

III

To whom is the narrator of this story talking or writing? As in all such cases of first person narration, it is not easy to answer that question. A first person narration differs from third person narration, with its convention of an anonymous narrating voice. In the case of a first person narration like 'The Aspern Papers', it is as though we as readers, or, better, I as reader, since it is an intimate and singular experience, had been made the overhearer of a murmuring internal voice of narration that is going over and over the facts of the case as remembered, trying to put them in order, above all trying to justify itself. This voice seemingly speaks in response to a demand for an accounting. Someone, it seems, has said to the story-teller: 'Account for yourself.' The narrator of 'The Aspern Papers' speaks as a witness. As James's preface to *The Golden Bowl* says, he is 'witness of the destruction of "The Aspern Papers" ' (*The Golden Bowl*, 1:vii).[19] James's capitalization and punctuation here identifies the Aspern papers themselves and the story of that title. In what way the story itself is 'destroyed' or what that might mean remains to be seen. The reader, in any case, is put by the narrator's deposition in the position of the conscience, the judge or jury. It is as if we had demanded this accounting and had taken upon ourselves the responsibility of evaluating it for plausibility and credibility, then judging it. We have to pronounce, 'Guilty' or 'Innocent'. If the verdict is 'Guilty' we must decide on what punishment should be meted out.

Or rather 'I' am put in that position. The call is addressed to me, personally. I alone must act, must respond. I cannot let anyone else read for me. Perhaps, for example, I might think, the narrator is punished enough by being forced to think over and ove what he has done, for the story ends with his statement of suffering: 'When I look at it [the picture of Jeffrey Aspern] I can scarcely bear my loss – I mean of the precious papers' (143).[20] Or the reader might be led to ask whether the narrator must be held responsible for moral stupidity, for not having understood correctly the relation between narration and history. What is the proper punishment for that crime? So I must carefully sift the evidence, read between the lines, put two and two together. The effect of this is to make me read carefully (or it should be), paying attention to tiny details of language, to any other clues the narrator may give, perhaps in spite of himself. If he is that notorious personage, the 'unreliable narrator', then James may be speaking to me, ironically, through gaps and lapses in the narrator's language.

As in all such cases, I am myself on trial, for I am in danger of being unjust, insensitive, or inattentive. I may have missed something crucial. James excels in putting the reader in that situation, in putting the reader on trial. If the narrator has, it may be, treated Juliana and Tina badly, I may be in danger of treating *him* badly, of judging him wrongly. If he behaved badly, how should he have behaved? Where did he go wrong? How would I have behaved in his place? And of course beneath all that or around it I am judging James, whom I know is the author of the tale I am reading. Can I trust him as a moral guide or as someone who tells the truth about the human situation?

Is this putting of the reader on trial characteristic of James's stories and novels, or is it peculiar to this one or to a group like this one? Do all James's works put on the reader this heavy responsibility of judging, with an implied penalty if he or she makes an error? I think it can be said to be a general characteristic. In each story by James the characters behave in a certain way and the story comes out in a certain way. The reader is asked to evaluate that behaviour and that outcome morally. Usually the reader is asked especially to judge some climactic decision and act, almost always some act of (apparent) renunciation, of giving up, almost always a sexual renunciation. In 'The Aspern Papers' the narrator refuses Miss Tina's offer of herself in marriage. That precipitates the dénouement. In *The Portrait of a Lady* the heroine, Isabel Archer, returns to her cruel and egotistical husband, Gilbert Osmond. In *The Ambassadors* Strether refuses to get anything out of it for himself, that is, he refuses Maria Gostrey's offer of herself. In *The Golden Bowl* Maggie condones her husband's adultery with her stepmother. In *The Awkward Age* Vanderbank refuses to marry Nanda. In all these diverse cases the reader must pass judgement on the protagonist's decisive, life-determining act.

James always gives the reader abundant, even superabundant, evidence, lots of rope with which to hang himself or herself. But unfortunately the evidence is always in one way or another indirect. The rule is that James never tells me in so many words what I should conclude, how I should evaluate and judge the characters. This exasperates some readers, for example, Wayne Booth in *The Rhetoric of Fiction*. It is as though James were saying, with a faint ironic smile on his face, 'Here is all the evidence. I have kept nothing back. I have even given you, it may sometimes seem to you, a tedious superfluity of evidence. Now it is up to you to judge.' This is analogous to one of the imaginary visions the narrator of 'The Aspern Papers' has when he looks at the portrait of the dead poet, Jeffrey Aspern, whose life so obsesses him:

> I only privately consulted Jeffrey Aspern's delightful eyes with my own (they were so young and brilliant, and yet so wise, so full of vision). . . . He seemed to smile at me with friendly mockery, as if he were amused at my case. I had got into a pickle for him – as if he needed it! He was unsatisfactory, for the only moment since I had known him.
>
> (97)

Many readers have found James himself elusive and mocking. To read James is to be put in the pickle of being made responsible for judgement when the grounds for judgement are not at all certain. The reader is put on trial in a way that is not wholly pleasant. Certainly it is not relaxed or merely receptive. The reader's state is not at all consonant with the idea that the pleasures of reading James are pure irresponsible pleasures of aesthetic form, the pleasures of passive admiration. This is the case even though James himself in the prefaces to his work often seems to promise just that, in the form of what he calls 'amusement'.[21]

IV

Well, what is the evidence on which to base a properly responsive, responsible judgement of what 'The Aspern Papers' has to say about history and narration?

The preface to this story (written for the New York Edition) stresses in several ways the relation of the story to history. Thinking about its genesis brings back to James the history of his own past life in Italy, 'the inexhaustible charm of Roman and Florentine memories', not to speak of the 'old Venice' of the story itself (vi). Moreover, the story had its genesis, James says, in the way 'history, "literary history" we in this connexion call it, had in an out-of-the-way corner of the great garden of life thrown off a curious flower that I was to feel worth gathering as soon as I saw it' (v). This is

James's characteristically oblique way of saying that 'The Aspern
Papers' is based on a historical episode. This was the survival into
the late nineteenth century in Florence of Jane Clairmont, 'for a
while the intimate friend of Byron and the mother of his daughter'
(vii) and the attempt by a man from Boston, Captain Edward Silsbee,
to become a lodger in her house and thereby get hold of documents
about Shelley and Byron she was thought to possess.

James's account of how he came to write 'The Aspern Papers'
leads him to some general reflections about history and narrative.
The anecdote about Jane Clairmont appealed to him as the subject
of a story, he says, because it was just far enough in the past, but
not too far: 'And then the case had the air of the past just in the
degree in which that air, I confess, most appeals to me – when
the region over which it hangs is far enough away without being too
far' (ix). The eloquent passage that follows develops and explains
this appeal. Such a nearby past is visitable, recoverable. It combines
strangeness and familiarity in just the right proportions, whereas a
more distant past cannot be visited and reappropriated by the writer,
thereby made into a narrative. Too many other historical periods
intervene. These baffle the imaginative writer's attempts at an intimate
recovery:

> I delight in a palpable imaginable *visitable* past – in the nearer
> distances and the clearer mysteries, the marks and signs of a world
> we may reach over to as by making a long arm we grasp an object
> at the other end of our own table. The table is the one, the
> common expanse, and where we lean, so stretching, we find it
> firm and continuous. That, to my imagination, is the past fragrant
> of all, or of almost all, the poetry of the thing outlived and lost
> and gone, and yet in which the precious element of closeness,
> telling so of connexions but tasting so of differences, remains
> appreciable. With more moves back the element of the appreciable
> shrinks – just as the charm of looking over a garden-wall into
> another garden breaks down when successions of walls appear.
> The other gardens, those still beyond, may be there, but even by
> use of our longest ladder we are baffled and bewildered – the
> view is mainly of barriers. The one partition makes the place we
> have wondered about *other*, both richly and recognisably so; but
> who shall pretend to impute an effect of composition to the
> twenty? We are divided of course between liking to feel the past
> strange and liking to feel it familiar; the difficulty is, for intensity,
> to catch it at the moment when the scales of the balance hang
> with the right evenness.

(x)

This passage seems to promise that 'The Aspern Papers' will be a narrative about a successful visiting of the early nineteenth century, the time when Byron and Shelley lived in Italy. That James's definition of such a past (familiar and yet strange) corresponds exactly to Freud's definition of the uncanny (*das Unheimliche*) might give the reader pause. It would define such a recovery of the past as a raising of ghosts, the return of something repressed, something exposed and yet hidden, something known that nevertheless ought to be kept secret. This definition of the near past as an uncanny mixture of familiarity and strangeness may connect this story in some obscure way with James's ghost stories, such as 'The Jolly Corner' and 'The Turn of the Screw'. That, however, may be a false association, since what James here emphasizes is the possible successful recovery of history through narration. There seems nothing uncanny about this success.

In fact, however, the image of the ghostly resurrected revenant from the past has already appeared early in the preface when James speaks of his memories of Italy as 'haunting presences' (vi). And the figure of the ghost was already present in the story itself. Juliana Bordereau, the old woman in the story who corresponds to Jane Clairmont in the 'real life' historical events, seems to the unnamed narrator who has designs on her papers, 'too strange, too literally resurgent' (Penguin, 25). '. . . as she sat there before me,' he says, 'my heart beat as fast as if the miracle of resurrection had taken place for my benefit. Her presence seemed somehow to contain his, and I felt nearer to him at that first moment of seeing her than I ever had been before or ever have been since' (24–5). The resurrection of Juliana Bordereau is in a manner of speaking the resurrection of Jeffrey Aspern himself, James's fictional equivalent of Byron. Juliana's 'literal' resurgence generates Aspern's figurative resurrection. The narrator at various crucial moments in the story imagines himself confronting Aspern face to face, even talking with him and hearing his voice:

> That spirit [of Venice] kept me perpetual company and seemed to look out at me from the revived immortal face – in which all his genius shone – of the great poet who was my prompter. I had invoked him and he had come; he hovered before me half the time; it was as if his bright ghost had returned to earth to tell me that he regarded the affair as his own no less than mine and that we should see it fraternally, cheerfully to a conclusion. It was as if he had said, 'Poor dear, be easy with her; she has some natural prejudices; only give her time. Strange as it may appear to you she was very attractive in 1820 . . .'
>
> (37)

What the narrator says here employs the language that is ordinarily used to describe the invocation of a spirit. The rhetorical name for this is prosopopoeia, the ascription of a name, a voice, or a face to the absent, inanimate, or dead. To ascribe or inscribe a name or a voice is performatively to call into being, to invoke, to resurrect, to utter a new version of Jesus' 'Lazarus, come forth!' All historical story-telling depends on the efficacy of such performative prosopopoeias. These figures raise from the dead words on the page the illusions of the various personae, including the narrator. In that sense all historical stories are ghost stories.

One function of James's ghost stories proper, it might be argued, is to bring out into the open this basic aspect of all historical narration. 'I had invoked him and he had come.' The one who raises a ghost must then take responsibility for his or her act. That responsibility is most accurately figured in some demand the resurrected ghost makes on the one to whom he appears, as the ghost of Hamlet's father demands that Hamlet revenge his murder or as the narrator of 'The Aspern Papers' incurs a responsibility, by way of Aspern's ghost, for Juliana and Tina. The narrator wants knowledge. He does not get the knowledge he wants, but he does get responsibility. Is it possible that our situation as readers may parallel that of the narrator? We have been taught to read literary works, for example, 'The Aspern Papers', in order to understand them. Reading may rather put an unforeseen burden of obligation on our shoulders. The story, it may be, demands not that we know but that we do.

V

The narrator's failure to know is paralleled by the way the story by no means fulfils the retrospective promise of the preface to give the reader knowledge of history, of 'a palpable, visitable past'. 'The Aspern Papers' is rather a story of the impossibility of knowing and possessing the historical past through narrative.

Why is this? Why is it that 'The Aspern Papers' is a narrative of the failure of narrative to reach and possess history, even that charmingly close period of the early nineteenth century the preface promises the story will visit? The story is a brilliant putting in question of just that set of hermeneutic assumptions about the relation between narrative and history I began by describing as taken for granted, for the most part, in our tradition. Those assumptions are just the ones assumed in James's preface. By 'hermeneutic' I mean the presupposition that the truth about a set of historical events, like the truth about a document or set of documents, for example, a work of literature like 'The Aspern Papers', is inside the evidence and can by proper procedures be penetrated, reached, decoded, revealed, unveiled, and trimphantly brought out into the open where all may see it and where it may be told as a coherent narrative. Joseph Conrad expresses this assumption when he has the primary narrator in *Heart of Darkness* say that 'The yarns of seamen have a direct simplicity, the whole meaning of which lies within the shell of a cracked nut.'[22]

The narrator of 'The Aspern Papers' is a literary scholar who specializes in the work of an American poet of the early nineteenth century, Jeffrey Aspern. The narrator's basic professional assumption is that biographical facts will explain Aspern's poetry. He immensely admires the poetry, but James does not allow him the slightest insight into the possibility that the poetry might be worth reading for its own sake or that it might have any meaning that would exceed its biographical references. He assumes that the more he knows about Aspern's life the more he will have established solid grounds for decoding the poetry. In explaining this the narrator uses a religious metaphor that recurs in the story and provides another version of the hermeneutic structure. In one place the narrator says Juliana represented 'esoteric knowledge' about Aspern's life (38). Earlier he asserts, 'One doesn't defend one's god: one's god is in himself a defence' (12–13). This desire to get at the hidden facts of Aspern's life outweighs any compunction he might have about lying to Juliana and forcing his way into her intimacy, even though he says at one point, when he is trying to worm information out of Juliana's niece Tina: 'I felt particularly like the reporter of a newspaper who forces his way into a house of mourning' (64).

Later on, in a crucial discussion with Juliana, the narrator tells her he is 'a critic, an historian' and writes about 'those who are dead and gone and can't speak for themselves'. The interchange that follows identifies just what form the narrator's interpretative assumptions take. The narrator assumes that getting the full biographical facts about Jeffrey Aspern and then narrating them as a full history of his life will serve as a solid ground or *logos* by which to measure his works. He defends himself to Juliana by asking: 'What becomes of the work I just mentioned, that of the great philosophers and poets? It is all vain words if there is nothing to measure it by' (70). Juliana pours scorn on this idea by saying it is like applying a measuring tape to someone in order to make him a suit. 'You talk as if you were a tailor', she says (70). The truth, for Juliana, is inaccessible by the narrator's kind of search for historical truth.

Why Juliana is right and the narrator wrong, the working out of the story dramatizes. Juliana is so appalled when she catches the narrator in the act of trying to break into her secretaire to steal the papers that she dies of the shock. The narrator has in a manner of speaking killed her. Juliana's middle-aged niece, Tina, is right when she suspects that the narrator would have been capable of 'violating [her] tomb' (99). Tina has functioned throughout as an intermediary and go-between. She gives the narrator indirect access to Juliana, just as Juliana will give him indirect access, he hopes, to Aspern. After Juliana's death Tina offers to give him the papers if he will marry her: 'What in the name of the preposterous did she mean if she did not mean to offer me her hand? That was the price – that was the price!' (101). The narrator refuses to marry her and leaves. Tina then burns all the papers, telling him when he returns, in her inadvertently comic literalism: 'It took a long time – there were so many' (106). The narrator says 'a real darkness descended for a moment on my eyes' (106). He is left with the portrait of Aspern and with his chagrin: '. . . it hangs above my writing-table. When I look at it I can scarcely bear my loss – I mean of the precious papers' (142).

What does this dénouement mean? As many critics have noted, the unnamed teller of this story is unreliable not because he deliberately lies but because though he is intelligent he fails more or less completely to understand what has happened to him. The 'real darkness' that descends on him when he nearly faints is the correlative of the figurative blindness that has afflicted him all along. That other blindess keeps him permanently in the dark about the meaning (if that is the right word) of his experience. When he identifies his unbearable loss as being of the precious papers he almost recognizes, in the pause indicated by the dash, that he has brought on himself another worse and unrecognized loss. It is worse in part because it is unrecognized. 'The Aspern Papers' parallels in this another celebrated story by James, 'The Beast in the Jungle', though in that tale the narrator may get insight at the end of the story, when it is already too late.

The narrator of 'The Aspern Papers' has assumed that his only responsibility is to the historical biographical truth about Aspern. Any means, even a theft that is presented as a figurative sexual assault, even as a kind of necrophilia, 'violating a tomb', are justified in the name of finding out that truth. The narrator's responsibility to this kind of truth is underwritten by the entire institutional apparatus of literary history as a discursive practice in our culture. It is not an accident that *The New York Times Book Review*, for example, today routinely reviews literary biographies, good or bad, while passing by even distinguished critical readings of the same authors. This notion of literary history is institutionalized also in university study of literature. The search for literary historical truth is one version of the university's commitment to a selfless search for the bringing to light of knowledge. The motto of Yale University is 'Lux et Veritas'. The motto of Harvard is 'Veritas'. The motto of The University of California is 'Let There Be Light'. The university assumes that everything has its reason, its underlying explanatory 'Grund', its measure. Our primary and exclusive responsibility is to bring that truth to light. The commitment to the search for a narratable historical truth is only a version of a more inclusive commitment to truth-seeking in our culture. The university is one of this commitment's main institutional guardians.

What the narrator does not see and what his narration allows the reader to glimpse indirectly, to 'read between the lines', as one says, is that historical events are not open to this kind of knowledge and therefore cannot be narrated. All that can be narrated is the failure to see, know, possess, or uncover the actual events of the historical past. The paradigmatic example of an historical event in the story is the presumed affair between Juliana Bordereau and Jeffrey Aspern. Such an event, the story implies, cannot be known from the outside. It is not something that could ever have been known through research and then told in a narration. It can only be 'known', without being known, in an event that repeats it, that bears witness to it by doing something like it again.

Why can an historical event like the presumed love-making of Juliana and Aspern not be known? A true historical event, the story indicates, does not belong to the order of cognition. It belongs to the order of performative acts, speech acts or acts employing other kinds of signs in a performative way. Such an event makes something happen. It leaves traces on the world that might be known, for example, the Aspern papers if they were published and read, but in itself it cannot be known. Even if the narrator had taken possession of the papers and read them, he would not have known what he wanted to know.

Two kinds of knowledge may be distinguished. One is the kind obtained from historical research or from seeing something with one's own eyes. That kind can be narrated. The other kind is that blind bodily material kind that cannot be narrated. We can only witness to it, in another speech act. This kind is expressed in the Biblical formula: 'Adam knew his wife and she conceived.' The sex act is paradigmatic of this other kind of knowledge. All speech acts, for example, promises, are of the same order, as is the unknowable event of my own death. The connection among these three forms of non-narratable historical events is indicated in the way the three crucial events in Hyacinth Robinson's life, in James's great political novel, *The Princess Casamassima*, are not directly narrated. They are blanks in the text. These events are Hyacinth's act of promising the revolutionaries that he will commit a terrorist act, Hyacinth's experience of sleeping with the Princess, and Hyacinth's suicide.

In 'The Aspern Papers' the narrator can only 'know' what he wants to know by a present performative that repeats the earlier one. That 'knowledge' will not be the sort of clear retransmissible cognition that we usually mean when we think of historical knowledge. It will be the sort of knowledge that Adam had of his wife, an unknowing knowing. Such an event is unavailable to clear knowing in the same way as the performative side of speech acts cannot be known, or as the materiality of any inscription is not phenomenal, since it is instantly seen as a sign, or as the rhetorical dimension of language as it interferes with clear grammatical and logical meaning makes that language unreadable.

To repeat what Aspern did by marrying Tina, as the story makes clear, would put the narrator in an impossible double bind. It would be impossible at least from the point of view of his goal of revealing history through narration. In order to get possession of the papers the narrator must marry Tina. That this would repeat what Jeffrey Aspern did is made clear earlier in the story when the narrator says of Aspern: 'Half the women of his time, to speak liberally, had flung themselves at his head, and out of this pernicious fashion many complications, some of them grave, had not failed to arise. . . . [Nevertheless,] he was kinder, more considerate than, in his place (if I could imagine myself in such a place!) I should have been' (14). The narrator, as he says, 'had not the tradition of personal conquest' (24), that is, he has not been successful with women. In spite of that, he finds himself in a manner of speaking in Jeffrey Aspern's place before the story is done. Tina 'throws herself at his head', and he does get into a 'grave complication' with her. The difference is that Aspern did apparently sleep with at least some of the women who threw themselves at him. The grave complications that followed were, so the narrator hints, a result of that. The narrator, however, refuses Tina, even though for a moment his 'literary concupiscence' (105) leads him to think he might marry her: ' "Why not, after all – why not?" It seemed to me I was ready to pay the price' (105). His delay in deciding about that costs him the papers, since by the time he is ready to marry Tina, to 'pay the price', she has already burned them.

On the other hand, if he had married her he would have become, as Tina says, 'a relation'. 'Then,' she says, 'it would be the same for you as for me. Anything that is mine – would be yours, and you could do what you like. I couldn't prevent you – and you would have no responsibility' (99). If on the one hand he would have no responsibility of the sort he would have incurred if he had stolen the papers, rapt them away, on the other hand he would have the infinite responsibility Juliana incurred toward Jeffrey Aspern by becoming his mistress (if she did in fact do that, which can never be known), that is, the responsibility to keep their liaison secret. Married to Tina the narrator would have had the absolute responsibilty of a husband to keep his wife's family secrets. He cannot have the papers if he remains an outsider, so cannot publish them. He can have them if he becomes an insider, but then he cannot publish them because he will have incurred a family responsibility that will far outweigh his responsibility as a literary historian.[23] The knowledge he would have as Tina's husband would repeat the knowledge Jeffrey Aspern had, but it is not the kind of knowledge that can or should be narrated in a cognizable historical text. Such an event can only be repeated in another performative act. An example is the way Aspern's presumed affair with Juliana appears to be repeated in the poetry that Jeffrey Aspern wrote about her. The reader is given not one single word of that poetry. All we know is that the narrator wants to go straight through it to reach the biographical facts that will explain and 'measure' it. That poetry is both intimately connected to the historical events that 'generated' it and at the same time disconnected from them by an uncrossable breach, a chasm as wide as that between the 'sources' of James's story and the story itself. To understand 'The Aspern Papers', or to find out if it is intelligible, you have no recourse but to read it. Reading it, as I shall argue, may be another kind of performative repetition. The narrator's story in 'The Aspern Papers' is a parody of this kind of repetition. It repeats as a narrative of non-knowledge the non-event of the narrator's refusal to marry Tina. The narrator does indeed witness to the destruction of 'The Aspern Papers' as a truth-telling historical narrative as well as to the destruction of the Aspern papers.

VI

The line of analysis I have been following would seem to put the canny reader in a position of superiority to the unperceptive narrator. The narrator cannot read the data with which he is confronted, but the reader can at every point second-guess him. He or she can do this thanks to the abundant clues for the reader's enlightenment James has strewn throughout the story. But is this really the case? For one thing it would appear to reaffirm for the perceptive reader, the reader in depth, just that hermeneutic model of penetration within or behind the data to reach a hidden meaning that has been thoroughly discredited in the story itself. It has been discredited as the mistaken paradigm that not only prevents the narrator from achieving real knowledge but also makes him responsible for despicable acts toward Juliana and Tina, not to mention his desecration of the grave, so to speak, of Jeffrey Aspern.

The answer to this apparent contradiction is that what the reader learns is not a definite knowledge but at most a kind of bodily understanding of why he or she cannot in principle objectively and impersonally know, but can only do, perform, act. The new act in question would be an interventionist reading possibly repeating James's story in another mode but certainly not giving definitive knowledge of the meaning of James's tale. Or better, the reader does not even understand that, since it cannot be understood in the ordinary sense of that term. Reading, it may be, is a mode of doing, not a mode of knowing. I say 'possibly' because there is no way in principle to know whether a given reading works in that way. If it does work that way it belongs not to the order of truth and knowledge but to the order of non-cognizable speech acts. If it were a speech act it would be a new historical event repeating the previous one of James's writing the tale, just as the narrator of 'The Aspern Papers' would by marrying Tina have repeated Jeffrey Aspern's liaison with Juliana Bordereau, if that liaison did in fact exist. That the story keeps eternally secret, just as I cannot in principle have knowledge of the efficacy of speech acts I perform, since they are a doing not a knowing.

VII

Let me try to explain this further, in conclusion, by a brief discussion of four views of history that parallel to some degree the relation between narrative and historical events I have identified in James's 'The Aspern Papers'. The idea that history may be unknowable and non-narratable is difficult to grasp, understand, or accept, but four authors may help to approach apprehension of it.

Friedrich Nietzsche distinguishes in 'Vom Nutzen und Nachtheil der Historie für das Leben' between two relations to history. On the one hand there is the relation of those who write academic history, for example, that institutionalized literary history the narrator of 'The

Aspern Papers' wants to practise. On the other hand there is a paradoxical relation of forgetting to the historical past. It must be forgotten in order to make a space for present action. To turn history into the object of scientific knowledge is to neutralize it and to neutralize ourselves too, to make us all like universiy professors in the humanities (Nietzsche's main polemical target in this essay), learned men whose learning has no effect on the world. The paradox, as Nietzsche recognizes, is that we are what history has made us. To expunge our memory of the historical past in order to act freely in the present would be to expunge also ourselves. The past must be forgotten as objective narratable knowledge in order not so much to be remembered as to be repeated in vigorous inaugural present action that gives birth to the future. 'We need history, certainly,' Nietzsche says, 'but we need it for reasons different from those for which the idler in the garden of knowledge [der verwöhnte Müssiggänger im Garten des Wissens] needs it. . . . We need it, that is to say, for the sake of life and action (zum Leben und zur That), not so as to turn comfortably away from life and action.'[24]

In one way or another both Jacques Derrida and Paul de Man hold that historical events cannot be known in the way monumental historians claim to know and narrate them. For Derrida and de Man, the performative, therefore the non-phenomenal and non-knowable, aspect of literature, philosophy, and criticism, of language and other signs generally, makes history. This distinction between cognitive statements and performative speech acts has been the basis of my reading here, though it must be remembered that the separation can never be made absolute. There is always a cognitive side to performatives, and vice versa, even though these two sides of language can never be reconciled. The performative side of language is not something that can be known, even though there is an imperative need to know it in order to find out what we have done with words and to take responsibility for that doing. This impossibility of knowing speech acts is part of what Derrida means in recent seminars when he says 'the gift, if there is such a thing', 'the secret, if there is such a thing', 'witnessing, if there is such a thing'. Since the gift, the secret, and witnessing are kinds of speech acts or sign acts, they are not the objects of a possible verifiable cognition. They must remain a matter of 'if'.

De Man's way of putting this was to say that the performative force of language, its power to make something happen in history and society, is linked to its materiality, that is, to a non-referential non-cognitive side of language. In the so-far-unpublished lecture on 'Kant and Schiller', given at Cornell University a few months before his death, de Man discusses the sequence in Kant's *Third Critique* from a 'cognitive discourse as trope' to 'the materiality of the inscribed signifier'. He argues that only the latter is historical, a historical event. The regressive misreading of Kant initiated by Schiller is not historical, not a series of historical events. There is in Kant, said de Man,

> a movement from cognition, from acts of knowledge, from states of cognition, to something which is no longer a cognition but which is to some extent an occurrence, which has the materiality of something that actually happens, that actually occurs . . . , that does something to the world as such. . . . There is history from the moment that words such as 'power' and 'battle' and so on emerge on the scene; at that moment things happen, there is occurrence, there is event. History [has to do with] the emergence of a language of power out of the language of cognition.

He means by 'language of power' not just language that names aspects of power, but language that has power, language that does what it names, as 'I pronounce you man and wife', spoken in the right circumstances, brings it about that the couple is married. This conception of the materiality of inscription is worked out by de Man in 'Shelley disfigured', in 'Aesthetic formalization: Kleist's *Über das Marionettentheater*', and in 'Hypogram and inscription', as well as in the late essays on Kant and Hegel.

De Man, like Derrida or Nietzsche, argues for a potential performative, history-making power in language, including the language of literature, philosophy, and even 'practical criticism'. This potential power may or may not be actualized or effective in a given case. It would be a foolhardy person who would claim that what he or she writes is an historical event. It is in any case not of the order of cognition. To put this in de Manian terms, the 'linguistics of literariness' includes the performative dimension of literary language. Understanding it will help account for the occurrence of ideological aberrations, but knowing those aberrations will not change them. Only the performative, material, 'word-thing' side of language will do that. A rhetorical reading, registered in the most responsible critical terms, may actively liberate a past text for present uses. This new act is not engineered by a previously existing self-conscious 'I', the sovereign reader in full control of is or her knowledge of a text. The reading is constitutive of the 'I' that enunciates it.

Walter Benjamin describes in somewhat consonant terms in the seventeenth of the 'Theses on the philosophy of history' the way an 'historical materialist' sees 'a revolutionary chance in the fight for the oppressed past' when he finds a way to 'blast (*herauszusprengen*) a specific era out of the homogeneous course of history – blasting a specific life out of the era or a specific work out of the lifework'.[25] '*Herauszusprengen*' names here a speech act that has effects on the future, not a historical cognition that tells something true about the past. A historical event (as all these authors, including James in 'The Aspern Papers', posit) cannot be known through narration. It can only be performatively repeated, since it was a speech act in the first place. For that repetition the one who repeats must take responsibility. The doer must take responsibility, that is, for what he or she does not know but can only perhaps succeed in reinscribing. He reinscribes it in a new, singular, unheard-of way, with incalculable effects on the future.

University of California

Notes

1 See Stanley Cavell, *A Pitch of Philosophy: Autobiographical Exercises* (Cambridge, Mass: Harvard University Press, 1994).

2 I am thinking especially of the shift within *How to Do Things with Words* from the performative/constative distinction to the distinction among locutionary, illocutionary, and perlocutionary acts of language.

3 See especially *Speech Acts: An Essay in the Philosophy of Language* (Cambridge: Cambridge University Press, 1969).

4 See *Pragmatics: An Introduction* (Oxford: Blackwell, 1993).

5 *Proceeedings of the Texas Conference on Performatives, Presuppositions, and Implicatures*, ed. Andy Rogers, Bob Wall, and John P. Murphy (Washington, DC: Center for Applied Linguistics, 1977), pp. 27–45.

6 Derrida's two essays, a summary of Searle's and a new 'Afterword' were collected in Jacques Derrida, *Limited Inc* (Evanston, Ill.: Northwestern University Press, 1988).

7 'Psyche: Inventions of the Other', *A Derrida Reader*, ed. Peggy Kamuf (New York: Columbia University Press, 1991), pp. 207–8.

8 'Excuses *Confessions*)', in *Allegories of Reading* (New Haven, Conn.: Yale University Press, 1979), pp. 296, 299, 300.

9 *Aporias*, trans. Thomas Dutoit (Stanford, California: Stanford University Press, 1993).

10 See 'Déclarations d'indépendance', in *Otobiographies* (Paris: Galilée, 1984), pp. 13–32.

11 Jacques Derrida, 'Fourmis', in *Lectures de la différence sexuelle*, ed. Mara Negrón (Paris: Des femmes, 1994), p. 89, my translation. The passages I cite from Derrida are full of puns and wordplay that are difficult to translate, to say the least. 'Appeller' means call, while 'rappeler' means, among other senses, to call back, to summon up, to restore, and 'se rappeler' means to recollect, to remember, to recall to mind. 'Tu' means

you in the singular, thou, but it is also the past participle of 'taire', not to say, to keep hidden.

12 Jacques Derrida, 'Deconstruction and the Other', in Richard Kearney, *Dialogues with Contemporary Continental Thinkers: The Phenomenological Heritage* (Manchester: Manchester University Press, 1984), p. 123.

13 *Aporias*, p. 22. I have changed Dutoit's 'completely' to 'wholly'.

14 Jacques Derrida, 'Psyché: Invention de l'autre', in *Psyché: Inventions de l'autre* (Paris: Galilée, 1987), p. 60, my translation.

15 'Dehisce' is a botanical term meaning 'to burst or split open along a line or slit, as do the ripe capsules or pods of some plants', in order to release seeds (*The American Heritage Dictionary*).

16 *Psyché*, pp. 58–9; 60–1.

17 'L'autre appelle à venir et cela n'arrive qu'à plusieurs voix (The other calls [something] to come and that does not arrive except in multiple voices)' (*Psyché*, p. 61).

18 Henry James, *The Art of Fiction and Other Essays* (New York: Oxford University Press, 1948), pp. 59–60. I have discussed this passage in 'Narrative and history', *ELH*, vol. 41, no. 3 (Fall 1974), pp. 455–73.

19 Citations for all works of fiction by Henry James except 'The Aspern Papers' are from the *The Novels and Tales of Henry James* (Fairfield, NJ: Augustus M. Kelley, 1976). This is a reprint of the New York Edition of 1909. 'The Aspern Papers' is cited from Henry James, *The Aspern Papers and Other Stories* (Harmondsworth, Middlesex: Penguin Books, 1976). This is a convenient reprint of the New York Edition version. The preface to 'The Aspern Papers' is cited from the reprint of the New York Edition.

20 Thus in the revision of the story for the New York Edition of 1909. The first version (1888) has 'When I look at it my chagrin at the loss of the letters becomes almost intolerable' (Henry James, *The Complete Tales*, ed. Leon Edel (Philadelphia and New York: J. B. Lippincott Company, 1963), vol. 6, p. 382. James made a number of changes in this story for the New York Edition, for example, changing the name of Juliana Bordereau's niece (if she is a niece) from Miss Tita to Miss Tina. In general, where there are changes they seem to me usually to add important nuances. I have therefore cited the revised version. The changes act as a kind of reading of the story after the fact by its author, like the famous prefaces themselves. The preface to *The Golden Bowl* discusses the way re-reading is re-vision and revision.

21 See for example, the preface to *The Portrait of a Lady*, where James speaks of 'the anxiety of my provision for the reader's amusement' (vol. 1, p. xvi).

22 Joseph Conrad, *Heart of Darkness and The Secret Sharer* (New York: Signet, 1950), p. 68. Paul de Man works out the implications of this inside/outside figure for a hermeneutic way of reading in 'Semiology and rhetoric'. An admirable paper by Naomi Silver on 'The Aspern Papers' called my attention to the relevance of this paradigm for reading this story.

23 One critic has read the story as a disguised representation of James's feelings about his book on Nathaniel Hawthorne for the 'English Men of Letters' series. That book is in large part biographical. James had tried unsuccessfully to persuade Hawthorne's son Julian (perhaps obliquely referred to in the name 'Juliana' in 'The Aspern Papers') to give him

access to Hawthorne's private papers. Julian later published his father's intimate papers himself and was widely criticized for this as a 'publishing scoundrel' (p. 89), to borrow the words Julian Bordereau hisses at the narrator in the climax of the story. See Gary Scharnhorst, 'James, "The Aspern Papers", and the ethics of literary biography', *Modern Fiction Studies*, vol. 36, no. 2 (Summer 1990).

24 Friedrich Nietzsche, *Sämtliche Werke*, Kritische Studienausgabe, ed. Giorgio Colli and Mazzino Montinari (Berlin: Walter de Gruyter, 1988), vol. 1, p. 243; 'On the uses and disadvantages of history for life', in *Untimely Meditations*, trans. R. J. Hollingdale (Cambridge: Cambridge University Press, 1983), p. 59.

25 Walter Benjamin, *Illuminations*, trans. Harry Zohn (New York: Schocken, 1969; Walter Benjamin, *Illuminationen* (Frankfurt a. M.: Suhrkamp, 1955), p. 278.

Peter Nicholls

A conversation with Lynne Tillman

Abstract

The interview ranges across Tillman's published work, focusing particularly on *Haunted Houses* and *Cast in Doubt*. Reference is also made to Tillman's work with film. Topics explored include Tillman's expatriate experience and her use of travel as a motif in her fiction; her attitudes toward psychoanalysis and related theories of gender and sexual difference; her conception of narrative styles.

Keywords: Lynne Tillman; contemporary American fiction; gender

Lynne Tillman is the author of three novels – *Haunted Houses* (1987), *Motion Sickness* (1991), *Cast in Doubt* (1992) – and two collections of short stories: *Absence Makes the Heart* (1990) and *The Madame Realism Complex* (1992). With Sheila McLaughlin she co-directed and wrote the movie *Committed* (1984). Between October and December 1994, Tillman was Writer-in-Residence at the University of Sussex where the following interview took place.

(Abbreviations: *H: Haunted Houses, M: Motion Sickness, C: Cast in Doubt, A: Absence Makes the Heart, MR: The Madame Realism Complex*.)

PN: Your parents were first-generation Americans of families from Russia and Austria. Do you feel that the emphasis in your work on displacement and exile echoes in some way that earlier experience?

LT: My parents' experience, as first-generation Americans of the early twentieth-century variety, is unlike that of the immigrants coming to America now, many of whom want to keep their own

Textual Practice **9**(2) 1995, 269–284

language. My parents' generation wanted to be Americans, to assimilate entirely, to leave their parents' generation behind, to leave Europe behind – because, of course, their Europe, their Russia, their Austria, was a place of oppression, pogroms. So it's incredibly hard to get even any information from them. But whether or not my knowledge of their decision, unconscious or conscious, to suture over all of that plays a role in my thinking about displacement, is hard to say. Later I became conscious of their difficulty, but not from them.

PN: In *Motion Sickness* you have the narrator say, 'It will probably be my fate not to learn other languages but to speak my own as if I were a foreigner' (*M*, 51). There's a question that the novel keeps raising about access to other languages, other codes, with a parallel sense of being alienated in one's own.

LT: I think it's the frustration one feels being born into one's body, and one's body politic. I'm always amazed when people can move from one culture to another and adopt the customs of another culture. Some people can do this, some people can really transplant themselves. I don't think I could.

PN: The attention you've shown to cosmopolitan experience strikes me as somewhat unusual in writers of your generation. Perhaps it ties you more to a slightly earlier group – Burroughs, the Bowleses and others – for whom Europe was an indispensable reference point, not to say an escape route?

LT: I was certainly interested in them, but before that I was fascinated by the period of the teens and the twenties, by the expatriate groupings in Paris, London and Zurich. Anyone fleeing. I suppose the desire was first to leave home, and then discovering that home is bigger than family, than your own tribe – that it includes the nation. That was something I contended with.

PN: What do you think you gained from the metropolitan cultures of London and Amsterdam that you wouldn't have found in your native New York – or, indeed, in other American cities like San Francisco or Chicago?

LT: I think I needed, with my insecurity about writing, just to be in another place. To survive. All the otherness around me allowed me to express my difference, my Americanness. It was easier to be an American in a way and to find my own language in the midst of people who weren't. The paradox is that you come closer to discovering what home is when you're far away from it. And how it influences you so you can try to break from it, because at least you see it.

PN: This was the period of the Vietnam war and its aftermath, of course, so there's also the question of being an outsider politically.

LT: It was a very heady, weird time – traumatic – after all those assassinations. It was extremely disturbing sometimes.

PN: The motifs of travel, movement, the journey, the quest have a central place in your work. I was reminded of the way travel also figures in Jane Bowles's fiction. She describes it as 'a sensation that lay between suffering and enjoyment' and she adds that for her character Lila, 'it had a direct connection with her brother's lies' – it's as if the ambivalent feelings occasioned by travel have some fundamental relation to fiction.

LT: In a way writing, like travel, is uncomfortable. Even if you get pleasure from it, and I do, the desire to do it also probably comes from tremendous frustration and a peculiar kind of displacement that you want to pin down. I don't actually find travelling that enjoyable, but on the other hand I have a greater fear of stasis. I mean I have a real fear that if I sit in my apartment, for a very long time, I'll lose any kind of perspective I have, that I really won't be able to see my thoughts at all. They'll simply be the wallpaper everything else is and I'll just accept everything. My fear is that I'll just accept all the ways in which I'm limited because I won't any more see them as limits. You begin to recognize your limits when you're up against the unfamiliar.

PN: In *Motion Sickness*, you use a quotation from Julia Kristeva as an epigraph: 'The expatriate represents, in fact, the normal state of an average citizen in this last part of the 20th century.' Why is that notion so suggestive for you?

LT: Because of issues around alienation... and the alien nation within. I was trying to turn a so-called anti-anti-travel novel [*sic*] into something that's really about the place you're in. Turning it on its head. I wanted to turn it all around and say, OK, here's this travel business, but you can think about this differently. You can think that where you are is also not a secure place to be, and that you're maybe feeling as uprooted as somebody who's not in their own country. I mean, think about all the different populations in America who aren't exactly served by that system.

PN: You remember Orwell's essay 'Inside the whale' on Henry Miller. He argues that expatriates always have a superficial sense of what's going on, a limited perception of the place they're in.

LT: In England I cringe when they talk about something I've done

as 'expatriate'. I think Oh my God I've written an expat novel.
There's something really hideous about that. I think part of why I've
done what I've done is an in-your-face thing. There's a real distrust
in the States of people who choose to live somewhere else. They're
losers, they can't make it. Whatever the Romantic tradition used to
be at the turn of the century, that no longer exists and more and
more people don't understand why you would even want not to live
in the United States. And I think that's probably going to increase.

PN: You often use tourism and movement as figures of desire in
your work, In *Motion Sickness*, for example, the narrator says of her
relationship with Zoran that 'We're best when we're in motion.
Which is probably why we fuck most of the time' (*M*, 104). But the
title of the novel is *Motion Sickness*, and mobility seems to be
shadowed by forms of fixity – 'National identity is like armor', the
narrator concludes at one point (*M*, 127). Are there positive and
negative forms of tourism? The novel does at one point refer to 'a
true tourism in which you would find yourself outside your home-
land, and outside your body, and see yourself with emotional vivid-
ness, as you can't, and in the roles you play to others . . .' (*M*, 120–1).

LT: Obviously I'm being ironic about calling it a 'true tourism'. It's
not that you *find* yourself, but that you can *look* at yourself. When
you go somewhere else and see new things you're also trying to be
a different person in a new place. Of course you can't ever do that
really. But what you keep hoping for is getting outside yourself, your
country . . . so that in a way you wouldn't exist. That may be a
'positive' form of tourism. (*laughs*)

PN: What exactly is the 'sickness', then?

LT: I think that any desire indicates lack. If you say 'I want', even
if it shows some sort of agency – that the 'I' wants something – it
also indicates that you don't have what you want at the time. So
there's this curious movement between these two poles of desire and
lack, which obviously come out of each other. I think in the same
way we move because we want some kind of satisfaction; on the
other hand, the desire for movement may be the product of an
unbearable and never-ending kind of sickness, which is that you can
never fulfil all the need for motion that you've got.

PN: *Motion Sickness* seems to express something like the situationist
sense of drift – there's a reference to the idea of the *dérive* at one
point (*M*, 149) – but at the same time that sense of abandonment is
very ambivalent. 'When longing's absent, when I feel no specific

desire for anything, anything I can name, I vacillate, feel determined, content or empty' (*M*, 193) – isn't that kind of ambivalence actually rather different from what the situationists had in mind? It seems to inform much of the speculation about desire and identity which runs through your work.

LT: Yes, I think so. You move between and among all those different states. In a way desire, libido, that sort of drive, that energy – without it you probably wouldn't do anything. But when you have it, when you're experiencing it very, very strongly, so that it's pushing you in all sorts of ways, you're also at its mercy. You can feel content, maybe, in the moment when you're not feeling that, but you're also in a static state. You may have a period of equilibrium but you're always going to head toward a state of disequilibrium.

PN: There are several moments in *Cast in Doubt* where Horace finds himself 'without or separate from desire'; 'Indeed I felt blank', he says (*C*, 141).

LT: Yes – a desire not to desire. I'm working on a story now in which a woman likes to watch pornography. But to say 'I like this', or to say 'I want to see this', means that those things are not in her life. That's the implication. That's why nobody wants to be caught wanting. We're filled with desires, but you're not supposed to say that you have them. Because if you have them, it means that you're lacking.

At the ICA panel on *Straight Sex*, Lynne Segal in November talked about female heterosexual agency in so-called straight sex that everybody agrees is not so straight. Later all I could think about was that implied in the term 'I desire' is its own negation, a negation of agency. If you desire then you have a problem. But you can always say, 'I wanted him and I *got* him.'

PN: But he wasn't good enough!

LT: Then I wanted someone else!

PN: Can we go back to your first book, *Haunted Houses*? I gather the title comes from a passage in H. D.'s *Tribute to Freud* where she says that 'We are all haunted houses.' At the end of the novel that haunting is described as 'A bad feeling that someone or something is never going to let you alone' (*H*, 206). What kind of someone or something were you trying to get at in this novel?

LT: I guess it's a question of personal history, psychological history, of one's family, which never leaves you alone. The idea that you can be completely free of that is bogus. Moving from personal history into public history, your present is always inflected by your past. I believe one can move, with a lot of psychological work, further away from the neurosis of the family, but perhaps never completely.

PN: There's certainly a lot of interest in this first book in forms of recollection and repetition. The young women in the novel fear they will repeat the lives of their mothers, and it's as if the conventions of feminine behaviour are felt with the intensity of some sort of trauma. In other words, there's a memory of something you haven't experienced directly . . .

LT: Being a woman is a memory I haven't had. It's a cultural memory. It's extremely interesting that you pick this up because I think the way in which we're constructed as men and women is pretty violent. It's active, it's constant. . . . I remember reading about one of the early transsexuals who would say that it was very hard work being a girl, making sure that he did all of the right things . . .

PN: The idea that a gendered identity takes work connects with some of the things Judith Butler has been writing about recently. She talks, for example, of gender as something 'tenuously constituted in time' through 'a stylized repetition of acts'.

LT: Absolutely. I wonder if she also read people like Garfinkel, Sacks, and Goffman. Because that was their point, that this wasn't something simple, that doing gender was hard work.

PN: Perhaps this is where we get some sort of connection between gender and being haunted by memories which come from somewhere else? I mean it's your mother being feminine that you remember. Similarly, in *The Madame Realism Complex*, 'Paige suffers mainly from reminiscences', a phrase which refers us directly to Freud on hysteria. How did this psychoanalytic theme develop in your thinking?

LT: I came to Freud because a number of people in my extended family were being analysed in the fifties. Later, when I went to college in the mid-sixties I saw a psychotherapist who was a Freudian, not an analyst but who was taught by Freudians. I think my first way in was through practice, and then I began reading some Freud and arguing with my male psychotherapist about penis envy. Reading Juliet Mitchell's *Psychoanalysis and Feminism* was extremely important for me. And then there was film theory – Laura Mulvey, Peter Wollen, and others.

PN: May I ask, in parenthesis, how you came upon the Madame Realism persona? Why 'Realism'?

LT: She's not a persona. In 1983, I got a phone call from somebody asking me to contribute to a Surrealist magazine. I thought that that was idiotic, I thought people going around thinking they're Surrealists is crazy. Then I began thinking about Meret Oppenheim whom I'd interviewed in Paris in '73, then in New York in '78. I thought about how she had talked about being only twenty-one when she made the *Fur Tea-Cup and Saucer*, and how Max Ernst was her lover and she left him because she didn't want to be influenced by him. There was the problem of young women in the Surrealist movement, how difficult it was for them. 'Madame Realism' was a retort to Surrealism. It really doesn't have to do with realism.

PN: Going back to *Haunted Houses*, the three female characters seem almost permeable with each other. The reader finds it hard to pull them apart.

LT: That's what Paul Bowles said too. He said it was like a Russian novel, that he couldn't keep them apart, but that he liked that. It was deliberate. In so many novels characters were pitched against each other, to represent so many different ideas, and then there would be a clash. Lawrence is the perfect example of that. I was interested in the social as well as the psychological, how these interpenetrated. I thought if you took a particular moment you could find girls being turned into girls and there would be a lot of similarities, questions about virginity, their mothers, their fathers. So, yes, they would be as much like each other as unlike each other – maybe more so. It was so confusing to me I had to make a chart to remember the characteristics I had given to Emily, Jane or Grace.

PN: There's something similar about character in *Motion Sickness* . . .

LT: Yes, in the 'I' being unnamed, but I wanted to do the opposite there, which was to go from characters who never met each other, as in *Haunted Houses*, to ones who constantly meet. I wanted to play with that happening and see if I could get away with it.

PN: One major theme of the book seems to be summed up in a quotation you give from Simone de Beauvoir: 'It is a strange experience for whoever regards himself as the One to be revealed to himself as otherness, alterity.' That awkward passage from self to other seems to provide one of the main dynamics in your narratives.

LT: I think I'm more comfortable with 'identity' than with 'self'.

There's something historically about 'self' that assumes one owns it. With 'identity' or 'subjectivity' you have the sense that it's shot through with others already. There's something very painful about *Haunted Houses* and not painful about *Motion Sickness*. There is the anxiety of recognizing how really unstable your identity is in *Motion Sickness*. When you meet others on the road, your relation to yourself can change. *Haunted Houses* is more painful because the girls are trying to achieve some identity, as if they'll be able to. By the time I wrote *Motion Sickness*, my sense was that there was no use in trying. You're not going to achieve a stable existence, but that's not so terrible in a way. It might make you sick, though, once in a while, because of that motion.

PN: It reminds me that in the story called 'Madame Realism', the narrator decides that 'Anything can be a transitional object. No one spoke of limits, they spoke of boundaries. And my boundaries shift, she thought, like ones do after a war when countries lose or gain depending on having won or lost' (*MR*, 39). The reference to Winnicott's concept of 'transitional objects' seems to have a relevance to your sense of how fiction operates – perhaps as (to use another concept from Winnicott) a 'potential space' somewhere between psyche and world where a certain 'play' can take place?

LT: In criticism you always have to make one argument, and you have to support that argument against other arguments. In writing a novel or a short story there are arguments going on too, but there you have the possibility of different voices and different characters. You don't have to argue as if there's one truth, or one way to see something, you can allow for a lot of ambivalence. In some way writing fiction for me is about anxiety and being extremely insecure, and having between me – and maybe this is Winnicottian – between me and the world a space where I say, this is not me, and it is me, ambivalently, but this is also not Truth.

PN: *Motion Sickness* suggests that national identity is like armour; in *Haunted Houses* are we meant to conclude that gender is similarly a kind of defence and constraint?

LT: Yes, I think I very much felt that when I wrote *Haunted Houses*. All my books are in a way about limits, and about fighting those limits. *Haunted Houses* definitely was about the limits of gender and of being a girl, how you took it on, how you wrestled with it; then with *Motion Sickness* it was national identity and nationalism. But you never want to celebrate your limits, you don't want to celebrate being an American, to celebrate being a woman. That's making a virtue out of something that's neither a vice nor a virtue. It's a given. You're born into something and it's a matter of what you do with that.

PN: Relations between self and other seem to be played out visually a lot of the time – in *Haunted Houses*, for example: 'there was a chance of being looked at, which was better than being spoken to: it was as if she were being taken, unaware and involuntarily, and not taken' (*H*, 62).

LT: Being looked at – again this would be an interesting argument that pornography is not rape – looking at something and having a fantasy is different from being thrown into the bushes and raped. This could also lead into a discussion about aspects of female desire and whether a woman's desire to be looked at is passive or active. I tend to feel those terms, 'passive' and 'active', are – well, talk about permeable! There's a way, oddly enough, that you can be very active in being looked at. Being extremely aware of that. It's not a position of powerlessness. Women like to look too.

PN: The gaze, of flirtation or voyeurism, seems bound up with another major theme of this novel, which is the artificiality of gender. Early on, Grace is warned against promiscuity by her brother: ' "You did it when you were my age," she said. "I'm a guy," he said, "it's different." "Fuck difference," she said' (*H*, 37). The novel as a whole seems to 'fuck difference' in its play with forms of androgyny, transvestism, and so on. Would that be the right place to put the emphasis?

LT: In the sense of a binary division. It's a very hard thing to discuss. I'm such an anti-essentialist that while I recognize that there is difference, what that means will always be unknown for me. Why hierarchies come into being, how those kinds of differences are arrived at. And while you don't know, there's the area you can play. The space in which our ignorance of why things come to be the way they are can also give us the room and energy to fuck around, not to accept things for what they are.

PN: The characters are haunted by the seemingly absolute forms of sexual difference then? And the novel seems to gesture toward an opposite idea of gender as fiction. Your references in the novel to Susan Sontag's essay on Camp reminded me that she had proposed some of these ideas well before Judith Butler and others. Sontag says, for example, that 'the most refined form of sexual attractiveness . . . consists in going against the grain of one's sex'; and she defines Camp as 'the triumph of the epicene style. (The convertibility of "man" and "woman", "person" and "thing").' How important were these ideas to *Haunted Houses*?

LT: Haunted by difference, yes, and also by the possibility of agency. 'Camp' was a revelatory essay for me. Unfortunately Sontag pulled back from those concerns. You would have felt from that essay that in the seventies she could have been a very sophisticated feminist. But she wasn't, and in fact I think she's something of an anti-feminist. Those kinds of ideas were important. The first gay male friend I had was when I was eighteen. I thought of feminism and gay liberation as working the same terrain. To me at that point it was all about not accepting what you were being handed on the sexual platter – what roles.

PN: There's a passage from Andy Warhol which you quote in one of your new pieces called 'Love Sentence': 'Once you see emotions from a certain angle, you can never think of them as real again. That's what more or less has happened to me.' Has it happened to you?

LT: How do you deal with love? Is it a limit, or is it something that's so explosive it's not a limit? This thing we feel to be unique when we experience it is so common. Warhol did have love affairs. He did in the last years of his life live with somebody, I believe. I think the kinds of questions you set for yourself around what you're feeling can stop you from just being able to throw yourself into it. Also, there's the problem of emotional repetitiveness.

PN: There's a related interest here in breaking with conventional forms of narrative. In one of your later stories, Madame Realism writes in her notebook: 'Beware of premature closure' (*MR*, 147), and this distrust of narratives which are driven by a need for endings is already there in *Haunted Houses*.

LT: Yes, that's right.

PN: And a lot of this depends on how you think about memory. *Haunted Houses* offers at least two different views: Jane, for example, thinks that 'there was just as much invention in versions of the past as in what's written about the future' (*H*, 100), while Jimmy wonders whether 'remembering things keeps you from thinking new thoughts' (*H*, 103).

LT: I don't think you have a choice between these two. Memory is in fact very active. A sociologist who read *Motion Sickness* in manuscript said he was disgusted by it because the narrator was so passive. And I said what do you mean 'passive'? She thinks all the time.

PN: 'Grace thought her time in bars would lead to something but Lisa said she shouldn't expect anything to lead to anything' (*H*, 146). In *Motion Sickness* you describe a fight as 'much less conclusive' than a prizefight or a baseball game – 'It's much more like fiction' (*M*, 21). How does this inconclusiveness relate to the narrative desire to connect one thing with another?

LT: They're in bed together. You wouldn't have that desire to connect one thing with another unless there was all this inconclusiveness. Again, it's the absence of an ability to make a conclusion that draws you to want to make connections.

PN: That recalls Gertrude Stein's comment about any assemblage of heterogeneous things already containing implicit narrative links.

LT: I'm sure she was influenced by the Kuleshov experiment in film, that when you edit, you can put images together and no matter what, the viewer makes connections. Take what Tarantino does with narrative in *Pulp Fiction*. I began to think of it as a kind of time-line being stretched, and the end, what kind of end is that? They just walk out a door. It's circular, begins again. It's a very complicated handling of narrative. Going back to that fight in *Motion Sickness*, it has an ending in the sense that the two men separate, but who is the winner? You know that they're in a relationship with each other, but the question of who won or lost will depend on the version of the story you're going to hear from each of the participants. What does it mean to come to a conclusion? Jouissance, I suppose. Coming to a conclusion.

PN: In 'Madame Realism', we're told that 'stories do not occur outside thought. Stories, in fact, are contained within thought. It's only a story really should read, it's a way to think' (*MR*, 108). The point seems to be that narratives shouldn't be locked up in a distinction between true and false, but are actually ways of articulating ourselves.

LT: Yes, I was trying to take narrative out of the realm of untrue, irrelevant, not profound. . . . Some people say 'I never read a novel, I read theory', and so on. The same people might argue against a high/low split but say they don't read novels. You could say the novel's an old form; with the computer why should people read stories and novels? I wanted to argue that any form you use represents a way of thinking, ideas. Do you read things only because you identify with them or can you disidentify with them too?

PN: One of the interesting things about these stories is the connection you seem to pursue between narrative and the familial, the Oedipal. 'All ideas are married', says Madame Realism (*A*, 105), and in the story called 'Absence Makes the Heart', the death of the father seems somehow connected with the idea of the Woman as solitary and mystified – 'Her reluctance must be read as a mystery, a deception from one whose own creation was exampled in the stories he loved' (*A*, 69). It's not immediately clear to me whether the loss of the father signals the failure of narrative or freedom from it.

LT: What if the loss of the father, her recognition of him as now symbolic, in fact enables her to see herself in the story, a story that men have of her?

PN: She becomes the narrator instead of being just the Woman?

LT: That's right. It's like saying: you're placing me in the story in certain ways but I have needs, I have desires. I'm the subject of my own story, I'm not just the object in your story.

PN: There's a passage in *Motion Sickness* where the narrator remembers her father's voice: 'It's my father's voice at the Leaning Tower, distracting me just the way he does when I eat veal parmigiana and it sticks in my throat because I know how much he loved it. I'm eating for two, if indeed I've incorporated him à la 'Mourning and Melancholia' (*M*, 69). I keep coming up against this network of references in your fiction: the loss of the father, the idea of mourning as a lump in the throat impeding communication, and above all a sense of resulting perplexity and confusion. It seems important that Paige's harrowing recollection of her father in 'To Find Words' leads to her feeling 'lost at sea and cast in doubt' (*MR*, 25). It's a question of narrative again . . .

LT: Writing is always about loss in some way. Maybe for me my father's loss became the loss that took in all loss, which made me want to write in the beginning. But there's a way in which death is too easy, because death is everyone's conclusion. Death is the closure that's never closure. Because even if someone dies there are those alive who remember him or her. So the impact of that person's life is still felt in the people living after. I'm thinking about the AIDS epidemic. There's nothing conclusive about death except that it's something we all do. That's the curious thing about the paradox of using death – in a way I know that whenever I put death in my work it's the most vital thing to do, because we all feel so connected to it.

PN: In interviews you've often talked about *Cast in Doubt* in terms of a collision of modernist and postmodernist perspectives. Does the difference again have to do with conceptions of narrative?

LT: I wanted to do many things in that book, including figuring out how to tell a story that reflected on story-telling and on how we read stories.

PN: It does seem that Horace can only reach a sense of self by seeing himself as a character in a story. There's a curious passage where he says 'While I accept the Greek version of destiny, or fate, as in tragedy, when one's end flows from one's flaws, from hubris, I abhor the idea that one's life is fated' (C, 160). But the Greeks couldn't dissociate those ideas, and are you suggesting that Horace ultimately can't either (his novel is, after all, called *Household Gods* . . .)?

LT: That is a strange passage. I think I wanted, because I was playing off the Greek material, the notion of an inevitability, certain things set in motion, from x to y to z. But as a modernist, Horace also wants to think about progress and about his own ability to insert himself in the story and make a change. There's a certain kind of optimism in that, but it's confused. He's confused by two kinds of narrative, the narrative of inevitability and the narrative of change.

PN: Horace is caught up in this web of imagined plots, whereas Helen and Gwen function with 'no plan, no plot' (C, 160), they pursue no ideal or truth, they are a 'new breed' (C, 147). Again it seems relevant that Horace tries to understand Helen in terms of 'some family tragedy' (C, 97), and that the graffiti in her room reads 'OEDIPUS WRECKS'. Has the 'new breed' achieved some sort of freedom from the Oedipal guilt-trip?

LT: This is from Horace's point of view . . .

PN: He's trying to embed them in an Oedipal plot that the reader can see they somehow evade. Especially in Helen's case because she does disappear.

LT: She disappears and we don't know what her history is. We do know in the sense that everyone has a father or mother, we know there's an Oedipal drama. Can we avoid that? No. The question is how do you work with that in a story. How conscious of that are you in your own story-telling and in your life?

PN: Horace says, 'I also believed that in our souls we were in deep and profound unity . . . she was, I assumed, like me' (C, 148). But the reader knows they really have nothing in common, and Horace's fantasy about Helen's 'special androgynous quality' (C, 148) is actually more Platonic than it is postmodern . . .

LT: One of the problems in Horace's life is that he would believe that he should not experience any kind of lack. He would think that there was a wholeness there for him to have. Whereas, in my mind, a Helen or a Gwen would understand that that's always an illusion. Let's say, no cure.

PN: Are you suggesting some sort of fundamental difference between this fantasy of androgyny – as original, prior to sexual difference – and the sort of thing Warhol and the Factory explored? Gwen, for example, 'admires Warhol precisely because of the falsity of his work, which actually makes it true, to her way of seeing and thinking, which is not mine' (C, 155).

LT: I subscribe more to a notion of bisexuality than to one of androgyny. I was also trying to think about homosexuality not as a fixed sexual position, so that a man who was a homosexual could also have desire for a woman at some moment, just the way a heterosexual man might have a desire for homosexual experience. Desire is pretty wild, and can move around, and be very unsettling. Horace wants to think she's androgynous rather than thinking that he might be more bisexual – unfixed – than he thinks. In other words, rather than seeing it – instability – in himself he's seeing it in her.

PN: We've talked quite a bit about narrative; maybe we should think too about tone and about your exploitation of particular figures of speech. *Cast in Doubt* is tonally rich, of course, but that's partly parodic. Other books, particularly *Haunted Houses*, seem to cultivate a certain lack of tone; sometimes the style reminded me of forms of naturalism. Whole passages of flat, short sentences which made me think of Dos Passos in the way one thing or event is simply placed against another. An emphasis on the local and contiguous rather than on some overall structure or plot, perhaps . . .?

LT: I don't think of the style of *Haunted Houses* as flat. It's angular, sharp. The edges between sentences are tough – take no prisoners. The structure too is angular – three characters who never meet, three chapters for each of the five sections, no greased transitions. I was interested in how gaps make meanings, how juxtapositions work. I'm always involved in that, pushing one set of ideas up against another. That's maybe what you think of as naturalistic. And all that makes strange disturbances. *Haunted Houses* is grimly funny sometimes.

Motion Sickness is more fluid, playing off a stream of words, associations; its structure is almost circular, with the first chapter, to my mind, a trailer for the upcoming feature. *Cast in Doubt* is arch, even toying with being precious. The structure is filled with holes, anxious ones. Each work is supposed to have its own integrity.

PN: And the style is always aware of itself, of the effects it's aiming for. At first glance it just seems witty, but there's another layer where you start stripping away the cottonwool of metaphor: 'She chooses a piece of silverware as if it were a weapon. But she does not attack her food' (*A*, 106). This kind of effect reminds me of Brecht's advice to his actors, to speak their lines as if they were bracketed within quotation marks.

LT: Books are made of words, characters are made of words. I like to call attention to that. To me it's pleasurable. It's like watching a movie. If the film-maker isn't using the camera well, using that medium as if there weren't a camera, or if the editing isn't really interesting, what are you watching? You're not actually watching something that's taking advantage of the medium.

PN: What I called 'bracketing' is also something that I think you've explored in your work with film. In an interview about *Committed* you say that you 'used certain narrative codes but then veered away from them sharply and used other, more avant-garde ones – deliberately going back and forth.' There's certainly an emphasis in the movie on construction – of image, identity, of power – which is deeply unsettling . . .

LT: It's very disturbing to recognize how constructed things are and to find yourself in a set-up you never made. In *Committed*, Frances Farmer is shown as trapped in different narratives or languages – family, love, law, psychiatry, femininity. That's why I was attracted to her life. She was a tragic, famous figure, her plight was dramatic but not really unusual. How do you get to all that, as a writer or film-maker, and make it extreme, let's say, visible and visceral, which we wanted to do? One way is to upset the delivery system, the codes.

PN: In the same interview you observe that 'A very important effect of feminism on psychoanalysis has been in talking about the institution as being descriptive rather than prescriptive.' You go on to say that the discovery that 'through speaking you can undo things, has made a big difference'. That seems to tie together your various interests in psychoanalysis, film and language, and to set up the narrative and stylistic techniques we've talked about as a means of 'undoing' things. Could you comment on that ten years on, in the light of what you have written since that interview?

LT: I'm less certain now about what can be undone, though I still believe in talking and writing, making things or unmaking them if possible. Seeing ideas as descriptive not as prescriptive is still important to me. That's why I'm against censorship and interested in offensive jokes. I'm using them in the novel I'm working on now, *No Lease on Life*. I'm questioning notions of outer and inner, public/ private, how each of us – how I – exist in a framework in which we are affected, bombarded, by the world, and still manage to think, feel, have our own worlds. Writing becomes more important to me even if it sometimes feels more futile. (*laughs*) More feudal.

University of Sussex

Jo-Ann Wallace

Technologies of 'the child': towards a theory of the child-subject

Abstract

This article argues that 'the child' and 'childhood' function as points of aporia and anxiety in the field of subject theory and it outlines the possibilities for a theory of the 'child-subject'. The paper describes the current historical moment as one of 'child panic', outlines existing scholarship on constructions of childhood, points to the blindness of theory to the foundational category of 'the child', suggests how some of poststructuralist theory's insights can be turned to the question of 'the child', and asks what light a consideration of the 'child-subject' can shed on emerging theories of citizenship. It concludes by drawing a parallel between late nineteenth-century anxieties regarding childhood 'white slavery' and current instances of child panic, suggesting that 'the child' becomes a site of increased anxiety and surveillance in response to the dismantling of the humanist subject by, e.g., evolutionary theory, early psychoanalytic theory, or poststructuralist theories of the subject. The paper is informed by the following questions: what kinds of activities does an idea of 'the child' authorize? and what kinds of symbolic management does an idea of 'the child' enable?

Keywords: child; childhood; children; subject

'There can be no concepts of childhood which are socially and politically innocent.'[1]

The title of my paper implies a brave Foucauldian promise, 'technologies of "the child"' seeming to suggest an exploration both of the disciplinary apparatuses by which children are simultaneously

Textual Practice **9**(2) 1995, 285–302   © 1995 Routledge 0950–236X

produced and subjected, *and* those practices by which children come to recognize themselves as desiring subjects. Its subtitle, however, expires into a fainthearted deferral. Not only will the paper *not* attempt a coherent theory of the child-subject, though it will point *towards* the need for one, it will not discuss children as historical agents. These two gaping holes – no theory, no children – reflect, on the one hand, the relative absence of theoretical sophistication in the field of, for example, children's literature criticism and, on the other, the continuing absence of children in theories of subjectivity, particularly in emerging theories of citizenship.[2] Although this paper cannot *fill* either of these holes, it will attempt to trace the contours of the second.

What I want to suggest here is that 'the child' and 'childhood' function as points of aporia and anxiety *in the field of theory*. That is, the category of 'the child', a foundational product of the modern episteme, remains an unacknowledged and therefore unexamined organizing principle – *not only* of the modern nation-state in its relations with many of its own citizens and those of the so-called *developing* world, but *also* of what we might call, borrowing a term from Ross Chambers, 'oppositional' theory. In the remainder of this paper, I want to outline the possibilities for what we might call a future theory of the 'child-subject'. As my use of quotation marks here and elsewhere indicates, I am using the term 'the child' to denote a subject-position rather than an identity based on biological immaturity. Historically, 'the child' has never been a subject-position available to all, or even most, children; moreover, it has frequently been a subject-position imposed on colonized adults. The remainder of my paper will touch on some of the scholarship to date on constructions of childhood, point to the blindness of theory to 'the child', and suggest how some of theory's insights can be turned to the question of 'the child'. In other words, I want to look not only at what theory – particularly theories of the agential subject – can offer to an analysis of the category of 'the child', but also what light that category can shed on theory. The questions informing such a project might be: what kinds of activities does an idea of 'the child' authorize? and what kinds of symbolic management (to use Mary Poovey's term) does an idea of 'the child' enable?

Child panic

This paper is written in an historical moment of massive anxiety in the West about the capacities, the safety, and the status of children.

We are all familiar with the ways in which images of 'the child' are deployed to stand in for humanitarian concern regarding crises of war and famine in the world 'out there'; however, 'the child' is also the increasing focus of anxious regard *at home*.[3] This is nowhere more evident than in representations of 'the child' in the news media. In February 1993 in Liverpool two ten-year-old boys abducted and murdered a two-year-old. The crime reverberated not only because of the age of the participants, but because it had been carried out, as it were, *under surveillance*: two sets of security cameras and various passersby had observed the crying and resisting two-year-old with his abductors.[4] This event overshadowed another which had occupied the British media: in Wales a fifteen-year-old schoolboy had been found guilty of raping a classmate; the judge awarded him a suspended sentence on condition that he pay his victim five hundred pounds to enable her to take 'a good holiday'.[5] Callers to radio phone-in shows suggested that the *parents* of such children – that is, the parents of murderers and rapists – should be tried for their children's crimes. Others, including Prime Minister Major, suggested that the age of criminal responsibility should be lowered – 'Society needs to condemn a little more and understand a little less.'[6] At what age is a child fully agential? What is the relationship between agency and culpability?

In 1989 and 1990 in Canada a nine-month royal commission meeting in St John's, Newfoundland, heard evidence of the sexual abuse and torture of boys practised by the Christian Brothers who ran the Mount Cashel orphanage during the mid-1970s. At that time, twenty-six boys complained of abuse; a 1975 report by a detective with the Royal Newfoundland Constabulary was altered, the investigation was quashed, and no charges were laid.[7] The continuing social repercussions of the Mount Cashel story – for the individual boys, now men, and for the community – prompted the Canadian media to question to what degree children, folded away in the privacy of such institutions as the orphanage, the school, the family, are vulnerable to sexual and physical abuse by their adult guardians. One might also ask whether the domestication of 'the child' has contributed to such abuse?

A recent issue of *The New Yorker* documents the case of Baby Clausen whose Iowa biological parents and Michigan adoptive parents have been engaged in a two-year custody battle. At issue are such fundamental questions as the rights and legal status of a child: Iowa law dictates that the rights of birth parents supersede those of their children; the Michigan court 'ruled that [the child] was a resident of Michigan, and that, since the Iowa courts had been unable to consider her best interests, [it] would'.[8] As *The New Yorker* reporter put it, 'By the child's second birthday, she would be in an unprotected limbo, treated by the courts not as a person but as a disputed possession. She would have no legal mother, no legal name.'[9] What is the legal status of children? Can they represent themselves? Are they citizens?

Although there is alarming evidence that more children than we thought possible are sexually abused by adults and other children, one can none the less argue that the events I described above do not represent the lives of *most* children, that they are 'news' precisely because they are atypical, and that children today are under no more – and possibly less – threat than children of earlier historical periods.[10] However, this would miss the point that 'childhood', like 'femininity', stands in for and mediates larger social anxieties. This is true not only in the news media but increasingly in sectors of academic scholarship. The Winter 1993 issue of *Daedalus*, the journal of the American Academy of Arts and Sciences, is a special issue ambiguously titled 'America's Childhood'. Its cover design – which features lines of brightly coloured stick-people on which is superimposed the special issue title in crude, or child-like, scrawl – evokes in visual shorthand that which is typically attributed to childhood: the attraction to primary structures and colours, the still uncertain mastery of fine motor skills, the undeveloped but growing grasp of language – in short, it evokes a subjectivity-in-formation, a subject-to-be-educated. The articles include, among others, the following: 'Child poverty and public policy: towards a comprehensive antipoverty agenda'; 'Towards sustainable development for American families'; 'America's children and their elementary schools'; 'Thief of time, unfaithful servant: television and the American child'. In the words of the editor's preface, 'the articles examine what children are experiencing [socially and culturally] in the United States today.'[11] That is, the focus of the issue is on *children* – particularly children disadvantaged by race, ethnicity, and class – not on the more generalized and universalizing notion of *childhood* as suggested by the issue title. Given the focus and reform politics of the issue (which calls for 'study linked to action'), why is it called 'America's *Childhood*' rather than 'America's *Children*' or even (more accurately though less pithily) 'The Children of Disadvantaged Americans'? The editor calls the title 'an intentional pun' but does not explain its valencies. Obviously we can read it as referring to 'childhood in America', or as evoking the childhood *of* America (as a way, perhaps, of signifying a *new*-world set of social problems). What we cannot escape, however, is that the title refers not to a historically specific group of people (children) but to a state of being (childhood). To draw a couple of blunt analogies, it would be as if *Daedalus* had devoted a special issue to 'America's Femininity' or 'America's Negritude'. To be fair, this was not the intention of the editor who devotes most of his preface to criticizing the universalizing, middle-class assumptions and language of the 1992 report of the National Commission on Children. How is it, then, that the problems attached to children can still be subsumed under this kind of rhetoric? Why do children's advocates continue to appeal to the child's 'right' to a 'childhood'? What does the fact of advocacy tell us about the social and legal status of children? Can 'theory'[12] shed any light on these issues?

Constructing 'childhood'

This paper has an epigraph which is derived from a recent article by two sociologists of childhood, Alan Prout and Allison James: '[T]here can be no concepts of childhood which are socially and politically innocent.'[13] In what has been called an 'age of theory' this statement should provoke nothing more than a yawn of recognition; surely, by now, the discursive category of 'childhood' – like the categories of 'femininity' or 'the primitive' – has been unhooked from a discourse of 'the natural'. To a degree, of course, this unhooking *has* begun. In what follows I want to look at three locations in which this has happened – social history, radical pedagogy, and literary theory – and speculate a little about why these instances have not been more effective in furthering cross- , or trans- , or inter-disciplinary theoretical studies of 'the child' and 'childhood'. I want to leave in suspension for a moment the question of whether unhooking a discourse of 'the child' from a discourse of 'the natural' necessarily means unhooking it from children.

As Prout and James point out, 'A key concept in the dominant [social sciences] framework surrounding the study of children and childhood has been *development* and three themes predominate in relation to it: "rationality", "naturalness", and "universality" '.[14] The developmental model of childhood studies is, of course, most closely associated with developmental psychology – in particular, the foundational work of Jean Piaget – which elaborates an essentially biologistic and universalist paradigm of childhood 'based on the idea of natural growth'.[15] According to this model,

> Childhood . . . is important to study as a presocial period of difference, a biologically determined stage on the path to full human status i.e. adulthood. The naturalness of children both governs

and is governed by their universality. It is essentially an evolutionary model: the child developing into an adult represents a progression from simplicity to complexity of thought, from irrational to rational behavior.[16]

It may be useful to see Piaget's articulation of cumulative developmental stages as the place in which various knowledges of 'the child' – in formation since the Enlightenment – accumulate in a newly hegemonizing, because 'scientific', discourse. Prout and James point to Piaget's influence by, on the one hand, Comte's theory of social evolution in which 'the "savage" was seen as the precursor of civilized man' just as the child is precursor of the adult, and, on the other hand, Levy-Bruhl's work on 'primitive' thought. An idea of 'the child' develops in tandem with an idea of 'the primitive' and, as I have argued elsewhere, makes thinkable the European move from a mercantile to a colonial form of imperialism.[17] The concept of 'allochronism' which Johannes Fabian develops in *Time and the Other: How Anthropology Makes Its Object* has explanatory purchase in relation to constructions of 'childhood' as well as the 'other' of anthropological discourse. Allochronism, or the 'denial of coevalness', is 'a persistent and systematic tendency to place the referent(s) of anthropology in a Time other than the present of the producer of anthropological discourse'[18] – either by situating the referent *outside* of time and history, in the realm of the natural, or *prior to* the time of the anthropologist, that is, at an earlier stage of development.[19] Discourses of 'the child' are posited on both forms of allochronism, with the added complication that – as Philippe Ariès has observed – in Western culture 'the child' is also the repository of outmoded fashions, games and even genres.[20]

In fact, it was the 1960 publication of Philippe Ariès' important and controversial study, *Centuries of Childhood [L'Enfant et la Vie Familiale sous L'Ancien Régime]*, which inaugurated new interest in childhood *as a social construction*.[21] In it, Ariès argued that the West's idea of 'childhood' – as a separate stage in life characterized by the need for protection and education – is largely an invention of the early Renaissance. Born, in part, from the humanist revival of interest in theories of education and in vernacular languages, the idea of childhood was given philosophical grounding in such Enlightenment texts as Locke's *Some Thoughts Concerning Education* (1692), which famously described 'the child' as 'white wax', a *tabula rasa*, ready to receive any impression, any inscription, and Rousseau's *Emile* (1762), which sought to protect the fully 'natural' child from all writing, all texts save one – *Robinson Crusoe*. As I shall discuss below, the category of 'the child' remains caught in this tension between what one might call the empty and the full, between lack (of personality, attributes, and history) and excess (full natural presence). The idea of childhood was firmly consolidated by the middle of the nineteenth century as evidenced by a rising discourse of child management and discipline, together with a series of legislative reforms focusing on child welfare. Althusser has noted that in the nineteenth century the school replaced the church as the dominant ideological state apparatus,[22] and Ariès is most polemical – but also, I think, most moving – when he describes the effect, not only of the European movement towards universal and compulsory schooling, but of the relationship between the school and various *repressive* state apparatuses:

> Traditional apprenticeship was replaced by the school, an utterly transformed school, an instrument of strict discipline, protected by the law-courts and the police-courts. . . . Family and school together removed the child from adult society. The school shut up a childhood which had hitherto been free within an increasingly severe disciplinary system, which culminated in the eighteenth and nineteenth centuries in the total claustration of the boarding school. The solicitude of the family, Church, moralists and administrators deprived the child of the freedom he had hitherto enjoyed among adults. It inflicted on him the birch, the prison cell – in a word, the punishments usually reserved for convicts from the lowest strata of society. But this severity was the expression of a very different feeling from the old indifference: an obsessive love which was to dominate society from the eighteenth century on.[23]

This passage reminds us, of course, of Foucault's *Discipline and Punish*, and one could argue that (along with the family, perhaps) the school is a primary site of the kind of 'technology of power' that calls 'the child' into being.[24] Just as 'the criminal' is produced by the prison and 'the madman' is produced by the insane asylum, so 'the child' is produced by the school. This is true, of course, not only for children but for the production of colonized others as child-subjects through their schooling in the oppressor's culture, as Gauri Viswanathan has argued in her analysis of the beginnings of English literary study in India.[25]

One can, of course, discover other explanatory narratives for the emergence and development of an idea of childhood. Neil Postman, for example, argues that 'childhood' emerged in the West with the invention of the printing press which created literacy as a new criterion for fully social adulthood.[26] Thus it was a newly defined notion of the literate 'adult' that called into being a notion of the unschooled 'child'. Moreover, the rise of a print culture meant that children – the preliterate – could be protected from an adult knowledge, specifically knowledge about violence and sex, encoded in print. According to Postman, the rise of a television culture threatens the disappearance of childhood (which he describes as one of the 'great inventions' of the Renaissance) by eliminating the need to acquire special skills in order to have access to 'adult' culture and information. When we consider the historically unwavering association throughout Western modernity between 'the child' and various forms of schooling and discipline – much of it aimed at producing, in Foucault's terms, a 'docile body' – Postman's work on 'the child' seems to me less interesting than that of other educational theorists, particularly those articulating the field of critical or radical pedagogy. Here the work of Michael Apple and Henry Giroux is especially promising in its analysis of the ways in which, for example, the overt school curriculum legitimates certain knowledges while the 'hidden curriculum' – which works to distinguish between work and play, which disciplines the body through the imposition of rules governing its functions, and which inures the child to periods of inactivity and boredom – interpellates the child-subject as the worker-in-formation.[27] Ironically, however, as Giroux's work becomes more unapologetically 'theoretical', the figure of 'the child' seems increasingly under erasure.[28] In *Border Crossings: Cultural Workers and the Politics of Education*, for example, Giroux locates pedagogy as a 'form of cultural production', noting the ways in which 'schools function in the shaping of particular identities, values, and histories by producing and legitimating specific cultural narratives and resources'. He argues that 'critical pedagogy needs to develop a theory of educators and cultural workers as transformative intellectuals who occupy specific political and social locations.'[29] What seems to me *missing* from this important project is a more specific consideration or theory of what we might clumsily call pedagogy's *addressee*; that is, there seems to be no theory of 'the child-subject' to replace the more traditional developmental model of childhood. Giroux makes it clear that the product of radical pedagogy is ethical, critical, radically democratic citizenship – but whether the child is always-already a citizen (and what, outside a discourse of natural rights, this might *mean*) or whether citizenship is only *produced* through pedagogy (as it is, for example, in Locke's and Rousseau's treatises on education) is unclear.[30] On the one hand, Giroux's ideal of 'postmodern citizenship' is represented as dynamic and productive, a radically democratic *goal* born out of a 'discourse of hope';[31] progressive cultural workers, like their students, continually reaffirm their citizenship through dialogic engagement with their communities. On the other hand, students – as subjects-in-formation – are *prepared for* citizenship *by* their educators, the process of 'preparation' suggesting that citizenship is a privilege one *accedes to* rather than an engagement one continually reworks and reclaims.[32] Giroux's notion of critical 'literacy' further complicates the question of whether or not children are 'citizens' by suggesting that within critical democracy the 'political subject' must possess a degree of knowledge and experience which is simply unavailable to young children.[33]

'The child' in theory

To express this suspension of the citizen we are obliged to search in history and literature for categories that are unstable or express instability.[34]

In response to the philosophical question 'Who comes after the subject?' Etienne Balibar proposes the historico-political answer, '*After the subject comes the citizen*'; in 1789 'politics destroys the "subject" of the prince, in order to replace him with the republican citizen.'[35] Citizen Subject, as Balibar denotes him, is both subject and citizen, 'a *subject of the law*, the strict correlative of the citizen who *makes the law*'.[36] For Balibar, as for Giroux, the figure of 'the citizen' defined by the principle of equality – 'not only the actor of a founding revolution, a *tabula rasa* whence a State emerges, but the actor of a *permanent* revolution'[37] – represents utopic possibility. However, Balibar's use of the '*tabula rasa*' metaphor to indicate the site or suspension of 'the citizen' *prior to* the republican state suggests that 'the child' may be figured as the shadow cast by the Enlightenment figure of 'the citizen'. In the republican state, the child comes before the citizen as the citizen-in-formation, the citizen-in-training, not always subject *to* the law (one mark of an 'advanced' state being the degree to which it protects its 'young offenders' from the full weight of 'adult' law) and never able to represent him/her self (hence the growth of child advocacy movements).

The emergence of a discourse of childhood in Western Europe and Britain coincident with the emergence of a discourse of citizenship and Enlightenment rationality suggests the need for both a theory of the child-subject *and* a consideration of the ways in which 'the child' marks an aporia in many current theories of the subject. Admittedly, it is difficult at this stage to imagine how a theory of the child-subject might proceed, particularly since 'the child' is everywhere in representation (on Bennetton's billboards, on television shows, in the news) but almost nowhere in public *self*-representation. One might argue, to extrapolate from Jacqueline Rose, that in public culture 'the child' is nothing more than the site of the adult's representation and discursive address. As suggested by the title of her brilliant, but unfortunately least read, book – *The Case of Peter Pan or The Impossibility of Children's Fiction* – Rose explores ways in which 'the child' is produced *by* and *for* adult desire, specifically as a way of holding the unsettling question of sexuality at bay.

> I am using desire to refer to a form of investment by the adult in the child, and to the demand made by the adult on the child as the effect of that investment, a demand which fixes the child and then holds it in place. A turning to the child, or a circulating around the child – what is at stake here is not so much something which could be enacted as something which cannot be spoken.[38]

The 'something which cannot be spoken' is the adult's investigation, through the child, of origins – that is, of the ways in which our own identities are implicated in language, in sexual difference, in the constant reworking of our own memories of ourselves as children. On the one hand, 'childhood' offers a consoling fiction of development and eventual coherence; to quote Rose, 'Children are no threat to our identity because they are, so to speak, "on their way" (the journey metaphor [in children's fiction] is a recurrent one). Their difference stands purely as the sign of just how far we have progressed.'[39] On the other hand, 'childhood' unsettles our sense of self-presence and self-coherence. The fact that 'the child's' sexuality is, to use Rose's phrase, 'fragmented, component, and perverse'[40] reminds us of the fragility of our own mastery of sexual identity; 'the child's' body is similarly *in excess* – its unmanageability, its changes, its growth spurts, remind us that our own bodies are similarly unstable, in process, changing. One way, then, of understanding what I earlier described as the fullness and emptiness of the category of 'the child' is to argue that we evoke 'the child' and then empty the category of its material specificity as a way of regulating anxieties about somatic and psychic instabilities.

However, this explanation is only partly satisfying; it does not account for 'the child' as a category of social thought – that is, it does not account for the kinds of political, ideological *work* an idea of 'the child' authorizes. Nor does it account for the open question of 'the child's' political and legal status. Ultimately, the question that a theory of 'the child-subject' must address is the question of agency. Developmental models of childhood cannot allow for productive resistances, but if we look to contemporary theories of 'the subject' we are confronted once again with the mystery of the missing child. Moreover, the category of 'the child' destabilizes many of the premises of theories of the agential subject. Paul Smith's *Discerning the Subject*, which attempts to account for the possibilities of historical agency and resistance within theories of subjectivity, is a useful case in point. Smith argues that the human agent – which he defines as 'the place from which resistance to the ideological is produced or played out' – 'exceeds the "subject"' as it is constructed both by poststructural theory and 'the discourses against which ... theory claims to pose itself'.[41] He suggests that agency or resistance is possible but only within 'the interstices of the subject-positions which are offered in any social formation'; resistance here is 'regarded as the by-product of contradictions in and among subject-positions'.[42] The fact that within Western modernity children have fewer subject-positions available to them – they are not, for example, 'allowed' to work, to have sexual relations, to withhold their labour at school – complicates their possibilities for agency in Smith's theory. *How many* subject-positions does it take to create enough contradiction to allow for agency? Smith continues by arguing that

> it is perfectly possible that interpellation should be resisted - that it should fail, simply. What produces such a failure is history itself, embodied in the person who lives it and who makes it beyond as it were the immediate and direct call of ideology. A singular [or personal] history always mediates between the human agent and the interpellations directed at him/her.[43]

But *how much* personal history, how much experience, is enough? Six months? Two years? Eighteen years? What is clear from Smith's otherwise convincing theory of agential subjectivity is that, first, it is (to use an unfortunately fatuous term) 'adultist' in its assumptions and, second, our thinking in regard to the category of 'the child' is largely unchanged from the time of Locke. What are the repercussions of this for the child's political and legal status? Can children represent themselves – culturally, socially, politically – or is advocacy the only means by which their well-being can be safeguarded?

The (post)modern Babylon

At the beginning of this paper I suggested that we are in an historical moment of massive anxiety which organizes itself around problems of 'the child'. The question I left unasked was 'why now?' However, a more accurate question might be 'why again?' In 1885 W. T. Stead published a four-part series of sensational articles in the *Pall Mall Gazette* under the title 'The maiden tribute of modern Babylon'. The series was intended as an exposé of white slavery and child prostitution in London, and it claimed to uncover the degree to which working-class girls were sacrificed – often by their mothers and other women of their neighbourhoods – to the sexual appetite of 'the dissolute rich'. In Stead's hyperbolic words:

> London's lust annually uses up many thousands of women, who are literally killed and made away with – living sacrifices slain in the service of vice. That may be inevitable, and with that I have nothing to do. But I do ask that those doomed to the house of evil fame shall not be trapped into it unwillingly, and that none shall be beguiled into the chamber of death before they are of an age to read the inscription above the portal – 'All hope abandon ye who enter here.'[44]

This passage is of interest for its appeal to typically modern constructions of 'the child' as outside or prior to language and therefore presocial and without agency – in other words, as a figure of pathos. And yet, as Deborah Gorham and Judith Walkowitz have shown, in their anxiety to stabilize recognizably middle-class boundaries between childhood and adulthood in the face of an emerging category of adolescence, Stead and other late nineteenth-century purity reformers frequently misread the texts of these girls' lives. The evidence suggests that the actual incidence of white slavery was small; most prostitutes 'moved onto the streets in their late teens' and most 'had already had sexual relations of a noncommercial sort with a man of their social class'.[45] Many chose prostitution as the best of an admittedly limited set of options. And yet, Stead's series had significant juridical and social effects: two months after its publication, a new social purity organization – the National Vigilance Association – had formed 'to devote itself to the protection of young girls';[46] that same year, the Criminal Law Amendment Act raised the age of consent *for girls* from thirteen to sixteen. Working-class girls found themselves the objects of an increased technology of surveillance intended not only to protect them from wealthy male predators, but to inculcate in them habits of self-control.[47] I have argued in this paper that 'the child' is a mobile subject-position; in mobilizing the figure of 'the child' in their agitation, and in emphasizing active male sexual licence in contrast to the passivity – the emptiness – of the child-victim, middle-class social purity reformers ignored 'their own complicity in a more generalized exploitation of girls and young women',[48] that is, their own very material investment in manageable girls to serve as domestic labour. However, they also effected lasting changes in working-class culture through, for example, changes in child-rearing practices. As Walkowitz notes:

> The prescriptive literature distributed by social purity groups also seems to have influenced the child-rearing practices of the time. Edwardian working-class parents were notable for their strict schedules, puritanical treatment of masturbation, and for the severe restrictions they placed on their teenage daughters' social and sexual behavior.[49]

That is, the mobilization of the figure of 'the child' in response to a perceived set of social problems, regardless of whether children as a specific group are at 'real' risk, has 'real' effects on our productions of 'childhood' and the child-subject, and ultimately on the lives of children.

Walkowitz suggests that Stead's 'Modern Babylon' series was so spectacularly successful in part because it provided a narrative of sexual danger which 'both highlighted and managed the boundary disputes paradigmatic of metropolitan life';[50] that is, it worked in part to exploit and regulate social anxieties regarding the consolidation of women's access to various public spaces. Inaugurating the New Journalism, Stead's series was the first of a number of late nineteenth-century sensational sex stories which would culminate in newspaper coverage of the Jack the Ripper murders. The 'Modern Babylon' differed from its progenitors in its strategic deployment of the figure of 'the child' – thirteen-year-old 'Lily' (Eliza Armstrong), purchased for five pounds, silent in Stead's account but for a small 'bleat' of fear. I want to open up the scope of Walkowitz's analysis to suggest that the mobilization specifically of the figure of the child, today as a century ago, is *also* in anxious response to our two most recent 'ages of theory' – the first of which, in the mid to later nineteenth century, gave us evolutionary theory, Marxist theory, the first glimmerings of psychoanalytic theory, and the first wave of feminist agitation; the second of which, particularly since 1968, is newly working through the full repercussions of the first. At the end of *The Order of Things*, Foucault anticipates the coming-to-an-end of man – that is, Enlightenment man, 'man' as the product of a 'fundamental arrangement of knowledge'.[51] 'The child' as, in a sense, the repository *and* projection of all that is repressed by that 'arrangement' is the forgotten shadow cast not only by Enlightenment man but by poststructural man. 'The child' remains a mobile subject-position implying, as Fabian says of anthropology, a subject out of time; 'the child' is the subject to come – *not yet* literate, *not yet* capable of reason, *not yet* fully agential – but also the subject before now – the primitive, the prehistoric, the presymbolic, the presocial.[52] The mobility of the child-subject is evident, for example, in the rhetoric of (neo)imperialist expansion which still describes colonial others, in almost Piagetian terms, as occupying a stage of (economic or political) 'development', but also in the self-help movement's appeal to 'the child within', the older, truer self who coexists with us. Foucault speculates that a rearrangement of knowledge might mean 'that man would be erased, like a face drawn in sand at the edge of the sea'.[53] Is 'the child' similarly under erasure? Are there significant points of coincidence between discourses of 'the child' and the lives of children? How do we raise children in an 'age of theory' and radical uncertainty? If nothing else, we need to begin with an interrogation of the ways in which our practices and our theory either invoke and position the child-subject or altogether elide the figure of 'the child'.

Notes

An earlier version of this paper was presented at the 'Human Sciences in the Age of Theory' Conference at the University of Western Ontario in April 1993. I am grateful for the questions and comments of those who attended the session in which it was presented; I am also grateful to my research assistant, Mary Beth Wolicky, and to Len Findlay for his encouraging interest in the larger project of which this paper is a part. This project is funded by the Social Sciences and Humanities Research Council of Canada.

1 Alan Prout and Allison James, 'A new paradigm for the sociology of childhood? Provenance, promise and problems', in Allison James and Alan Prout (eds), *Constructing and Reconstructing Childhood: Contemporary Issues in the Sociological Study of Childhood* (London: The Falmer Press, 1990), p. 22.

2 I want to stress my use of the term '*relative* absence' since there has clearly been some significant work in the area (the work of Peter Hunt, Jacqueline Rose, and Jack Zipes comes immediately to mind). However, the field of children's literature criticism has been more resistant to 'theory' than other fields of literary and cultural study; where 'theory' has made incursions, it has normally been as a template applied to individual texts.

3 See, for example, Patricia Holland, *What is a Child? Popular Images of Childhood* (London: Virago, 1992).

4 See Ronald Faux, 'Mother's fears are confirmed as video boy is found dead', *The Times*, 15 February 1993, p. 3; Tim Rayment, 'Two boys face charges on Jamie's murder', *The Sunday Times*, 21 February 1993, p. 1.

5 See Andrew Alderson, 'Rape girl spurns attacker's £500', *The Sunday Times*, 7 February 1993, p. 9; 'Teenage rapist gaoled on appeal', *Guardian Weekly*, 21 March 1993, p. 3.

6 See Paul Koring, 'Stiffer sentences proposed for adolescent lawbreakers', *Globe and Mail*, 22 February 1993, p. A7.

7 See Nora Underwood, 'Scandal on the Rock', *Maclean's*, 2 October 1989; 'Sex and scandal', *Maclean's*, 30 October 1989; 'Charges of a coverup', *Maclean's*, 4 December 1989.

8 Lucinda Franks, 'The war for Baby Clausen', *The New Yorker*, 22 March 1993, p 69. As Franks also notes, 'On December 27th, Judge Paul J. Kilburg, of the Iowa District Court, ruled that, although the DeBoers had provided "exemplary care" for the baby, they had not proved that Schmidt had abandoned her. If established legal principles did not favor the rights of biological parents in such cases, even above those who could provide better homes, he said, then "the court would be engaged in uncontrolled social engineering." The court ordered the DeBoers' adoption petition denied and instructed them to return custody of Jessica to Daniel Schmidt' (p. 66).

9 ibid., p. 58.

10 See Ian Hacking's 'The making and molding of child abuse', *Critical Inquiry* 17 (Winter 1991), pp. 253–88, which argues, in part, that a discursive shift from a nineteenth-century emphasis on 'cruelty to children' to a late twentieth-century emphasis on 'child abuse' – seen within a framework of normalcy and pathology – can be traced largely to the medicalization of the phenomenon. See also Joel Best, *Threatened Children: Rhetoric and Concern About Child-Victims* (Chicago and London: University of Chicago Press, 1990).

11 *Daedalus* vol. 22, no. 1 (Winter 1993), p. vi.

12 I am using the term 'theory' much as it was used at the 1993 'Human Sciences in the Age of Theory' conference; that is, as shorthand for the academic field of post structuralist theory.

13 Prout and James, p. 22.

14 ibid., p. 10.

15 ibid., p. 10.

16 ibid., pp. 10–11.

17 Jo-Ann Wallace, 'De-Scribing *The Water-Babies*: "The child" in postcolonial theory', in Alan Lawson and Chris Tiffin (eds), *DeScribing Empire* (London: Routledge, 1994).

18 Johannes Fabian, *Time and the Other: How Anthropology Makes Its Object* (New York: Columbia University Press, 1983), p. 31.

19 See also Irving Hallowell, 'The child, the savage, and human experience', in Arlene Skolnick (ed.), *Rethinking Childhood: Perspectives on Development and Society* (Boston and Toronto: Little, Brown & Co., 1976), previously published as 'The recapitulation theory and culture', in *Culture and Experience* (Philadelphia: University of Pennsylvania Press, 1955).

20 In *Centuries of Childhood: A History of Family Life*, trans. Robert Baldick (New York: Vintage Books, 1962), Philippe Ariès calls this tendency 'archaizing' and notes the ways in which it connects ideas of childhood and ideas of class. See, for example, his discussion of children's costume (p. 57) and of children's games (p. 99):

> In every case the same evolution takes place with repetitious monotony.
> At first the same games were common to all ages and all classes. The phenomenon which needs to be emphasized is the abandonment of these games by the adults of the upper classes and their survival

among both the lower classes and the children of the upper classes. . . .
It is important to note that the old community of games was destroyed
at one and the same time between children and adults, between lower
class and middle class. This coincidence enables us to glimpse already
a connection between the idea of childhood and the idea of class.

21 Prout and James, pp. 1, 16. For a summary of Ariès' thesis and of critical
responses to it, see Chapter 1 of Linda A. Pollock's *Forgotten Children:
Parent–Child Relations from 1500 to 1900* (Cambridge: Cambridge University Press, 1983). See also Chapter 9 of Lawrence Stone's *The Family,
Sex and Marriage in England 1500–1800* (London: Weidenfeld & Nicol-
son, 1977) for an analogous examination of a new attitude towards childhood in England.

22 See Louis Althusser, 'Ideology and ideological state apparatuses', in *Lenin
and Philosophy and Other Essays*, trans. Ben Brewster (London: New
Life Books, 1971).

23 Ariès, p. 413.

24 Michel Foucault, *Discipline and Punish: The Birth of the Prison*, trans.
Alan Sheridan (New York: Vintage Books, 1979). For a discussion of the
ways in which institutional discipline produces the appropriately docile
child body, see Jo-Ann Wallace, 'Subjects of discipline: the child's body
in the mid-Victorian school novel', in Anthony Purdy (ed.), *Literature
and the Body* (Amsterdam: Rodopi, 1992).

25 Gauri Viswanathan, 'The beginnings of English literary study in British
India', *Oxford Literary Review* 9 (1987), pp. 2–26.

26 Neil Postman, *The Disappearance of Childhood* (New York: Dell, 1982).

27 In *Ideology and Curriculum*, 2nd edn. (New York: Routledge, 1990)
Michael Apple argues that schools 'play a rather large part in distributing
the kinds of normative and dispositional elements required to make
[socio-economic] inequality seem natural. They teach a hidden curriculum
that seems uniquely suited to maintain the ideological hegemony of the
most powerful classes in this society' (p. 43). Elsewhere he defines
the 'hidden curriculum' as 'the tacit teaching to students of norms, values,
and dispositions that goes on simply by their living in and coping with
the institutional expectations and routines of schools day in and day out
for a number of years' (p. 14).

28 In his introduction to *Border Crossings: Cultural Workers and the Politics
of Education* (New York and London: Routledge, 1992) Giroux notes
what he calls a 'rising anti-intellectualism' among US educators which
masks as 'calls for "real" practice, accessible language, and grassroot-level
politics' (pp. 1–2). Giroux rejects the 'binary opposition between theory
and practice' and argues that 'creating a new language is both an urgent
and central task today in order to reconstitute the grounds on which
cultural and educational debates are to be waged' (pp. 2–3).

29 Ibid., pp. 3, 76, 78.

30 Michael Apple similarly elides 'the child' when, in his introduction to
Ideology and Curriculum, he articulates what he calls three 'aspects' of
his programme: 'the school as an institution', 'the knowledge forms', and
'the educator him or herself', p. 3.

31 Giroux, p. 240.

32 '[E]ducators must prepare students for a type of citizenship that does not
separate abstract rights from the realm of the everyday and does not define

community as the legitimating and unifying practice of a one-dimensional historical and cultural narrative' (Giroux, pp. 133–4).

33 'Literacy in its varied versions is about the practice of representation as a means of organizing, inscribing, and containing meaning. It is also about practices of representation that disrupt or rupture existing textual, epistemological, and ideological systems. Literacy is critical to the degree that it makes problematic the very structure and practice of representation; that is, it focuses attention on the importance of acknowledging that meaning is not fixed and that to be literate is to undertake a dialogue with others who speak from different histories, locations, and experiences' (Giroux, p. 244). Chantal Mouffe's description of radical democratic citizenship, grounded in 'the political identity that is created through identification with the *respublica*', would also seem to preclude the possibility of the child-citizen since it assumes a degree of social and political sophistication of which the very young child is not yet capable. Within a paradigm of radical democracy, 'the citizen is not, as in liberalism, someone who is the passive recipient of specific rights and who enjoys the protection of the law'; instead, radical citizenship is 'a common political identity of persons who might be engaged in many different purposive enterprises and with differing conceptions of the good, but who accept submission to the rules prescribed by the *respublica* in seeking their satisfactions and performing their actions. What binds them together is their common recognition of a set of ethico-political values. In this case, citizenship is not just one identity among others – as in liberalism – or the dominant identity that overrides all others – as in civic republicanism. It is an articulating principle that affects the different subject-positions of the social agent . . . while allowing for a plurality of specific allegiances and for the respect of individual liberty.' See Mouffe, 'Democratic citizenship and the political community', in Chantal Mouffe (ed.), *Dimensions of Radical Democracy: Pluralism, Citizenship, Community* (London and New York: Verso, 1992), p. 235. For a more extended discussion of the denial of citizenship rights to children, see Bob Franklin, 'Children's political rights', in Bob Franklin (ed.), *The Rights of Children* (Oxford and New York: Blackwell, 1986), and Part II of David Archard's *Children: Rights & Childhood* (London and New York: Routledge, 1993). Chapter 8 ('Embryonic sexual citizenship: children as sexual objects and subjects') of David T. Evans's *Sexual Citizenship: The Material Construction of Sexualities* (London and New York: Routledge, 1993) describes the ways in which 'rights discourses for children . . . have crystallised around the conjunction of sexual, economic and political independence in ways usually concealed when the dimensions of adult sexual citizenship are discussed' (p. 239).

34 Etienne Balibar, 'Citizen Subject', in Edouardo Cadava, Peter Connor, and Jean-Luc Nancy (eds), *Who Comes After the Subject?* (London and New York: Routledge, 1991), p. 52.

35 ibid., pp. 38, 39.

36 ibid., p. 48.

37 ibid., p. 54.

38 Jacqueline Rose, *The Case of Peter Pan or The Impossibility of Children's Fiction* (London: Macmillan, 1984), pp. 3–4. This book has recently been republished (1993) with a new introduction, 'The return of Peter Pan',

which situates *Peter Pan* within the context of Conservative underfunding of public institutions (like the Great Ormond Street Hospital for Sick Children) and 'the crisis of child sexual abuse in the 1980s' (p. xvii).

39 ibid., p. 13.

40 ibid., p. 14.

41 Paul Smith, *Discerning the Subject* (Minneapolis: University of Minnesota Press, 1988), pp. xxxv and xxx.

42 ibid., p. 25.

43 ibid., p. 37.

44 W. T. Stead, 'The maiden tribute of modern Babylon', *The Pall Mall Gazette*, 6 July 1885, p. 2. See Judith Walkowitz's brilliant reading of 'Maiden tribute' – particularly its debts to other cultural forms like melodrama, myth, the literature of urban exploration, and late-Victorian pornography – in Chapters 2 and 3 of *City of Dreadful Delight: Narratives of Sexual Danger in Late-Victorian London* (Chicago: University of Chicago Press, 1992).

45 Judith Walkowitz, *Prostitution and Victorian Society: Women, Class, and the State* (Cambridge: Cambridge University Press, 1980), p. 19.

46 Deborah Gorham, ' "The maiden tribute of modern Babylon" re-examined: child prostitution and the idea of childhood in late-Victorian England', *Victorian Studies*, vol. 21, no. 3 (1978), p. 361.

47 ibid., p. 377. Walkowitz describes the 'political effects' of the 'Maiden tribute' as 'startling' and notes that the Criminal Law Amendment Act of 1885 'not only raised the age of consent for girls from thirteen to sixteen' but 'made indecent acts between [consenting] male [adults] illegal, thus forming the basis of legal proceedings against male homosexuals until 1967'. Walkowitz, *City of Dreadful Delight*, p. 82.

48 Gorham, p. 377.

49 Walkowitz, *Prostitution and Victorian Society*, p. 253.

50 Walkowitz, *City of Dreadful Delight*, p. 80.

51 Michel Foucault, *The Order of Things: An Archaeology of the Human Sciences* (New York: Vintage Books, 1973), p. 387.

52 See, for example, Julia Kristeva's 'Place names' in *Desire in Language: A Semiotic Approach to Literature and Art*, trans. Thomas Gora, Alice Jardine, and Leon S. Roudiez (New York: Columbia University Press, 1980) which proposes 'the child' as 'the real from which we begin our analysis . . . of our (any) language's *infantile* attributes' (p. 278). The essay opens (p. 271) with the following description of the West's repression of and return to 'childhood':

> Twice during the past few centuries Western reason perceived that its role of being a servant to meaning was imprisoning. Wishing to escape, it turned toward and became haunted by childhood. Witness Rousseau and Freud – two crises of classical and positivist rationality. And two revolutions loomed on its horizon: one in political economy (seeking its status in Marx), the other in the speaking subject (articulated today by modern literature's disruption of the Christian Word). Before Sade and Solzhenitsyn, who spell out jouissance and horror, analytic discourse was given a privileged foil, a nexus of life and language (of species and society) – the child.

53 Foucault, *The Order of Things*, p. 387.

Harriet Guest

The dream of a common language:
Hannah More and Mary Wollstonecraft

Abstract

This essay considers the similarities in the arguments of
Wollstonecraft's second *Vindicaton* and More's *Strictures* of 1799,
which were remarked on by readers in the late eighteenth and
early nineteenth centuries, and have received some recent critical
attention. Similarities between the two texts focus on the representation of the corruption perceived to be endemic among middle-
class women. The essay argues that this representation can best
be understood in the context of concerns about the role of women
as consumers and commodities in relation to the model of the
division of labour which dominated conceptions of commercial
culture in the period.

Keywords: Wollstonecraft; More; femininity; commerce; sexuality

I

'Have you read that wonderful book, The Rights of Woman', wrote
Anna Seward to Mr Whalley, on 26 February 1792. 'It has, by turns,
pleased and displeased, startled and half-convinced me that its author
is oftener right than wrong.'[1] Seward's enthusiasm for Wollstonecraft's
work, and sympathy for the trials of her life, seem to have endured
despite her passionate antagonism to political radicalism in England.
By August of 1792, she writes, with what is clearly a deeply felt
sense of personal as well as political alarm, of:

Paine's pernicious and impossible system of equal rights, [which]
is calculated to captivate and dazzle the vulgar; to make them

Textual Practice **9** (2) 1995, 303–323   © 1995 Routledge 0950–236X

spurn the restraints of legislation, and to spread anarchy, murder, and ruin over the earth.[2]

But neither Wollstonecraft's use of the discourse of natural rights, nor the scandal of her personal career, seem to have dismayed her. In 1798 she reports that Wollstonecraft's 'death shocked and concerned me',[3] and, in a letter to Humphry Repton, she writes in praise of Godwin's *Memoirs* that:

> Bearing strong marks of impartial authority as to the character, sentiments, conduct, and destiny of a very extraordinary woman, they appear to be highly valuable. Since, on balancing her virtues and errors, the former greatly preponderate, it is no disgrace to any man to have united his destiny with hers.[4]

Seward seems to have found in Wollstonecraft's work and life principles she could continue to admire even though she recognized the sympathy between Wollstonecraft's political opinions and the radicalism she hated and feared. She went on to explain, in her discussion of the *Vindication* of 1792, that:

> Though the ideas of absolute equality in the sexes are carried too far, and though they certainly militate against St Paul's maxims concerning that important compact, yet they do expose a train of mischievous mistakes in the education of females; – and on that momentous theme this work affords much better rules than can be found in the sophist Rousseau, or in the plausible Gregory. It applies the spear of Ithuriel to their systems.[5]

What's intriguing about Seward's comments, I think, is the implication that Wollstonecraft's arguments about the education of women are somehow separable from the politics of her *Vindication* of their rights. Seward links her admiration for Wollstonecraft as an educational theorist with her feeling for her as a woman victimized by what she described as her 'basely betrayed attachment to that villain Imlay,' rather than with arguments for rights to sexual and political equality.[6] Now, I don't want to suggest that it was commonplace for women who rejected Wollstonecraft's political views to see her theories on the education of women as a distinct body of beliefs, uncoloured by her radicalism, and capable of being uncoupled from the claim to sexual equality. Writing in July 1792, Sarah Trimmer, for example, remembered the second *Vindication* exclusively as a claim for 'a further degree of liberty or consequence for women' within marriage; a claim which, she felt, threatened her own 'happiness in having a husband to assist me in forming a proper judgement, and in taking upon him the chief labour of providing for a family'. Trimmer regretted that Wollstonecraft had not employed her 'extra-ordinary abilities ... to more advantage to society'.[7] In August of the same year, Horace Walpole wrote congratulating Hannah More on not having read the *Vindication*. Apparently confident of More's agreement, he observes that:

> I would not look at it, though assured it contains neither meta-physics nor politics; but as she entered the lists on the latter, and borrowed her title from the demon [Paine]'s book, which aimed at spreading the *wrongs* of men, she is excommunicated from the pale of my library.[8]

More herself claimed to find the notion of the rights of woman both absurd, and a regrettable staining of 'domestic manners ... with the prevailing hue of public principles'.[9] Whether or not they had actually read the second *Vindication*, these writers clearly perceived it in the context of a polemical genre associated primarily with the discourse of rights – they perceived it as a political text.

What I do want to suggest, however, is that for a surprising range of readers the educational theories of Wollstonecraft's work did represent a common currency apparently uninflected by political differences. These readers seem to identify substantial parts of the text, at least, with a subgenre of educational conduct books and satires on social morality which they do not perceive to be appropriate to the articulation of political views. They seem, perhaps, to see gender as a category of concern that cuts across political differences. Mary Berry, the society hostess and correspondent of Walpole and More, acknowledges this possibility most directly. She writes, in a letter of 1799:

> I have been able ... to go entirely through Hannah More, and Mrs Woolstonecraft immediately after her. It is amazing, but impossible, they should do otherwise than agree on all the great points of female education. H. More will, I dare say, be very angry when she hears this, though I would lay wager that she never read the book.[10]

In Hannah More's *Strictures on the Modern System of Female Education*, first published in 1799, and Wollstonecraft's *Vindication of the Rights of Woman: with strictures on political and moral subjects*, of 1792, Mary Berry detects an agreement on 'all the great points of female education' that would be amazing if it were not inevitable. And her observation may point up, I think, that aspect of the *Vindication* that seemed to Anna Seward to remove the text from political controversy, and to make it praiseworthy despite its arguments for sexual equality.

In a footnote to *The Unsex'd Females: A poem*, published in 1798, Richard Polwhele wrote that: 'Miss Hannah More may justly be esteemed, as a character, in all points, diametrically opposite to Miss Wollstonecraft.'[11] The polarization of the public and private characters of the two women is evident in the texts they produced, but nevertheless what seems to be common to them is the language, the discourse in which they characterize the corruptions of femininity. Their texts propose, on the whole, different remedies for that corruption, and identify its causes in markedly divergent terms. But the figure of the corrupt woman produced in these texts seems indistinguishable, and she seems characterized in terms that can stand independent of what Walpole and Polwhele saw as the absolute moral and political opposition of their views. That figure is, of course, familiar to any student of eighteenth-century writing on women. But I want now to examine her familiar features again, and to consider how they may illuminate the politics of feminism in the 1790s.[12]

II

Both More and Wollstonecraft allude, early in their arguments, to Hamlet's speech to Ophelia – 'You jig, you amble, and you lisp, and nickname God's creatures.'[13] And the allusion seems to trigger, in their very different polemical texts, strikingly similar rehearsals of an apparently misogynistic discourse. Wollstonecraft argues that women – and particularly middle-class women – are encouraged to acquire 'a kind of sickly delicacy ... a deluge of false sentiments and over-stretched feelings, stifling the natural emotions of the heart'(10). More similarly believes that 'unqualified sensibility' has been cultivated in affluent women, 'till a false and excessive display of feeling became so predominant, as to bring into question the actual existence of ... true tenderness' (VII, 79–80). It should be enough here to sketch only the outlines of the discursive construction of corrupt femininity that both texts then elaborate. In both, the feminine subject is represented as peculiarly the creature of her material circumstances, which absorb her perceptions and adapt or accommodate them to their own nature. More writes that:

> Women too little live or converse up to the standard of their understandings. .... The mind, by always applying itself to objects below its level, contracts its dimensions, and shrinks itself to the

size, and lowers itself to the level, of the object about which it is conversant.

(VIII, 57)

As a result of their preoccupation with trivial and unconnected phenomena, women are unable to generalize their ideas, are peculiarly localized, and cannot maintain a coherent train of thought. They are enthralled by novels, fascinated by manners, superficial appearances, surface ornamentation, distracted by isolated incidents and random, occasional events. The desire for continual and easy stimulation that these habits of mind entail results in a debilitating absorption in the sensible body, in the addictive pleasures of luxury, the lowest forms of taste. Women are slaves to the demands of the fashionable body for adornment, for epicurean and sexual sensation, for an endless diet of ever novel and artificial stimuli. . . . More writes that:

> To attract admiration, is the great principle sedulously inculcated into [a woman's] young heart; and is considered as the fundamental maxim; and, perhaps, if we were required to condense the reigning system of the brilliant education of a lady into an aphorism, it might be comprised in this short sentence, *To allure and to shine.*

(VII, 98)

Corrupted femininity is all surface, all display, lacking the detachment, the critical distance, necessary to the production of a continuous consciousness or integrity of identity capable of deferring its gratifications.

In Wollstonecraft's *Vindication* the analogy of travel provides a peculiarly revealing figure for the incoherence of feminine subjectivity. She argues that:

> A man, when he undertakes a journey, has, in general, the end in view; a woman thinks more of the incidental occurrences, the strange things that may possibly happen along the road; the impression that she may make on her fellow-travellers; and, above all, she is anxiously intent on the care of the finery that she carries with her, which is more than ever a part of herself, when going to figure on a new scene; when, to use an apt French turn of expression, she is going to produce a sensation. – Can dignity of mind exist with such trivial cares?

(60)

It may be worth noting that, in this passage, Wollstonecraft's writing seems almost to yield to the pleasures of the narrative that's afforded by the feminine attraction to incidental events and details, and almost to acknowledge that the woman does have an 'end in view' in her desire to produce a sensation, though it's an end that could only be appropriate to genres more amenable to sentiment, such as travel letters or the novel. But the point is that feminine lack of purpose is represented here as producing a kind of dissipation of subjectivity into a succession of accidents, so that feminine identity becomes indistinguishable from the finery, the things which 'are more than ever a part' of what it is that constitutes its tenuous and apparent continuity. More argues, in an intriguingly similar image, that:

> The female . . . wanting steadiness in her intellectual pursuits, is perpetually turned aside by her characteristic tastes and feelings. Woman in the career of genius, is the Atalanta, who will risk losing the race by running out of her road to pick up the golden apple; while her male competitor, without, perhaps, possessing greater natural strength or swiftness, will more certainly attain his object, by direct pursuit, by being less exposed to the seductions of extraneous beauty, and will win the race, not by excelling in speed, but by despising the bait.
>
> (VIII, 31–2)

In the *Strictures*, the analogy of masculine direction and feminine aimlessness provides what is a much more explicit image of the feminine incapacity to regulate desire for tangible and immediate gratifications. But for both Wollstonecraft and More, corrupt femininity is characterized by its attachment to what is incidental or extraneous, and by the absence of the sense of purpose and direction that seems to them necessary to self-possession and moral control.

The image of corrupt femininity, abandoned beyond all coherence or control, is familiar enough. In the *Appeal to the Men of Great Britain in Behalf of Women* (which was published in 1798, but largely written earlier in the decade), for example, Mary Hays (who seems the most probable author[14]) implies that it is unnecessary to detail the character of immoral femininity again. It seems enough, on the whole, merely to allude to women's 'state of PERPETUAL BABYISM' (97), and occasionally to flesh out the fascination with dress, the slavery to fashion, the addiction to what she calls 'the idle vagaries of the present moment' (82), that characterize the image. In general terms, corrupt femininity represents the obverse side of all that is valued in the dominant moral discourses of the eighteenth century. But in the 1790s it has a distinctive character, the implications of which I want to consider. For it is peculiarly an image of the feminine role in commercial culture – of the feminine consumer. In what seems to me to be one of the more striking passages of the *Vindication*, Wollstonecraft writes:

> The conversation of French women ... is frequently superficial; but, I contend, that it is not half so insipid as that of those English women whose time is spent in making caps, bonnets, and the whole mischief of trimmings, not to mention shopping, bargain-hunting, &c. &c.: and it is the decent, prudent women, who are most degraded by these practices; for their motive is simply vanity. The wanton who exercises her taste to render her passion alluring, has something more in view.
>
> (75–6)

The real crime here, Wollstonecraft is careful to emphasize, is that attention to 'the frippery of dress' weakens the mind, and distracts it from social duty. These women deprive the poor of employment, and themselves of the leisure necessary to self-improvement, for, she writes, they 'work only to dress better than they could otherwise afford' (75). But the most remarkable feature of this characterization must be that suggestion that the absorption in self-adornment, in the almost unmentionable folly of shopping and bargain hunting, is more contemptible and degrading than the behaviour of the sexually voracious woman, who at least has 'something more in view'.

What Wollstonecraft's comments here serve to confirm is that by the 1790s economic considerations have taken priority in the characterization of corrupted femininity. The problem is not that absorption in self-adornment may encourage an insatiable sexual rapacity disturbing to the social confidence placed in the system of propertied inheritance, though that remains an important ingredient of the discursive construction at issue. In these years, when fortunes may be more likely to be acquired through commercial speculation than as a result of inherited landed estates, the dangers of social disruption that cluster and find focus in the familiar figure of feminine excess, at least in the context of the polemical genre of vindications, appeals and strictures, result from the vices of consumerism, rather than the more colourful sins of bad sexuality. The figure of corrupted femininity, I suggest, needs to be understood primarily as a set of gendered characteristics appropriated to the requirements of the discourse of commerce and its feared inverse, the anti-commercial horrors of profiteering, greed and consumerism run riot. In the late eighteenth century, the discourse of commerce projects out of itself the image of its own amoralism, producing the figure of insatiable feminine desire that shadows the morality of middle-class men and women, and that, in its confirmed and acknowledged immorality, works to consolidate the shaky moral values of commerce itself. The vices of commerce are embodied in the figure of immorally desirous femininity, which serves, as it were, to draw that poison off from the system of commerce itself. But in this context, of course, the poison is also the antidote – commerce needs the image of corrupt femininity to account for the consumption of its commodities, to represent the ceaseless stimulations to desire in the marketplace, and to figure, in its own shining form, the radiance of the commodity. It needs corrupt femininity to moralize and masculinize its own self-image.

Wollstonecraft's shoppers are caught up and implicated in the changing nature of the retail trade – they hunt for bargains in violation of the code of trust that was believed to have existed between tradesmen and their customers. They are implicitly promiscuous in awarding the favours of their custom, responding to the seduction of window displays and cut-price offers, undercutting traditional channels of supply with the industry of their busy fingers, rather than participating in those steady and trusting relationships of reciprocal recognition between consumer and supplier that are imagined to have characterized the more paternalist society of the past.[15] In Hays' *Appeal*, in particular, these shoppers and stitchers are reprimanded for their failure to fulfil the obligations of their class and gender, their failure to provide poor women with steady employment.[16] They are the counterpart of those men Wollstonecraft describes to Imlay in her *Letters written during a short residence in Sweden, Norway, and Denmark* (1796). She writes that:

> men entirely devoted to commerce never acquire, or [they] lose, all taste and greatness of mind. An ostentatious display of wealth without elegance, and a greedy enjoyment of pleasure without sentiment, embrutes them till they term all virtue, of an heroic cast, romantic attempts at something above our nature; and anxiety after others, a search after misery, in which we have no concern. But you will say that I am growing bitter, perhaps, personal. Ah! shall I whisper to you – that you – yourself, are strangely altered, since you have entered deeply into commerce ... never allowing yourself to reflect, and keeping your mind, or rather passions, in a continual state of agitation.[17]

Imlay here is represented as partaking in those feminized qualities that the second *Vindication* attributes to corrupted femininity. What is personal, what strikes home to his self-image, she suggests, is the moralized and gendered discourse of anti-commerce, rather than the reflections produced by the discourses of sentiment, on the one hand, or civic humanism, on the other. Wollstonecraft's letter implies that Imlay the dealer in alum and soap will recognize and wish to reject the gendered and impassioned image of its own amoralism that commerce has produced.

Hannah More, it is no surprise to find, is prepared to locate value and virtue in the feminine image of the good consumer much more straightforwardly and explicitly than are Wollstonecraft and Hays – both of whom might be seen as more concerned to define middle-class women as something other than consumers. More's prose seems to register no flicker of doubt, none of the hesitancy that might point to a sense of incongruity, as she invests the figure of the good housewife with many of the virtues necessary to public spirit. She writes that:

> ladies whose natural vanity has been aggravated by a false edu-
> cation, may look down on *oeconomy* as a vulgar attainment,
> unworthy of the attention of a highly cultivated intellect; but this
> is the false estimate of a shallow mind. OEconomy ... is not
> merely ... the shabby curtailments and stinted parsimony of a
> little mind, operating on little concerns; but it is the exercise of
> a sound judgement exerted in the comprehensive outline of order,
> of arrangement, of distribution; of regulations by which alone
> well-governed societies, great and small, subsist.... A sound
> oeconomy is a sound understanding brought into action; it is
> calculation realized; it is the doctrine of proportion reduced to
> practice; it is foreseeing consequences, and guarding against them;
> it is expecting contingencies, and being prepared for them. The
> difference is, that to a narrow-minded vulgar oeconomist, the
> details are continually present.... Little events and trivial opera-
> tions engross her whole soul.
>
> (VIII, 5–7)

The argument that the practice of the good consumer indicates that More identifies as 'real genius and extensive knowledge' (VIII, 8) can clearly only be supported in juxtaposition to the representation of the 'vulgar oeconomist', endowed with the narrow-minded absorp-tion and capacity for engrossment in the physical that characterize corrupted femininity.

More writes of properly domesticated women that:

> Both in composition and action they excel in details; but they do
> not so much generalize their ideas as men, nor do their minds seize
> a great subject with so large a grasp. They are acute observers, and
> accurate judges of life and manners, as far as their own sphere of
> observation extends; but they describe a smaller circle. A woman

> sees the world, as it were, from a little elevation in her own
> garden, whence she makes an exact survey of home scenes, but
> takes not in that wider range of distant prospects which he who
> stands on loftier eminence commands.
>
> (VIII, 29–30)

The good domestic economist seems, on the one hand, to perceive
with the kind of commanding and comprehensive grasp that distinguishes the vision of public men, from their loftier eminences. But
on the other hand, within her 'smaller circle', she excels in her
attention to detail. Her 'survey of home scenes', in other words,
seems ambiguously 'exact' – it seems to be true and right, in the
sense that the perceptions of great men are imagined to be true,
disinterested and unbiased, and it seems to be exact in the sense that
it is precise, and preoccupied with detail. Those qualities, I think, can
only be represented as though they were compatible, and the notion
that women do not generalize their ideas 'so much' as men can only
be represented as though it made sense, as a result of the introduction
of the contrasting figure of the vulgar economist, who as it were
neutralizes the problem, by absorbing into herself what are seen as
the more degrading implications of engrossment in the physical detail
and menial drudgery of housekeeping.

III

The appropriation of the image of corrupted femininity to an anti-
commercial discourse is thoroughly problematic, as both More's *Strictures* and Wollstonecraft's *Vindication* demonstrate. The very currency, the power and resonance of the image in so many eighteenth-
century texts serve to indicate the extent to which it has hoovered
up the available languages of desire. It acts as a magnet for gendered
characteristics in excess of those necessary to its function as a guarantee of the moral discourses from which it is projected and excluded.
It can seem to have assumed the power to characterize not only what
is excessive, corrupted, and feminized, but those qualities which seem
in terms of the discourses of the period to be necessary to the
distinction of gender, to be those essential to femininity itself. In
the particular, anti-commercial form which I have suggested is specific
to the 1790s, the image of corrupted femininity can seem to embrace
and to represent all femininity, and thus to identify anti-commercial
discourse as misogynistic. This can be seen in many of the polemical
texts of the period, but is perhaps most unmistakably marked in

More's *Strictures*. Writing of women's fashionable publicity, she argues:

> If, indeed, women were mere outside, form and face only ... it would follow that a ball-room was quite as appropriate place for choosing a wife, as an exhibition room for choosing a picture. But, inasmuch as women are not mere portraits, their value not being determinable by a glance of the eye, if follows that a different mode of appreciating their value, and a different place for viewing them antecedent to their being individually selected, is desirable. The two cases differ also in this, that if a man select a picture for himself from among all its exhibited competitors, and bring it to his own house, the picture being passive, he is able to *fix* it there: while the wife, picked up at a public place, and accustomed to incessant display, will not, it is probable, when brought home, stick so quietly to the spot where he fixes her; but will escape to the exhibition-room again, and continue to be displayed at every subsequent exhibition, just as if she were not become private property, and had never been definitively disposed of.
>
> (VIII, 178–9)

More's argument is remarkable because of the twist, the change of direction that registers the problematic instability of discourses of gender. In the first place it seems that women are more valuable than portraits because they are more enigmatic, because they conceal hidden depths that cannot be known at a glance. The association of corrupt femininity with surface display seems to be what is established by portraiture, which can only paint the superficial appearance suitable for the exhibition room. But as More develops the image, that very addiction to surface, that sense in which femininity is fully manifested in its exhibitable and commodified form, becomes the valued and apparently uncorrupted site. Women who fail to recognize that they have become private property, which has been definitively disposed of, women who continue to desire to be seen, but unlike commodities do not apparently desire to be possessed, become identified as corrupt. They seem corrupt, shop-soiled, because of their suspect motivation and mobility – because, unlike portraits, they are not all surface. The analogy between women and their portraits, in More's argument, makes it clear that the identification of femininity with surface and display which is central to the discourse on feminized corruption has become ambiguous. The stable but superficial image which respects its status as private property is here a marker of relative purity and value.

Mary Hays' argument, in her *Appeal*, runs into similar difficulties in employing the analogy between women and works of art. She writes of corrupt women as 'mere automatans' [*sic*] who 'put on the semblance of every virtue', and may appear 'as captivating – perhaps even more so, than women of real sensibility'. She contrasts their 'varnish of surface' with 'real, unaffected, unassuming goodness', which is analogous to 'marble of the most exquisite quality, – which, without flaw or blemish, admits of an equal polish through all its parts as on its surface; and on which the sculptor may lastingly impress the sublimest efforts of his art' (255–6). What is curious about this contrast between automata and sculpture, what seems excessive to the familiar language of surface and depth, is the emphasis on the sculpted image of virtuous femininity as a production, lastingly impressed by the hand of its maker. Both the automaton and sculpture, that emphasis on production serves to point up, afford pleasure to the spectator because of their visible surfaces and polished finish. The fact that marble statuary has a more enduring polish does not call into question the characterization of both corrupt and virtuous femininity in the desire to excite desire, in qualities common to commodities. What seem to distinguish corrupt from virtuous femininity are the aesthetic criteria which articulate discrimination between different kinds of art, between the value of different kinds of private property. The analogy between women and painting or sculpture makes explicit the commodification of femininity, while veiling that commercial form in the decent and acceptable drapery of aesthetic value, but the analogy also elides the distinction between virtue and corruption that it is apparently called upon to support. In this context, all femininity is identified as spectacle, and caught up in those transactions of desire that characterize both consumers and commodities.

The perceived erosion of what was imagined to have been the clear distinction between virtuous and corrupt femininity is a matter of explicit concern and alarm for conservative writers of the later eighteenth century. John Bowles, for example, in his *Remarks on Modern Female Manners* of 1802, laments that women of unblemished character 'No longer ... pride themselves ... on the distinction which separates them from the abandoned part of their sex'.[18] He argues that virtuous women should not tolerate the society of known adultresses – a point of etiquette that Hannah More also stressed in her *Strictures* of 1799, although in her *Essays for Young Ladies* of 1777 she had argued for the exercise of Christian forgiveness and tolerance. Bowles advances his case with an excessive strength of feeling that borders on panic. He writes that:

Honour, especially in women, can admit of no compromise with dishonour; no approaches from one towards the other must be suffered; the boundary between them must be considered as impassable; the line by which they are divided is the RUBICON of female virtue.[19]

His insistence can be taken as an indication of the frailty of definition, the discursive instability, of the categories of feminine virtue and corruption – categories which cannot be kept distinct by the mere device of social manoeuvring that he advocates. The blurring of these categories, he argues, represents 'a much more formidable enemy than Buonaparte himself, with all his power, perfidy, and malice'.[20] It indicates a social change which, he writes:

> would be more tremendous than even the suspension of those wonderful powers of nature, which confine the planets to their respective orbs, and maintain, from age to age, the harmony of the universe.[21]

Bowles believes that apocalyptic chaos will result from virtuous women adopting immodest fashions of dress. Confronting the discursive confusion this represents, he exclaims that:

> compared with such a woman, the bold and abandoned profligate, who with dauntless effrontery, appears publicly in her true character, is less disgraceful to her sex, and less injurious to society.[22]

Like Wollstonecraft contemplating the horrors of shopping, he finds himself welcoming the unambiguously scandalous woman as a more socially acceptable and useful figure than the fashionable woman of indeterminate morality. For, as I suggested earlier, it is the feminine image of corrupt desire, of bad sexuality, that is necessary to inoculate the morality of commercial culture. The danger represented by the confusion of the signs of vice and virtue, or by the possibility that anti-commerce might be recognized as a feature of commerce itself, is greater than the danger represented by the bold and abandoned face of bad sexuality or Napoleonic perfidy.

IV

The problem that I believe these texts of the late century respond to and articulate in their shared and apparently misogynistic discourse is clearly set out in Anna Laetitia Aikin or Barbauld's essay of 1773, 'Against Inconsistency in our Expectations'. She explains that:

> We should consider this world as a great mart of commerce, where fortune exposes to our view various commodities, riches, ease, tranquillity, fame, integrity, knowledge. Every thing is marked at a settled price. Our time, our labour, our ingenuity, is so much ready money which we are to lay out to the best advantage. Examine, compare, choose, reject; but stand to your own judgement; and do not, like children, when you have purchased one thing, repine that you do not possess another which you did not purchase.[23]

It is perhaps apparent from this initial image of society that Barbauld's essay attempts to wed a moral discourse on the use of talents, on those differences of character that may result in tranquillity, fame, or integrity, to a discourse on the division of labour concerned to explain the diverse specializations of commercial society in a way that seems also to justify its inequalities. Barbauld concludes that:

> There is a cast of manners peculiar and becoming to each age, sex, and profession. . . . Each is perfect in its kind. A woman as a woman: a tradesman as a tradesman. We are often hurt by the brutality and sluggish conceptions of the vulgar; not considering that some there must be to be hewers of wood and drawers of water, and that cultivated genius, or even any great refinement and delicacy in their moral feelings, would be a real misfortune to them.[24]

The inclusion of women here, as though gender were a category immediately comparable to occupation or class, is thoroughly problematic. What women in their capacity as The Sex bring to the great mart of commerce is, most obviously, their sexuality. They may figure in the great mart as consumers or commodities, but as I have tried to show, those roles are at least morally ambiguous.

What women are more commonly valued for by the late century is precisely their exclusion from the marketplace – the marginal position from which, according to John Bowles:

> they soften, they polish, the rougher sex, which, without their mild and genial influence, would never exhibit any thing better than a race of barbarians. . . . They constitute the very ties of those family connections, those domestic societies, which can alone foster in the human heart those tender sympathies, the social affections. . . . In short, they adorn, they harmonize the world.[25]

That image of women as social glue is common to many of the polemical texts of the 1790s, including Wollstonecraft's and More's.

But in Barbauld's essay it's clear that even this vague notion of a social function for virtuous femininity is incompatible with the model of society that the division of labour articulates. Barbauld laments that in modern society:

> Every one is expected to have such a tincture of general knowledge as is incompatible with going deep into any science; and such a conformity to fashionable manners as checks the free workings of the ruling passion, and gives an insipid sameness to the face of society, under the idea of polish and regularity.[26]

The qualities that Barbauld here regrets, because they militate against specialization and against the division of labour on which the great mart of commerce is perceived to depend, are precisely those of polish and regularity which it is the business of women to instil. Barbauld acknowledges that the idea of society which it is the function of women to harmonize and polish is made redundant by the more powerful and persuasive model of the great mart described by political economy. In the context of that commercial model, there is no moral or professional language available to articulate feminine virtue. It has no place and no value. By the 1790s, I think, that perception has become inadmissible. The problem of feminine virtue, the problem of what women are wanted for, has become an issue capable of producing that anxiety about policing the division between good and bad women that John Bowles articulated – an anxiety that animates the spate of conservative and radical texts on the education of women in the 1790s. The most obvious function of women in the 1790s is to fuel the discourse of anti-commerce – a discourse that I have suggested shows an alarming tendency to become fully misogynistic, and to become the only available, or at least the dominant discourse on femininity.

V

Wollstonecraft, Hays, and More might all be understood, in their polemical writing, to respond to the impossible demands placed on femininity in commercial culture, and they all look to the possibility of professionalization to reclaim respectability for the notion of virtuous femininity. Hays and Wollstonecraft both argue strongly that the exclusion of women from the division of labour as anything but consumers means that the terms in which they can be represented are restricted almost completely to those of corrupt feminine desire made available by what I have called the discourse of anti-commerce.

Emphasizing the dominance of the model of society produced by political economy, Wollstonecraft writes:

> Taught from their infancy that beauty is woman's sceptre, the mind shapes itself to the body, and, roaming round its gilt cage, only seeks to adorn its prison. Men have various employments and pursuits which engage their attention, and give a character to the opening mind; but women, confined to one, and having their thoughts constantly directed to the most insignificant part of themselves, seldom extend their views beyond the triumph of the hour.
>
> (44)

What women are perceived to be for, the character of femininity, is for Wollstonecraft produced by their allocated place and employment within the division of labour, which dictates that they will consume goods for their personal adornment, goods which the middle-class woman finds become 'more than ever a part of herself' (60), and constitute her social identity.[27] Hays' *Appeal* is more explicitly concerned than is the *Vindication* with the issues raised by differences of class. She argues that what she identifies as the 'misemployed talents' that middle-class women expend on 'ribbons, gauze, fringes, flounces and furbelows . . . might have placed thee on the woolsack, or have put a mitre on thy head, or a long robe on thy back, or a truncheon in thy hand' (79). The vanity of corrupt femininity is ambition misemployed, she claims. She argues strongly for the reappropriation to women of trades and professions that had become masculinized in the course of the eighteenth century. Significantly, Hays emphasizes that the masculinization of women's work had left prostitution as the only available professional course open to poor women obliged to compete in the marketplace.

More, in contrast, employs the language of professionalization to characterize both corrupt and virtuous femininity. The life of fashionable women, she argues, 'formerly, too much resembled the life of a confectioner', but 'it now too much resembles that of an actress; the morning is all rehearsal, and the evening is all performance' (VII, 120–1). The passions women bring to their public performances resemble those that 'might be supposed to stimulate professional candidates for fame and profit at public games and theatrical exhibitions' (VII, 123). More argues that:

> Most *men* are commonly destined to some profession, and their minds are commonly turned each to its respective object. Would it not be strange if they were called out to exercise their profession,

or to set up their trade, with only a little general knowledge of the trades and professions of all other men, and without any previous definite application to their own particular calling. The profession of ladies, to which the bent of *their* instruction should be turned, is that of daughters, wives, mothers and mistresses of families. They should therefore be trained with a view to these several conditions, and be furnished with a stock of ideas, and principles, and qualifications, and habits, ready to be applied and appropriated, as occasion may demand, to each of these respective situations.

(VII, 111–12)

More's suspicion of those who are equipped 'with only a little general knowledge' echoes Barbauld's distrust of the 'tincture of general knowledge' that is valued 'under the idea of polish and regularity'. It is a suspicion of what has come to seem an anachronistic lack of specialization, appropriate to an idea of society innocent of commercial progress. In More's *Strictures*, women can only become properly modern and professional by subjecting themselves to an extraordinary degree of restraint – by accepting the confinement of their different presence within the 'smaller circle' of domesticity. More argues that fashionable men are peculiarly subject to the allure of the ambiguously public world of clubs, which 'generate and cherish luxurious habits, from their perfect ease, undress, liberty, and inattention to the distinctions of rank' (VIII, 184). Clubs, she argues, 'promote . . . every temper and spirit which tends to *undomesticate*' (VIII, 185). It is the duty of the wife to correct what More represents as the democratical spirit of club life by cultivating in her husband the 'love of fireside enjoyments' (VIII, 186). By confining her own circle of understanding and activity to the domestic, More suggests that the wife will be able to produce in herself and her husband the belief that 'those attachments, which . . . are the cement which secure the union of the family as well as of the state' (VIII, 187) are those which are nourished in the asocial world of the family, of domesticity. The kind of limited publicity and professionalism to which Wollstonecraft and Hays wish to secure women access is associated in More's argument with 'inattention to the distinctions of rank', with the blurring of the boundaries of public and political space – boundaries which are for More secured by the polarization of family and state, and confirmed by the antagonism that she and John Bowles wish to see between virtuous and immoral women. Whereas for Wollstonecraft and Hays, women seem left with the possibility of entering more fully into the political and economic marketplace. As Wollstonecraft observes: 'The world cannot be seen by an unmoved spectator, we must mix in the throng, and feel as men feel' (112).

What is problematic about that statement is of course its apparent denial of the value of gendered difference. And that is a problem which, I hope to have shown, is produced by the specific historical moment in which the *Vindication* participates. The apparently misogynistic discourse that is common to both Wollstonecraft and More, and to a less marked extent to Hays, in their polemical texts if not in their writing in other genres, needs to be understood, I think, as peculiar to the late century. As I have mentioned, the general terms in which it characterizes corrupt femininity are common to writing about women throughout the eighteenth century. Mary Astell, for example, has some very similar things to say about fashionable women at the beginning of the century. But in Mary Astell's writing the image is not misogynistic, it is not a representation of all femininity. It is a set of terms appropriated, broadly speaking, to those women who are seen to be surplus to the marriage market, marriageable women who may be made redundant by the newly emerging relationship between the city and the landed gentry. By the late century, however, the requirements of anti-commercial discourse appropriate the image of corrupt femininity, and extend it into the nightmare of a language that represents all women, and all forms of feminine desire. It is important, I think, to recognize the specific uses to which the notion of feminine corruption is put, in the course of the eighteenth century. For if we accept its terms as common to all forms of femininity, then, in a sense, we accept their status as somehow essential to gender difference. We then tend to privilege from among the cluster of characteristics that make up the image those which we most nearly accept as essential to femininity ourselves – such as sexuality – and overlook the extent to which feminisms of the past have changed their nature to suit the specific historical circumstances in which they operate. We overlook the flexible self-image which is surely necessary to feminist polemical texts.

University of York

Notes

1 *Letters of Anna Seward: Written between the years 1784 and 1807. In six volumes* (Edinburgh: G. Ramsay & Co., 1811), III, p. 117.
2 To Lady Gresley, 29 August 1792, III. p. 160.
3 To Mrs Jackson of Turville-Court, 13 February 1798, V, p. 47.

4 13 April 1798, V, p. 73.

5 To Mr Whalley, 26 February 1792, III, p. 117.

6 To Humphry Repton, 13 April 1798, V, p. 74.

7 *Some Account of the Life and Writings of Mrs Trimmer, with original letters, and meditations and prayers, selected from her journal. In two volumes* (London: R. & R. Gilbert, 1814, this 2nd edn 1816), To Mrs M., 12 July 1792, II, pp. 60–1.

8 *The Letters of Horace Walpole Earl of Orford*, 9 vols, ed. Peter Cunningham (London: Bohn, 1861), 21 August 1792, IX, p. 385. Walpole's remark about the absence of politics in the text implies the absence of direct or explicit comment on the political events of the day. In the preceding paragraph of the letter he describes 'The *second* massacre of Paris' in some detail, and suggests that these events have confirmed his 'abhorrence of politics' (p. 384).

9 *Strictures on the Modern System of Female Education. With a view of the principles and conduct prevalent among women of rank and fortune* (1799), in *The Works of Hannah More. In eight volumes: Including several pieces never before published* (London: A. Strahan, 1801), VII, pp. 172–3.

10 *Extracts of the Journals and Correspondence of Miss Berry, from the year 1783 to 1852*, 3 vols., ed. Lady Theresa Lewis (London: Longmans, 1865), To Mrs Cholmeley, 2 April 1799, II, pp. 91–2. On perceptions of Wollstonecraft as an educational theorist see Regina M. Janes, 'On the reception of Mary Wollstonecraft's *A Vindication of the Rights of Woman*', *Journal of the History of Ideas*, 39 (1978), pp. 293–302, and Virginia Sapiro, *A Vindication of Political Virtue: The Political Theory of Mary Wollstonecraft* (Chicago: Chicago University Press, 1992), p. 28.

11 In Vivien Jones (ed.), *Women in the Eighteenth Century: Constructions of Femininity* (London: Routledge, 1990), p. 191.

12 The relation between More's *Strictures* and Wollstonecraft's second *Vindication* has been explored most fully by Mitzi Myers, in her important article, 'Reform or Ruin: "A revolution in female manners" ', in *Studies in Eighteenth-Century Culture*, no. 11 (1982), pp. 199–216. Myers argues that Wollstonecraft and More are united, despite or across their political differences, in 'perceiving a society infected with fashionable corruption, [to which] both preach a militantly moral middle-class reform grounded in women's potentiality' (p. 211). As will I hope become apparent, my essay is concerned to unpack – to specify and complicate – what is involved in those rather generalized notions of fashionable corruption and middle-class morality. But I also question Myers's reading of the second *Vindication* as primarily concerned with reforming women's domestic role, as well as her assumption that middle-class and affluent women are, in some sense, really corrupted by fashionable amusements. My approach is more extensively (if indirectly) indebted to Cora Kaplan's reading of Wollstonecraft in her brilliant and influential essay, 'Wild Nights: pleasure/sexuality/feminism', in *Sea Changes: Essays on Culture and Feminism* (London: Verso, 1986). Kaplan's essay (which was first published in 1983) argues that Wollstonecraft's text is 'interested in developing a class sexuality for a radical, reformed bourgeoisie' (p. 35), through the reform of something resembling Myers's 'fashionable corruption', but Kaplan argues that this reforming drive 'expresses a violent

antagonism to the sexual' (p. 41). Her essay questions this 'negative construction of the sexual in the midst of a positive and progressive construction of the social and political' (p. 36). My essay attempts to extend this questioning, and to reconsider the polemical uses of the figure of negative sexuality, in the context of concerns about feminine morality that are, I think, specific to the cultural politics of the 1790s.

13 See *Strictures*, VII, pp. 78–9; and Mary Wollstonecraft, *A Vindication of the Rights of Woman*, ed. Carol H. Poston (New York: Norton, 1975), p. 10. The subtext here may be Burke's notorious use of Hamlet's speech. He writes that in 'sensible objects', 'so far is perfection... from being the cause of beauty; that this quality, where it is highest in the female sex, almost always carries with it an idea of weakness and imperfection. Women are very sensible of this; for which reason, they learn to lisp, to totter in their walk, to counterfeit weakness, and even sickness. In all this, they are guided by nature.' *A Philosophical Enquiry into the Origin of our Ideas of the Sublime and Beautiful*, ed. J. T. Boulton (London: Routledge & Kegan Paul, 1958), p. 110.

14 William Thompson attributed the *Appeal* to Mary Hays in the Introductory Letter to Mrs Wheeler, in their *Appeal of one-half of the human race, Women, against the pretensions of the other half, Men* (1825). The attribution may also be indirectly supported by the apology for writing in the first person that is appended to the *Appeal*. See *Appeal to the Men of Great Britain in behalf of Women* (London: J. Johnson, 1798), pp. 295–300. Wollstonecraft wrote to Mary Hays on 12 November 1792, commenting on a draft of her *Letters and Essays, Moral and Miscellaneous*, which was to be published in 1793. She argued that the text was 'too full of yourself... true modesty should keep the author in the back ground'. Ralph M. Wardle (ed.), *Collected Letters of Mary Wollstonecraft* (Ithaca: Cornell University Press, 1979), p. 220.

15 On the changing nature of consumption see Neil McKendrik, 'Introduction. The birth of a consumer society: the commercialization of eighteenth-century England', and Chapter 1, 'The consumer revolution in eighteenth-century England', in Neil McKendrick, John Brewer and J. H. Plumb, *The Birth of a Consumer Society: The Commercialization of Eighteenth-Century England* (London: Europe, 1982); and E. P. Thompson's essay of 1971, 'The moral economy of the English crowd in the eighteenth century', reprinted in his *Customs in Common* (London: Merlin, 1991).

16 See, for example, *Appeal*, pp. 242–3.

17 In Janet Todd and Marilyn Butler (eds), *The Works of Mary Wollstonecraft* (London: Pickering, 1989), 7 vols. VI, pp. 340–1.

18 *Remarks on Modern Female Manners, as distinguished by indifference to character, and indecency of dress; extracted chiefly from 'Reflections political and moral at the conclusion of the war. By John Bowles, Esq.'* (London: Woodfall, 1802) p. 4.

19 Bowles, p. 6.

20 ibid., p. 16.

21 ibid., p. 20.

22 ibid., p. 15. Bowles's discussion may echo Hannah More's account of modern dress. She argues that as a result of excessive cultivation the arts have become 'agents of voluptuousness' (VII, p. 91), and comments: 'May

we not rank among the present corrupt consequences of this unbounded cultivation, the unchaste *costume*, the impure style of dress, and that indelicate statue-like exhibition of the female figure, which, by its artfully disposed folds, its seemingly wet and adhesive drapery, so defines the form as to prevent covering itself from becoming a veil? This licentious mode, as the acute Montesquieu observed on the dances of the Spartan virgins, has taught us "to strip chastity itself of modesty" ' (VII, p. 92).

23 In *The Works of Anna Laetitia Barbauld, With a Memoir by Lucy Aikin* (London: Longman, 1825), 2 vols, II, p. 185.
24 Barbauld, II, p. 194.
25 Bowles, p. 18.
26 Barbauld, II, pp. 193–4.
27 For a fuller discussion of Wollstonecraft's views on the employments appropriate to middle-class women, see Sapiro, pp. 158–61.

Correction

In Stephen Orgel's essay 'Insolent Women and Manlike Apparel', published in the last issue (TP 9:1), the title-page of *Pleasant Quips for Upstart Newfangled Gentlewomen*, illustrated in Figure 13, was supplied to the author in error. It is a nineteenth-century facsimile, and the original title-page has a different woodcut on it; the point, therefore, is no point at all: the woodcut is not a picture of the queen. The paragraph beginning 'What are the limits of social imitation' should be ignored.

Laurie E. Osborne

Filming Shakespeare in a cultural thaw:
Soviet appropriations of Shakespearean treacheries in 1955–6

Abstract

Though most critics of Shakespearean film know the work of
Kosintzev, Shakespeare first appears on film in Russia well
before Kosintzev turns to film in the 1960s. Between 1954 and
1956, the Soviet Union plunged headlong into representing Shakespeare's plays on film with the unusual production of four
Shakespearean films. During 1955 alone, two major Russian film
studios produced full-length feature films of Shakespearean plays:
the Lenfilm Studios produced and released Y. Frid's *Twelfth Night*,
entitled *Dvenadtsataia noch'*, and the Moscow Film Studio was
completing Yutkevich's *Otello*. This essay concentrates on how
these productions reproduce and rework Shakespeare's texts in
response to an important period in the Soviet Union's cultural
and political development, the time just after Stalin's death in 1953
when he was revealed to have betrayed both his people and his
commitment to Marxism.

As both Frid and Yutkevich invoke the violence provoked
by betrayal of trust, their characters' intense responses to failures
of loyalty in both films suggest that these particular Shakespearean
texts were especially suited to the overt interests of the Soviets
during the thaw: the elimination of double-dealing and the effects
of the transition. However, for both *Dvenadtsataia noch'* and
Otello, the overt purposes of the film-makers are exceeded by the
materials these plays offer for Soviet appropriation. In *Otello*,
Othello becomes a sacrifice which frees the state from the lies and
double-dealing of Iago, while the filming works to defuse Othello's own misguided violence against the innocent. In *Dvenadtsataia noch'*, those who are most threatened with punishment, like
Antonio, escape to freedom, as all failures of trust are forgotten

Textual Practice **9(2)** 1995, 325–347   © 1995 Routledge 0950–236X

in the celebration of the reunited family. However, *Twelfth Night* offers no place for and no appropriation of guilt. Given the complex Soviet response to their own victimization, *Otello* proved the more compelling film.

Keywords: Shakespeare; film; *Othello*; *Twelfth Night*; Russia; Stalin

Though most critics of Shakespearean film are familiar with the much-praised work of Kosintzev, Shakespeare first appears on the Russian film scene well before Kosintzev turns from stage to film in the 1960s. Between 1954 and 1956, the Soviet Union plunged headlong into representing Shakespeare's plays on film with the unusual production of four Shakespearean films.[1] Late in 1954, *Romeo and Juliet*, a film of the Bolshoi Ballet production, was released. During 1955, two major Russian film studios produced full-length feature films of Shakespearean plays: the Lenfilm Studios produced and released *Twelfth Night*, entitled *Dvenadtsataia noch'*, and the Moscow Film Studio was completing Yutkevich's *Otello*. In 1956, yet another production, a film of a theatrical performance of *Much Ado About Nothing* was released. The four films together reproduce and rework Shakespeare's texts in response to an important period in the Soviet Union's cultural and political development, the time just after Stalin's death in 1953.

My analysis of Soviet appropriations of Shakespeare has crucial similarities to the post-colonialist work of critics such as Robb Nixon, Barbara Bowen and Jyotsna Singh.[2] Nixon has explored African and Caribbean appropriations of *The Tempest* in terms of the post-colonialist subject's reworking of a dominant British cultural icon in an effort to establish a distinct identity, whereas Bowen treats the history of post-colonialist approaches to this play since Nixon's, emphasizing how Shakespeare's work becomes a site which international writers take up for their own purposes. Singh examines African appropriations of the Othello story which resist Western readings of Desdemona's innocence within the play's racist configurations, thus marking the significance of revisions which oppose standard Western readings. The local details of these analyses – identity construction, contestatory revisions, the significance of national histories – are relevant in my approach to these films but less important than the larger conceptual similarity.

Like recent post-colonial analyses, my work on the Soviet Shakespeare of the 1950s rejects the assumption of Shakespeare's universal appeal or relevance as the basis for analysing cross-cultural productions. Rather the amendments and revisions to these Shakespearean texts mark their cultural uses for negotiating varying constructions of identity and relationship, especially to Western culture. In my view, both post-colonialist and post-Stalinist productions of Shakespeare make use of his cultural capital through revisions and choices which speak to moments of great social turmoil and self-redefinition. In the Soviet Union, the period after March 1953 was just such a moment.

After Stalin's death came an array of startling reversals in the ways Soviets understood themselves. Most obviously, Stalin, who had enforced his image as the benevolent father to his country and a true Marxist leader, was revealed to have betrayed both his people and his commitment to Marxism. Nikita Khrushchev revealed Stalin's criminality in the special report to the 20th Congress of the Communist party, 24–5 February 1956.[3] To add to the unsettling, though not necessarily surprising revelations that Stalin had condemned, exiled and executed his enemies (real and imagined) without fair trials, Khrushchev began releasing political prisoners just after Stalin's death – as many as 12,000 by 1956 according to some analysts.[4]

The complex effects of these changes are evident in the urban stories which begin to circulate about these *politzeki*. In *The Thaw Generation*, Ludmilla Alexeyeva describes one such story:

> They had been forgotten, written off, and now they were out there, in the streets, like the walking dead. And in their honor Moscow wags invented tales of betrayal and repentance. Thus, thousands of Muscovites claimed that their friend or a distant cousin had witnessed a truly remarkable scene: A released convict walking through Moscow, ran into the investigator who had put him in prison fifteen years earlier. The investigator froze in his tracks . . . then fell to his knees and pleaded: 'Forgive me for putting you in prison for nothing. Forgive me, friend, forgive me.'[5]

These *politzeki* returned to a society still full of those who had betrayed and sentenced them under Stalin. Not all of the blame for Stalin's acts could be laid solely at his door since the desire for advancement or imperatives of survival led much of the populace into roles as informants, prosecutors, etc. To make matters still more complex, Khrushchev also initiated the rehabilitation of those who were summarily executed and stripped of Party status under Stalin. Reassessing Stalin's actions also revised the very categories of loyalty and betrayal for many Soviet citizens. The formerly loyal exposure and prosecution of Stalin's enemies became a betrayal of communist principles as well as of the Soviet people. As a result, the tenuous boundary between patriotic loyalty and criminal complicity becomes a pervasive concern in Soviet culture, articulated and in some ways projected on to the Western 'other' through the Soviet film productions of *Twelfth Night* and *Othello*.

Along with the liberation of political prisoners and the reassessment of Stalin's relationship with his country came a lessening of restraints on cultural expression, resulting in works like the 1954 novel, *The Thaw*, by Ilya Ehrenburg whose symbol for the post-Stalin era ultimately became its name.[6] The Soviet interest in Shakespeare, expressed in the four films released during this period, tellingly surfaces during this time. While acknowledging the ballet and the filmed stage productions, I wish to focus most closely on the two feature films, *Dvenadtsataia noch'* and *Otello*, which were released almost simultaneously in late 1955 and early 1956, respectively. I argue that the two films must be considered in relationship to each other, rather than ignoring *Dvenadtsataia noch'* in favour of the more well-known and critically acclaimed *Otello*. Taken together, they not only underscore each other's uniquely Soviet approach to presenting Shakespeare, but also reveal the significant choices involved in producing these two plays during Russia's cultural thaw.[7]

Both films stand in relationship to a tradition of Soviet Shakespeare developing around Boris Pasternak's translations. With the rigours of WWII, Pasternak retreated into what Elliot Mossman terms 'the anonymity of translation',[8] earning a living through translations while many writers were finding it very difficult to survive. Understandably under the circumstances, Pasternak offered his translations as 'the original's fruit and historical consequence' rather than just 'the correspondence of text to text [which] is too weak a link to guarantee that a translation achieves its aim'.[9] Rejecting the idea of word-for-word translation, Pasternak chose instead to preserve the features of poetry and prose in Shakespeare while keeping the same number of lines and syllables in the verse.[10] This correspondence of line rather than word necessitated considerable cutting because the Russian language, in contrast to English, typically contains predominantly polysyllabic words. The result was a briefer text in terms of meanings though of comparable length in syllables. Although the scholarly community often harshly criticized the liberties taken in Pasternak's translations, their popularity on stage and, later, on screen was remarkable.[11]

Yutkevich, director of the Mosfilm production of *Otello*, fully allied himself with the stage canon, selecting his Shakespearean script from among Pasternak's translations. Yutkevich even echoes Pasternak in saying that Shakespeare must affect the film-maker as 'something far deeper [than an academic exercise], indispensable, compelling and stirring his own creative consciousness . . . the ideas of the author become his own.'[12] Thus, he adopts not only Pasternak's script but also his logic of making a translation – this time into film. After thinking about directing a film of *Otello* since 1937, during one of Stalin's most repressive periods, Yutkevich finally got to film Pasternak's text only in 1955, two years after Stalin's death.

At LenFilms Studios, Y. Frid, also known as Iakov Borukhovich Friedland, took the opposite strategy, selecting a Shakespearean play which Pasternak had not translated and choosing comedy over tragedy. *Twelfth Night*, which had not been presented on film since the 1910 Vitagraph silent film, offered Frid the opportunity to play with a carnivalesque world where the Russian folk songs favoured by Stalin became part of the comic hilarity in the below-stairs plotting of Toby, Aguecheek and Feste.[13] More to the point, Frid could show the aftermath of *Twelfth Night*'s storm and its apparent destruction of family in a recuperative vision of confusions and reunions within an idyllic setting, offering a positive vision for the outcome of Soviet turmoil. In fact Frid himself emphasizes this goal in his comments on the film just after its release: 'The inexhaustible and life-giving optimism of *Twelfth Night* attracted us.'[14] The comic indulgence of *Twelfth Night*'s vision of relationships restored is a stark contrast to the utter destruction of people and family relationships in Yutkevich's *Otello*.

Although Yutkevich's *Otello* draws more attention than Frid's production, the two films are strongly connected. Both draw on Shakespeare's overall popularity in Russia, reappearing together in a 1956 Shakespeare Soviet film festival.[15] Both are also clearly designed to renew and promote cultural exchange with the West; *Dvenadtsataia noch'* appeared in New York in March 1956, almost immediately after its Soviet release, and Yutkevich's *Otello* reached the United States by May of 1960. Moreover, these film-makers exercise unusual and distinctive choices for appropriating Shakespeare's works. Avoiding the tragedies more commonly chosen for film representation like *Hamlet* or *Lear*, they single out plays whose situations resonate with the emotions released after Stalin's demise.

Othello was a more popular film subject, but it had only been filmed three times, as Yutkevich notes. Even within the eight translations Pasternak did, *Othello* was a somewhat unusual choice – Pasternak himself was not enamoured of the play. He wrote to his cousin about translating *Othello* while he was working on it: 'I am translating *Othello* against my will; I never liked it. I am working with Shakespeare now almost semi-consciously. . . . I am over-simplifying him terribly.'[16] Pasternak's 'oversimplification' served Yutkevich well; he, like Orson Welles, won best director at Cannes and world-wide recognition, because of his vivid conception and production of Shakespeare's *Othello*.

Yutkevich used an *Othello* already shortened by Pasternak's translation principles and further cut his screenplay so that he achieved without much controversy the requisite 90 to 100 minutes allowed to Soviet feature films. Frid's film, in contrast, drew a lot of criticism for cutting and especially for rearranging *Twelfth Night*.[17] His style of filming comes under as much attack as his alterations to the text. Paradoxically, his film work is viewed as unadventurous in comparison with *Otello*, despite the distinctive strategy of 'combinatory filming' which he used to show Katya Luchko as both Viola and Sebastian in the same frame.[18]

Peter Morris, who critiques especially Frid's curtailment of Malvolio's role, inevitably views the film's flaws in relationship to Yutkevich's *Otello*. He claims that, given Soviet interest in Shakespeare, it is 'not surprising to find another Shakespearean film following hard on the heels of the Russian *Othello*'.[19] Morris's comment itself is surprising, especially since all the evidence indicates that *Dvenadtsataia noch'* was released first in December of 1955 while *Otello* was released in 1956. The two films even appeared in that order on American screens. As Morris's evaluation suggests, the artistic stature accorded Yutkevich's film obscures the fact that, at its release, it followed rather than led the production of *Dvenadtsataia noch'*.

Because these two films appeared practically in the same year, from different state-owned film studios, they are produced in relationship to each other from the start. This much is clear from Frid's own assertions that 'For us, the creators of the film, the public opinion about this first screening of a Shakespearean play is very important. It can also be helpful to our friends in Mosfilms who are filming *Otello* at the moment.'[20] For his part, Yutkevich recalls the criticism of Frid's changes by insisting that not only did his production maintain 'the dramatic sequences of the original, preserving not only the action of the text, but all the main monologues', but also his work was even filmed 'by the method of taking the scenes in sequence'.[21] Yutkevich's remarks in the 1957 essay suggest the lingering relationship with the other film, further emphasized by *his* assertion that his work is a 'first but modest beginning' among Soviet film-makers fascinated with Shakespeare.

In promoting *Otello*, Yutkevich suggests that his production was doubly in order (as Frid's was evidently not) and that *Otello* was the first Soviet film of Shakespeare, dismissing *Dvenadtsataia noch'* even from consideration. Although Soviet socialism claims co-operation as its mode of production, the relationship between these two films – and between their film-makers – expresses a tension and a self-assertiveness which looks remarkably like competition to Western eyes. Subsequent critical assessments have only perpetuated this contestatory relationship.

Although the near-simultaneous release of the two films invited comparisons which inevitably seemed to favour Yutkevich's *Otello*, my concern here is not to determine which is the better film or which the better Shakespeare. The production of these two films in 1955–6 establishes them together as the products of the cultural thaw after Stalin's death in 1953. Presented in part as appropriations of Shakespeare which promote Russia's renewed cultural exchanges with the West, these films also interact with shifting models of Soviet identity developing in novels and debates over psychology during the thaw. Ultimately from their reflections of Soviet identity and its changes, they use Shakespeare's texts to meditate on the multiple betrayals and consequent turmoil the Russian people experienced under Stalin and hoped, however briefly, to escape after his death.

My cues for examining both *Dvenadtsataia noch'* and *Otello* in terms of the complex situation of the Soviet thaw comes from the film-makers themselves. As I have already mentioned, Frid favours *Twelfth Night* because of its 'inexhaustible optimism'. He also claims that 'the very theme of the comedy devoted to noble friendship and pure love is extremely in tune with Soviet spectators.'[22] The cheerful comedy of *Twelfth Night* will appeal to the Soviet people in 1955, according to its director. In 'My way with Shakespeare', Sergei Yutkevich analyses *Othello*'s central tragedy for the Western press in even more revealing terms:

> The tragedy of *Othello* is not that he possessed Desdemona and then lost her. The whole tragedy is the search for and loss of a tranquil spirit. . . . I dare to think that Shakespeare conceived of his tragedy of Othello not only as a tragedy of love and revenge. The tragedy of his hero is the tragedy of faith, the tragedy of trust and treachery; therefore the culmination of Othello's tragedy is reached at the moment when he learns of Iago's treachery.[23]

If anything, Yutkevich's comments to the *Moscow News* are more straightforward: 'It seems to me that from an emotional point of view the tragedy of Othello, the Moor of Venice centres [*sic*] around the fight for truth, against lies, against any kind of falsehood or double dealing.'[24]

Yutkevich's simplified view would clearly appeal during the period when the Soviet people were finally free of Stalin's deceptions and brutalities. In the *Moscow News* interview, he explicitly notes that the play 'gives the spectators a wealth of new ideas, it helps them to draw general conclusions from their own life's experience'. Yutkevich's claim that 'the genius of the play ... help[s] us to gain a deeper, more emotional understanding of our own life' reveals that features of the Shakespearean text resonate with the Soviets' ambiguous relationship to trust in the 1950s.[25]

As these remarks suggest, the Soviet interest in *Othello* diverges widely from the kinds of investments which critics like Barbara Hodgdon have traced in other reproductions of the play.[26] In consequence, the discourses of race and sexuality currently so visible in these plays are almost deliberately obscured in Yutkevich's and Frid's discussions and are certainly effaced in their film editing.[27] As these film-makers insist that their projects bear close relationships to the experiences of the Soviet people, they in fact refashion the plays' texts and images to promote the desired relationship. The strategies they use reveal the ideological imperatives which persist in cultural production even after Stalin's death.

Taken together, Frid's *Dvenadtsataia noch'* and Yutkevich's *Otello* offer some provocative similarities. The spectacular and extensive introductions of these films visually represent background only described in Shakespeare's plays. These scenes manipulate images of thresholds and imprisonment which would have special importance to the Soviet people in the 1950s. Not only do these films downplay differences which are not easily accommodated in Marxist or Stalinist approaches to class distinctions, but also they deliberately place more emphasis on the loyalty and betrayal of male bonds than on other motivations. For both films, the most provocative revisions of these plays and most striking filming centre around issues of trust and treachery.

The opening scenes establish strikingly similar contexts of turmoil, prominently represented in separation and storms at sea. *Dvenadtsataia noch'* begins with a lengthy representation of the storm which shipwrecks Viola and Sebastian, first seen clutching opposite sides of the mast on the heaving, drenched deck of their ship. After a particularly strong wave washes off Sebastian and then Viola, a number of dramatic shots of the storm, including the sinking of the ship, precede Viola's rescue. Then Frid contrasts the storm's turmoil and the untroubled weather and cheerful marketplace, clearly implying that upheaval has been passed and survived. This impression is reinforced because Frid not only rearranges the play to put Viola's rescue first but also intermingles her opening scene with Sebastian's first appearance. Displacing Sebastian to the play's opening demonstrates that the physical danger to both Viola and Sebastian is over, while establishing the crucial twinning from the start.

When Viola enters through multiple archways as she approaches Illyria, her liminal status and her association with boundaries establishes a visual pattern which persists throughout the film. Over and over again the Soviet production displays Viola crossing thresholds, usually through Olivia's various doorways. In Act 1, scene 5, she kicks the closed portal to Olivia's castle before gaining entrance and later appears dwarfed by a doorway easily three times her height as she enters Olivia's great hall. In fact, she never meets Olivia without some archway or arched trellis in the frame. The visual terms of her introduction recur as her disguise establishes her constantly on the threshold of a host of relationships with the Illyrians. While clearly relevant to the Shakespearean Folio text, these images also reflect the film's own position on the threshold of an apparent revival of Soviet culture after Stalin's death in 1953. The idyllic world of Illyria, Viola's movement across boundaries, and the severing and reunion of families are all particularly important images in *Dvenadtsataia noch'*, connoting the positive possibilities of transition.[28]

In the Lenfilm opening, another series of scenic details introduces Sebastian and his 'noble friendship' with Antonio. The display of figures in the marketplace before the camera shows Sebastian anticipates the situations which he will face. A woman in red surrounded by men/suitors prefigures Olivia who first appears to Sebastian in a deep maroon dress surrounded by her kinsmen and followers. Similarly, the drunk who bumps into him and ends up fighting Sebastian and Antonio foreshadows Toby's and Aguecheek's various assaults, establishing Antonio's role as protector. Viola, whose character is more completely explored throughout the play and the film, is not so thoroughly defined by *mise-en-scène*, while the relative paucity of information about Sebastian is augmented and reinforced by Frid's manipulation of setting.

Just as important, the details of this scene distinguish between the twins, here played by the same woman, Katya Luchko. Viola is mobile, creating Illyria for the spectator as she herself discovers it; Sebastian reacts to surroundings which already contain and define his role in the scene in the restaurant. Although Sebastian does offer to fight, Frid uses only defensive aggression to establish his masculinity and to signal the loyal friendship between Antonio and Sebastian.

The omissions from this scene are as significant as the additions. The Lenfilm presentation of the scene effectively shifts the focus

away from Sebastian's mourning and Antonio's love. Antonio's com-
forting of Sebastian is unsentimental and interrupted – most of Sebastian's references to his sister and his tears disappear, replaced by the
physical encounter of the fight. Frid also omits Antonio's declaration
of love entirely: 'I have many enemies in Orsino's court,/Else would
I shortly see thee there:/But come what may, I do adore thee so,/
That danger will seem sport, and I will go.'[29] The film text initially
gives no hint here that Antonio faces any unusual danger in Illyria
and shows the two men going off together in amiable fellowship.
The careful elimination of any hint of Antonio's passion extends to
their other scene together. This editing reflects Soviet attitudes under
Stalin, when homosexuality was alternately denounced as a criminal
act or designated a medical condition to be 'cured' by marriage.[30]
Noble friendship between men was a worthwhile ideal, but sexual
love between men had become criminalized, associated with spies
and informers under Stalin.

In the opening and throughout *Dvenadtsataia noch'*, Frid establishes an idyllic world in Illyria where treachery is easily explained
away, violence is only temporary if vivid, and those who rule are
either made innocuous by love (like Orsino) or incompetent in the
face of true loyalty (like the constables who attempt to control
Antonio). Securing the twin roles becomes an essential part of this
project, as the distinctions in gender combined with double identities
allow Viola and Sebastian to resolve most of the play's conflicts.
From this perspective, Frid's choice to double-cast the roles of Viola
and Sebastian suggests that the danger of betrayal which *Twelfth
Night* imagines could be real – there is only one Katya Luchko,
deeply involved in double-dealing. However, her two roles actually
represent the film's use of duplicity to increase verisimilitude (the
twins really could be mistaken for each other) and to undo treachery.
The double role also resonates with one of the thaw writers' significant themes – 'the image of a dual Russia becomes here an image of
the Russian functionary as a dual personality. He has a role and self-
identity in official Russia, but also a hidden and unofficial existence
and identity.'[31] The doubling in the film's casting is crucial not only
because it echoes the writers of the period wrestling with a dual
Russia, but also because the film can neither effectively invoke the
image of treachery nor thoroughly dismiss its threat without that
duplicity.

As in Frid's film, Yutkevich's opening to *Otello* enacts a description and anticipates the issues and imagery of the film. The first
images render a dumbshow of Othello's speech to the Senate, displaying how Desdemona came to love him. After a silent scene between

Brabantio, Desdemona, and Othello (viewed only from the back), Desdemona faces the camera alone. Resting her hand where Othello did on a large metallic globe, she turns to the camera and the image of her face blurs from the bottom up as we finally get to see Othello's face, but as 'Othello's visage in [her] mind' (1.3.251).

Desdemona's thoughts thus establish the major imagery of the film, beginning with Othello standing on the bridge of a ship he clearly commands. Under fire from the land, the first volley is followed by a camera shot up at the ship's mast through the rigging. After a brutal battle during which Othello takes the helm, Othello's capture is signalled by the cloak drawn over his face and his immediate appearance in a cage with his hands chained together. He is forced to row as a galley slave, but even in this subjugated position, his force of character is evident when he deters the galley master from whipping him with a single severe glance over his shoulder. Just after this display, the ship capsizes in a rough storm and Othello escapes by holding on to a mast, much as Viola escapes her shipwreck in *Dvenadtsataia noch'*. Once on shore, he lies on the rocks washed by the surf until the scene cuts back to him now on the helm of a ship, once again in command.

This narrative and its imagery serve both to establish Desdemona's fascinated love and, at the same time, Othello's heroic nature as affirmed through her eyes. At the same time, the image shot through the ship's rigging prior to Othello's enslavement recurs even more pointedly throughout the film. For example, when Iago warns Othello about jealousy as they walk on the beach, a series of images recall that rigging. First just one net, draped on wreckage on the sand, intervenes as Iago expresses his doubts about Cassio. Here Yutkevich makes Iago's threat literal: 'So will I turn her virtue into pitch,/And out of her goodness make the net/That shall enmesh them all' (2.2.360–2). Later the two men walk through an increasingly intricate maze of netting and broken masts while Iago goes further and further in suggesting that Othello look to Cassio and Desdemona. Finally Othello rides off frantically and in effect confines himself again in the galley of the ship from which he watches Cassio and Iago through a barred window.

These images reinforce Othello's entrapment within Iago's lies, reproducing the psychological effects that Soviets of the period could easily associate with the debate over Stalin's commitment to a Pavlovian view of the human psyche. Stalin's insistence on a psychological theory which could promise his people's reactions to propaganda gave way after his death to a backlash among Soviet psychologists.

Early in 1955, Stalin's deterministic model was strikingly contradicted by Rubinstein in *Problems of Psychology*:

> The model of the state-directed man presupposes a one-to-one correspondence between the verbal propaganda stimulus and the individual's reflex response. . . . Such determinism, concluded Rubinstein, 'would signify the *complete disintegration of personality*'.[32]

As Rubinstein and the Soviet psychologists of the thaw give autonomy back to the individual, Yutkevich plays out both the 'disintegration of personality' caused in Stalin's determinist view of psychology and a redemptive individual autonomy in Othello's final actions once freed from Iago's 'verbal stimulus'. The imagery of imprisonment even echoes the treatment of the supposedly insane who disagreed with Stalin's policies. Given this network of associations, the deterioration of Othello's mind and the images used to represent that deterioration are especially evocative material for the Soviet audience of the 1950s.

When Shakespeare's dialogue finally begins, the arch/doorway becomes a prominent image in this film as well. When the two men back away while warning Brabantio to look to his daughter, Yutkevich establishes Iago's characteristic position as hidden within an archway, perhaps associating him with Janus, the two-faced god of doorways and lies. Certainly Iago has two faces in this scene as he raises a beaked mask when he calls out his most provocative line: 'Your daughter and the Moor are making the beast with two backs' (1.1.115–17).

This sexual slur is the only one which remains from Shakespeare's opening, as the production all but eliminates the sexual language of the play in order to focus on the 'doubling dealing'. In his emendations, Yutkevich goes even further than Pasternak's translation which tends to downplay the sexual language rather than simply removing it.[33] None of Iago's other explicit imagery remains here, just as later the film omits both his language and Othello's about Desdemona's presumed adultery. Moreover, in her appearance before the Senate, Desdemona herself does not claim that 'My heart's subdued/Even to the utmost pleasure of my lord' (1.3.250–1) or ask to follow Othello for 'those rites for which I love him' (1.3.257), but instead claims, 'The Moor I loved above all else to live with him in proud esteem, and in my husband's hand did I our fortunes place. My soul shall perish while he is gone to war. I beg you leave to be where he is, my lord.'[34] Given the chastity of this plea, Othello then has no need to reassure the senate that he 'beg[s] it not/To please the palate of my appetite' (1.3.261–2) and simply asks the senator to allow Desdemona her way.

Along the same lines, all the sexual bantering between Desdemona, Emilia and Iago before Othello arrives in Cyprus and all of Emilia's matter-of-fact comments about men teaching women to err are gone. Just as tellingly, given the Lenfilm treatment of Antonio's love, Yutkevich's production completely omits Iago's revealing recitation of Cassio's dream, complete with its homoerotic overtones as the sleeping Cassio supposedly 'pluck'd up kisses by the roots/That grew upon my lips' (3.3.429–30). As in *Dvenadtsataia noch'*, the muting of the homerotic imagery tends to reinforce the relationships based on loyalty and secured male hierarchy, perhaps even more pointedly since homosexuals were often used as informers or even spies to seduce foreigners into espionage.[35]

This elision of Desdemona's sexual self and muting of the volatile linking between that self and the Moor effectively denies some of the important current insights into *Othello* especially since Yutkevich also undercuts Shakespeare and Pasternak's translation in references to Othello's blackness. In the opening sequence, the film withholds the sight of Othello's blackened face until it can be framed within Desdemona's imagination. The respect of Brabantio and the love of Desdemona are clear before we ever see Othello's face. The full disclosure of his colour is completely subject to Desdemona's worshipping gaze and thoughts.

In fact, Yutkevich cuts almost all of Iago's references to Othello's race. The only direct reference that the film keeps, as far as I can tell, is Othello's own despairing acknowledgement as he looks down into the well into which Iago has just gazed and says 'I am black', although in the reflection he actually looks less dark than he does at several other points in the film. The 'actual' blackness of Othello's skin does not become such a prominent part of the film's verbal imagery as it does in either Shakespeare's play or Pasternak's translation. As a result, the threatening otherness of female sexuality and race which critics such as Karen Newman have seen operating together in *Othello* is only *visually* present in Yutkevich's film: Bondarchuk's face and body are darkened for the part and Desdemona both 'paddles her hand' with Cassio and embraces and kisses her husband (though usually in such a way that his face is obscured).[36] However, the language which places Desdemona's sexuality and Othello's blackness in the foreground as connected issues from Iago's first slur in Shakespeare's text is noticeably missing in the Soviet film.

Although Yutkevich may be deliberately singling out the issues which he feels are most important and avoiding aspects of the play which recall the difficulties of a Marxist state in dealing with ethnicity and sexuality, it is also true that these issues are indissolubly enmeshed in the play's concerns. However Iago's verbal manipulations of sexual and racial prejudice have been muted, Othello remains black in this film, or, more precisely, a darkened white actor. Thus the visual representations of the film often play off blackness versus whiteness in exploring how trust is manipulated – Othello's blackness, for example, is emphasized or de-emphasized by his dress, by lighting, by contrast with Desdemona or likeness to the night in ways which link his darkness with Iago's treachery. While spoken text masks the film's investment in blackness as thoroughly as it cuts the language demonizing Desdemona, the visual use of light and dark emphasizes Othello's exotic otherness, most often at moments where the betrayal of male relationships, not sexual betrayal, is the issue.

Beyond the alterations and additions to the introductions, *Dvenadtsataia noch'* and *Otello* also devote considerable attention to the consequences and resolutions of betrayal in these plays. In *Dvenadtsataia noch'*, the betrayals are readily solved when Viola and Sebastian are shown to be two people rather than one. As a result, Cesario maintains her position as loyal servant to Orsino, and Sebastian keeps faith with his friend Antonio and his new bride Olivia. Nonetheless, before the revelation that they are twins, the film offers a series of representations of loyalty and its failure. Antonio's selfless display of his loyal friendship leads him into battle with the local authorities of Illyria – whom he almost defeats en masse. Viola is similarly devoted to Orsino and his cause, although she herself is in love with him. In both cases, the attempt to maintain trust initially fails because of the doubled main character. Luchko in one role transgresses the pledge of Luchko in the other role. In a visual rewriting of Russian duality, Viola's treachery is resolved because there turn out to be two people, rather than one with a public role and a private identity.

When Antonio is captured, he offers his first claim on Cesario directly: 'This comes with seeking you' (3.4.340). The reaction shot which follows this appeal shows Viola not heeding his words. When the camera cuts back to Antonio, he moves forward as she says she will lend him something. The camera then cuts back as he decries 'this youth's' ingratitude. Frid compresses Antonio's complaint, omitting all the officers' speeches and allowing Antonio control:

ANTONIO: O heavens themselves!
This youth you see here
I snatch'd one half out of the jaws of death,
And to his image, which methought did promise

> Most venerable worth, did I devotion.
> But O how vile an idol proves this god!
> Lead me on.
>
> (3.4.366–81)

Cutting the officers' interruptions and seven lines from Antonio's speech condenses his challenge to Viola's loyalty. Its brevity thus contrasts the extended reactions of Olivia and Orsino when they each think Cesario has betrayed them.

In Frid's final scene, Olivia signals her devotion to Cesario even as she walks down her arched corridor to speak with Orsino in the great hall. When she looks over her shoulder and kisses her ring to reassure Cesario/Viola, Viola is merely confused by the gesture. Orsino, however, catches on even as he speaks to her that her amorous glances are all for Cesario. As in Yutkevich's *Otello*, sexual jealousy is here positioned as a lesser concern than loyalty and betrayal, as Orsino orders Cesario to leave with him. Viola pauses only to swear her eternal loyalty to Orsino, as Sebastian has sworn his to Olivia. Thus, Olivia's subsequent lament that she has been beguiled also signals a breach of faith, one that she hopes to heal by calling him husband. That name, however, provokes Orsino to outright violence as he literally grabs Cesario by the neck and starts to strangle 'him' for 'his' betrayal. His aggression draws a reaction of shock and fear from Olivia, who enters the fray to rescue her 'husband' by biting Orsino's wrist, apparently the only action which will interrupt the throttling of Cesario. The violent assault which Frid stages, unique among all the *Twelfth Night* films I have seen for the sheer aggression Orsino demonstrates, is specifically a response to Cesario's betrayal: Orsino offers no such gesture toward Olivia, simply calling her an 'uncivil lady' (5.1.110) and a 'marble-breasted tyrant' (5.1.122).

Cesario's vulnerability here lies both in her position as subordinate to the Duke and in her apparent betrayal of the most earnest protestations of loyalty. In this film, Orsino's claim to that loyalty is more vividly defended than even Olivia's claim on her husband, as Frid transfers to Orsino lines which Olivia speaks to Cesario in the Folio: 'Hold little faith though thou has too much fear' (5.1.169). Perhaps given the violence which he has just shown, it is appropriate that Orsino invokes fear, but the line also resonates with the dilemmas posed under Stalin to people poised between keeping faith and well-justified fear. Only the dual existence described in the thaw literature offers a sort of resolution to the paradox – a dual existence which becomes literal in *Dvenadtsataia noch'*.

In the play, of course, the seeming betrayals are really only illusions: Cesario has remained loyal to Orsino, and Sebastian does keep his promise to Olivia, even though he has defended himself vigorously against Sir Toby's attack. The 'madness' which Sebastian discovers in Illyria has the positive benefit of providing him with an obviously wealthy wife, and the falsely accused Viola, like the falsely imprisoned Malvolio, is freed from any taint of disloyalty. Such easy release from imprisonment, from mistaken accusation, and, most important, from the threat that trust has been betrayed, embodies in Illyria the perfect carnivalesque fantasy: Illyria defuses the array of Soviet experiences under Stalin and after Stalin's death, experiences which provide the film's cultural context.[37] The conclusion's touching revelation of families restored and peacefully created only completes the fantasy while Antonio, who flouted authority for his friend, rides off to freedom.

In *Otello*, however, there are no useful twins to rescue Othello from the fact that either his loyal ancient, 'honest Iago', is betraying his trust, or both Desdemona and Cassio are. The structure that Yutkevich adopts for the final scene concentrates on Othello's experience of betrayal. Whereas many details of Desdemona's preparation for death are cut – her conversation with Emilia, for example – the display of Desdemona's body on the bed and the enactment of Othello's suicide are drawn out and reworked. Michael Neill has analysed in detail how the staging of this scene throughout the nineteenth century reflects the fascination and rejection attendant on the 'object which poisons sight' (5.2.365), the bed bearing Desdemona and Othello and displaying the 'monstrous' union which Iago so persistently invokes throughout the play.[38] Yutkevich's filming of the scene successfully avoids such display, just as his screenplay has cut most references to Desdemona's and Othello's sexual union. His aim is the restoration of Othello, betrayed into the violent destruction of the innocent.

Basically the Soviet *Otello* divides the events following Othello's smothering of his wife into three separate segments. The first takes place in the bedroom. Immediately following the murder, Othello has drawn the curtain around the bed, as many nineteenth-century productions do, and speaks before it, concentrating the camera's attention on him rather than the bed. Even after Emilia enters and hears her mistress's voice, Desdemona remains hidden behind that curtain. Emilia actually joins her behind it, and Desdemona's final words to her admitting the guilt of her own murder are practically inaudible. The bed is displayed with its curtains closed around the two women and filmed from across the room where Othello stands by a pillar.

Desdemona's disappearance from the scene both signals and hides her death. Her muffled (and false) confession of guilt for her own unjust fate strongly evokes Soviet experiences of abrupt disappearances, followed by confessions of guilt which justified the hidden punishments of the supposedly guilty. In Desdemona's false confession, her inaudible words locate both her death and confession as hidden from sight, as so many murders and supposed suicides are hidden from view during Stalin's reign. When Emilia emerges and confirms Othello's assertion that his wife was not murdered, Othello beckons her across the room and confesses to her. Thus Desdemona's death is also rehabilitated, as were so many deaths during the post-Stalin period.

Nonetheless, the focus of the scene is *not* Desdemona. Even as Emilia calls in the officers and draws the curtain to reveal her mistress's body, her immediate action is to direct attention away from Desdemona by bringing Iago in to confront Othello. Consequently, the film dwells only momentarily on Desdemona before taking up at length Iago's role.

Yutkevich singles out Othello's reaction when he understands the extent of Iago's treachery by producing a striking contrast between Othello's glowing eyes, illuminated by a narrow band of light, and his darkened form in shadow. The camera holds that image for several concentrated beats, in direct contrast to the jump cuts which Yutkevich uses to indicate Othello's response to seeing and understanding his wife's supposed betrayal. As Desdemona's reputation (never in doubt for the audience) is restored after her death, Othello's understanding of self has altered as radically as the Soviet citizens' did upon meeting the rehabilitated *politzeki* they had condemned.

The intensity of Othello's stare at Iago and his failed assault on him mark the shift to the second segment of the scene. As soon as the officers have departed, Othello lifts his wife from the bed and carries her up the stairs which circle the outside of the tower. He lays her out on the raised block in the middle of the parapet; the camera reveals her upside down with her hair hanging off the edge of the raised stone, as it pans up her body from her head to her feet. There we finally see Othello. Yutkevich cuts the language of the scene while drawing out the imagery of the staging in order to revise and control the crucial punishment of Othello the Moor.

Most important, when Othello finally does speak again, he explicitly recalls his relationship to the state as an essential part of his tragedy. As the guards dragging Iago find him and Desdemona on the parapet, Othello stands and begins his speech before killing himself, 'I have done some service to the state' (5.2.340). The film focuses closely on him during this striking echo of Stalinist philosophy which 'was succinctly summed up by Georgi Malenkov in a speech in 1941: "We are all servants of the state." '[39] Despite the assertion that he has loved not wisely but too well, the focus of his suicide turns out to be Iago as his demeanour dramatically heightens when he declaims,

> And say besides, that in Aleppo once,
> Where a malignant and a turban'd Turk
> Beat a Venetian, and traduc'd the state,
> I took by the neck the circumcised dog
> And smote him thus.

> (5.2.353–7)

This assertion positions Othello doubly, as the loyal Venetian and as the Turk to be punished for traducing the state. Othello's self-sacrifice on these words marks their significance for the Soviets all the more clearly since Iago unexpectedly breaks free and heads further up the stairs, as if to stop Othello. His intrusion is quickly followed by Othello dying on a kiss, as he covers both himself and Desdemona with his white cloak. As he has placed Desdemona on a stone altar, Othello also recreates himself as a sacrifice, as the punisher and the victim of a betrayal linked to the state.

Yutkevich then concludes the scene with yet a third shift of image, to show Ludovico's promise to persecute Iago and his declaration that 'the object poisons sight'. Unlike in stage productions, that object is not the bed, but Desdemona's and Othello's bodies laid out side by side ceremonially on the deck of the mourning ship as it sets sail back to Venice. Peaceful, beautifully dressed and once again united, Desdemona and Othello are ferried back in dignified splendour. When Ludovico gestures towards their peaceful, distinctly non-erotic forms and says, 'The object poisons sight' (5.2.365), his words do not suggest disgust at the violated marriage bed, but horror at the ennobled tragedy embodied in their still forms. Moreover, Iago's sight is the one which is to be poisoned, since he has been tied to the mast so that he has no choice but to see those he has betrayed.

The tripartite deathbed scene which Yutkevich designs ennobles Othello, principally by manipulating Desdemona's disturbing presence on her marriage bed. Immediately after her death, her body and the bed are concealed, and Othello's interactions with the others take place all the way across the room. Secondly, the movement of her body from the bed up the stairs to the stone table on the parapet elevates Desdemona's death to the sacrifice which Othello initially claims it to be. Framed in that context, his suicide becomes a sacrifice as well, one whose interpretation Othello tries to assure by the resonant appeal to the service he has done the state. Their final 'bed' together, laid out formally on a Valhalla-like heroic funeral bier, contrasts their union in death to Iago's suffering on the mast as if he must watch what amounts to Othello's triumphal and heroic return to the state. The further the filming moves us from the bed, the more thoroughly the Russian *Otello* achieves the closure suggested by its opening sequence, where Othello is returned to command of a ship and full respect from his descent into slavery. Desdemona's profile paralleling his, but lying beyond him on their mutual bier, reinforces his restoration with her innocence.

In strikingly parallel ways, both Frid and Yutkevich invoke the violence provoked by betrayal of trust. The characters' intense responses to failures of loyalty in both films suggest that these particular Shakespearean texts were especially suited to the overt interests of the Soviets during the thaw: the elimination of double-dealing and the effects of the transition. However, for both *Dvenadtsataia noch'* and *Otello*, the overt purposes of the film-makers are exceeded by the materials these plays offer for Soviet appropriation.

Both plays supply representations of the betrayal and duplicity so recently acknowledged officially throughout Soviet society. Nonetheless, the solutions they present are very different and are thus used in distinct ways to reflect shifting ideas about Russian identity. In *Otello*, Othello's self-destruction grows directly from the verbal manipulations which Stalin's state-approved psychology argued could control the individual. As a result, he becomes a sacrifice which frees the state from the lies and double-dealing of Iago, while the filming ennobles his death in ways which defuse his own misguided violence against the innocent. The film seems to use the racial otherness unassimilable to Marxist notions of class as a marker of Othello's foreignness and the possible displacement of guilt on to the other rather than the Soviet self.

In the fantasy world of *Dvenadtsataia noch'*, those who are most threatened with punishment, like Antonio, escape to freedom, as all failures of trust are forgotten in the celebration of the reunited family. In Illyria, all betrayals turn out to be illusions, banished by the comic production of twins. The twinning of Viola's character thus both comments on the Russians' dual lives and stops the violent response to betrayal, substituting marriage and family reunion. This focus on the positive aspects of rehabilitation – for Viola is loaded down with accusations of betrayal – equates the restoration of good name

with the benign re-establishment of family ties. No troubling disloca-
tions accompany the restoration of Sebastian into Viola's life. Quite
the contrary, his reappearance frees her from any semblance of guilt.

However, the rosy world of *Twelfth Night* offers no place for
and no appropriation of guilt. Viola's complicity is entirely innocent, and no physical harm ensues from her apparent treachery. Yet
the Soviet attempts at self-redefinition through psychology and literature always encounter the irrevocable punishments of the innocent,
which, like the murder of Desdemona, cannot be undone however
the participants might wish it. Adam Hochschild's recent book, *The
Unquiet Ghost: Russians Remember Stalin*, testifies to the ongoing
negotiations of the Soviet people with the influences of Stalin, tracing
the reactions of both those who are dedicated to opening the KGB
files and those who live on river-banks which erode, revealing the
mummified bodies of Stalin's victims.[40] Like the scars of the post-
colonialist subject, the impact of Stalinism on the Russian psyche
continues. Given the complexity of the Soviet response to their own
victimization, it is hardly a surprise that *Otello* proved the more
compelling film.

Colby College, Maine

Notes

This essay is dedicated to my father-in-law, Arnold Beichman, whose
studies in Soviet history and politics have here inspired my interest
in Soviet representations of Shakespeare.

1 *Romeo and Juliet*, dirs L. Armstam amd L. Lavrovsky (Mosfilms Studios,
   1954), *Dvenadtsataia noch'*, dir. Y. Frid (Lenfilms Studios, 1955), *Otello*,
   dir. Sergei Yutkeyev (Mosfilms Studios, 1956), and *Much Ado about
   Nothing – Mnogo shuma iz nichevo*, dir. L. Zamkovoi (USSR, 1956).
2 See Robb Nixon, 'Caribbean and African appropriations of *The Tempest*,'
   Critical Inquiry, 13 (Spring 1987), pp. 557–8; Barbara E. Bowen, 'Writing
   Caliban: anticolonial appropriation of *The Tempest*', *Critical Writing*, vol.
   5, no.2 (1993), pp. 80–99; and Jyotsna Singh, 'Othello's identity, postcolonial theory, and contemporary African rewritings of *Othello*', in Margot
   Hendricks and Patricia Parker (eds), *Women, 'Race,' and Writing in the
   Early Modern Period* (London and New York: Routledge, 1994),
   pp. 287–99.
3 Nikita Khrushchev, 'The crimes of the Stalin era', *The New Leader*, 1956.
4 Roy A. Medvedev, *On Stalin and Stalinism* (Oxford: Oxford University
   Press, 1979), p. 163.
5 Ludmilla Alexeyeva and Paul Goldberg, *The Thaw Generation: Coming
   of Age in the Post-Stalin Era* (Boston: Little, Brown, 1990), p. 71.

6 Ilya Ehrenburg, *The Thaw*, trans. Manya Harari (Chicago: H. Regnery, 1955).

7 I am deeply indebted to Richard Stites's analyses in *Russian Popular Culture* (Cambridge: Cambridge University Press, 1992) which provide much of my background here. His work is as yet unique in taking up Soviet culture in the 1950s, a period which is more or less ignored by scholars of Soviet cinema outside of Mira and Antonin Liehm's work in *The Most Important Art: Eastern European Film After 1945* (Berkeley: University of California Press, 1977). Peter Kenez's recent *Cinema and Soviet Society: 1917–1953* (Cambridge: Cambridge University Press, 1992) also dramatically delineates the falling off of Soviet film production in the period just prior to Stalin's death, singling out 1945 to 1953 as the nadir of Soviet film (pp. 227–46).

8 Elliot Mossman (ed.), *The Correspondence of Boris Pasternak and Olga Freidenberg: 1910–54* (New York: Harcourt, Brace Jovanovich, 1982), p. xix.

9 *Pasternak on Art and Creativity*, ed. Angela Livingstone (Cambridge: Cambridge University Press, 1985), p. 187.

10 Olga Akhmanova and Velta Zadornova, in 'The present state of Shakespeare translation in the USSR (Russian translations of Shakespeare)', *Shakespeare Translation*, 2 (1975), pp. 38–47, call Pasternak's approach 'free' translation, associating it with other liberal translations designed for the stage.

11 *Pasternak on Art*, pp. 151–2.

12 Sergei Yutkevich, 'My way with Shakespeare', *Films and Filming*, 41 (1957), p. 8.

13 Though feature films of *Twelfth Night* are few and far between, the play has received numerous television treatments, especially in the 1960s when there were two German television productions and the British produced the noteworthy Joan Plowright production which doubles the roles of Viola and Sebastian as *Dvenadtsataia noch'* does.

14 'Screening Shakespeare', *Leningrad Pravda*, 20 November 1955, p. 4. I would like to acknowledge the help of Mary Ann Ryshina, who translated this article from Russian for me, and Sheila McCarthy, who helped me find the bibliographical reference.

15 Three of the Shakespeare films of this period were re-released together in this 'festival of Soviet Shakespeare films' in 1956. Yutkeyev's *Otello* was shown first, accompanied by 'older, but still popular films', *Dvenadtsataia noch'*, and *Romeo and Juliet* (*Moscow News* 23 (1956), p. 5).

16 *The Correspondence of Boris Pasternak and Olga Freidenberg: 1910–54*, p. 237.

17 I am indebted to Denise Youngblood for locating and telling me about a reference to the film being very controversial in its abbreviation in *Kino i Vremia* (Moscow: Gosfilmofond, 1963).

18 According to John Gillette's assessment of Fried's film in *Sight and Sound*, 'Perhaps the least satisfying aspect of the production is the actual direction. *Othello* is remarkable for Yutkevich's strongly personal conception of the play; here the handling is generally respectable and occasionally a little dull' (as quoted in Peter Morris, *Shakespeare on Film* (Ottawa: Canadian Film Institute, 1972), pp. 19–20).

19 Peter Morris, p. 19.

20 'Screening Shakespeare', p. 4.

21 Yutkevich, op. cit., p. 8. Yutkevich's logic for this filming – in order to allow the actors to grow in their roles – would have deeply satisfied Walter Benjamin who decries film in 'Art and the age of mechanical reproduction' both because it separates the actor's experience from the audience's and because it makes the actor's experience of his own role discontinuous (*Illuminations: Essays and Reflections*, ed. Hannah Arendt (New York: Schocken Books, 1968), pp. 217–51).

22 'Screening Shakespeare', p. 4.

23 Yutkevitch, op. cit., p. 8.

24 ' "Othello" film preview: famous Shakespeare tragedy on Moscow screen', *Moscow News*, 20 (1956), p. 7.

25 Certainly, the failure of trust Yutkevich sees echoes his own experience: he and several other directors were attacked in the anti-cosmopolitan campaign of the late 1940s, as Jewish directors particularly became enemies of the state because of presumed views that there was a world cinema independent of ideology. In *Cinema and Society: 1917–1953* (see note 7 above), Kenez describes this about-face in the treatment of directors, especially Jewish directors like Yutkevich, noting that the insistence on ideological and Soviet values in film as distinct from international aesthetic concerns further limited the available subjects for film and completed projects (pp. 222–5).

26 Barbara Hodgdon, 'Kiss Me Deadly, or the Des/Demonized Spectacle', in Virginia M. Vaughn and Kent Cartwright (eds), *Othello: New Perspectives* (Newark, NJ: Farleigh Dickinson University Press, 1991), pp. 214–55.

27 The interpretations offered in Frid's 1955 discussion of *Twelfth Night* and Yutkevich's 1956 commentary on *Othello* clearly ignore or avoid issues in these plays which draw our attention now. Recent considerations resist such totalizing views of noble friendship or the quest for a tranquil spirit. For example, the most powerful recent analyses of *Othello*, such as Karen Newman's and Barbara Hodgdon's, explore how racial and sexual otherness are linked in the play's representation of patriarchal power and reworked throughout its performance histories. *Twelfth Night* has offered rich material for recent explorations of Renaissance homoeroticism by critics such as Joseph Pequigney ('The two Antonios and same-sex love in *Twelfth Night* and *The Merchant of Venice*', *English Literary Renaissance*, 22 (1992), pp. 201–21); Bruce R. Smith (*Homosexuality in Shakespeare's England* (Chicago: University of Chicago Press, 1991); and Valerie Traub (*Desire and Anxiety: Circulations of Sexuality in Shakespearean Drama* (London and New York: Routledge, 1992)).

28 An entire section of Richard Stites' book addresses specifically the cultural thaw in the Soviet Union (pp. 123–48).

29 William Shakespeare, *Twelfth Night*, Act 2, scene 1, lines 44–7. In future references to *Twelfth Night* and *Othello*, I will cite act, scene and line numbers from the Arden editions of both *Twelfth Night*, ed. J.M. Lothian and T. W. Craik (New York: Methuen, 1975) and *Othello*, ed. M. R. Ridley (New York: Methuen, 1965).

30 For further detail about the attitudes towards homosexuality under Stalin and after his death, see Simon Karlinski's 'Russia's gay literature and culture: the impact of the October Revolution', in Martin Duberman *et*

al. (eds), *Hidden from History: Reclaiming the Gay and Lesbian Past* (Harmondsworth and New York: Penguin Books, 1990), pp. 347–64.

31 Robert C. Tucker, *The Soviet Political Mind: Stalinism and Post-Stalin Change* (New York: W.W. Norton, 1979), p. 140.

32 ibid., pp. 168–9.

33 Anna Kay France, *Boris Pasternak's Translations of Shakespeare* (Berkeley: University of California Press, 1978), pp. 52–77.

34 The adaptation is listed to be by Nancy Macguire, who presumably approved the translation which is actually a retranslation back into English from those portions of the Pasternak text which Yutkeyev used. I do not claim that the dubbed language which I offer here exactly represents the Russian version, but the striking variations from the Shakespearean text must surely originate in the Russian speeches.

35 Karlinski, op. cit., p. 362.

36 Karen Newman, ' "And wash the Ethiope white": femininity and the Monstrous in *Othello*', in *Fashioning Femininity and English Renaissance Drama* (Chicago: University of Chicago Press, 1991), pp. 71–93.

37 There are numerous descriptions of the uncertainties of life under Stalin's rule. For a sense of the hardships, disappearances, and betrayals of that period, see *The Correspondence of Boris Pasternak and Olga Freidenberg*.

38 Michael Neill, 'Unproper beds: race, adultery, and the hideous in *Othello*', *Shakespeare Quarterly*, 40 (Winter 1989), pp. 383–412. See also James R. Siemon, ' "Nay, that's not next": *Othello*, V, ii in performance 1760–1900', *Shakespeare Quarterly*, 37 (1986), pp. 38–51.

39 Tucker, op. cit., p. 134.

40 Adam Hochschild, *The Unquiet Ghost: Russians Remember Stalin* (Harmondsworth and New York: Penguin Books (USA Viking), 1994).

Review article

Antony Easthope
History and psychoanalysis

Malcolm Bowie, *Psychoanalysis and the Future of Theory* (Oxford, UK, and Cambridge, Mass.: Blackwell, 1993), iii + 176 pp., £35.00 (hardback) and £11.99 (paperback)

Teresa Brennan, *History After Lacan* (London and New York: Routledge, 1993) vi + 288 pp., £35.00 (hardback) and £10.99 (paperback)

Catching his foot on a stone in the road his lover would soon ride down, Freud's Ratman felt obliged to move it but almost immediately felt obliged to put it back. The question of the relation between history and the process of the unconscious, between ideology and phantasy, like Ratman's obsessive stone, is something we seem unable either to resolve or forget. There are two approaches to the issue, one from the side of history, the other from the side of psychoanalysis.

Psychoanalysis viewed by history

Marx, right from the *Economic and Philosophical Manuscripts*, is concerned to show how the objective conditions of estranged labour are lived out subjectively as alienation, just as Weber in his study of the connection between capitalism and religion wants to stress the effect of deferred gratification as a structure internalized by the individual. Reading objective causes for their subjective effects – even if the *mechanism* by which one affects the other remains shadowy or merely assumed in the way of common sense – forms a tradition continued in a series of dazzling insights by Lukács when, in *History and Class Consciousness*, he writes of the subject of laissez-faire capitalism as seeking to find an imaginary personal totality in a movement of compensation for loss of a sense of social totality.

When this mainly Marxist line of development comes directly up against the psychoanalytic account of subjectivity two sub-tendencies emerge and diverge. In one, represented by Wilhelm Reich, generally by the Frankfurt School, and by work such as the now somewhat neglected Erich Fromm in *The Fear of Freedom* (1942), the project is to maintain the priority of historical analysis but to tack psycho-analysis on to it as an optional extra, an additional form of explana-tion for fleshing out detail. These, in his 1964 essay on 'Freud and Lacan', are very much the terms in which Louis Althusser, on the grounds of its claims to being a science and another materialism, appropriates psychoanalysis as supplement to historical materialism. We have learned since to distrust such supplements, and there is an instructive history to be written of the developing interaction here between host and parasite from Althusser on.

While that tendency within Marxism aimed to contain psycho-analysis by finding a home for it, another strand meant to expel the idea of the unconscious altogether on the grounds that it is inherently universalizing and ahistorical. Voloshinov (with whatever prompting from Bakhtin) drew on a theorization of inner speech to argue, in *Freudianism: A Marxist Critique* (1927) and again in *Marxism and the Philosophy of Language* (1929), that even the most intimately subjective meaning, insofar as it appears as a sign, is by that feature rendered transindividual, ideological, social. Leaning on this, Ray-mond Williams robustly denies that 'Freud and Marx could be com-bined', and takes the hard-line position that 'There can be no useful compromise between a description of basic realities as ahistorical and universal, and a description of them ... as modified by a changing human history'.[1] As is well known, his proposed alternative is a collective 'structure of feeling' (in the same spirit, more recently, Jonathan Dollimore has refused psychoanalysis the qualification of being a 'materialism').[2]

More subtle than Williams – and more wary of the psycho-analytic warning that the repressed returns – Foucault and Jameson in their different ways try to domesticate psychoanalysis by changing it into another animal, setting up their own system and then explain-ing psychoanalysis from a basis within that. For Foucault in *The History of Sexuality* psychoanalysis is variously a rational discourse like science (though a science which also performs well as an *ars erotica*), an effective practice of moral prohibition, an incitement to confession – anything, in fact, so long as it is not the study of the unconscious. For Jameson in *The Political Unconscious* the real unconscious is the historical process that works behind our backs; and so psychoanalysis is relegated as an adjunct to the development of the privatized family and the isolation of sexual experience. The repressed returns nevertheless. Both Foucault for his conceptualization of power as deflection and deferral and Jameson for his notion of history as unconscious are profoundly indebted to psychoanalysis as a theoretical model.

History viewed by psychoanalysis

Psychoanalysis, of course, does indeed begin with a version of 'the human', and then reads the social formation and its institutions as a more or less direct expression of psychic needs and desires; or, accepting as autonomous the existence of such institutions, assesses how far they provide satisfaction for human wishes. Its basis is to consider the social formation itself in relation to the *species*.

Lacan remarks that he may be accused of 'turning the meaning of Freud's work away from the biological basis he would have wished for it towards the cultural references with which it is shot through' (106 – all pages references are to the 'English' *Ecrits*). Sympathy now widely felt for this re-reading masks the degree to which, as Frank Sulloway showed in *Freud, Biologist of the Mind* (1980), Freud did his thinking within a Darwinian matrix, in an essay on Darwin noting that we are 'more closely related to some species and more distant to others'[3] (the note of secular detachment sounded here is exceptional for someone born in 1856).

In the just-so story of *Totem and Taboo*, in *The Future of an Illusion* and *Civilization and its Discontents*, Freud exhibits an unmistakable commitment to Darwinian time, the life of our species in comparison and contrast with others. He sustains the anti-Utopian argument that the social formation itself ('civilization') compensates for the act of repression necessarily entailed to bring it about; and in *Group Psychology* (a major text surprisingly neglected) he outlines the unconscious basis for human collectives in shared identification ('fantasy', as Teresa Brennan well says, 'has a physical force in history', 28). Except for occasional comments (can the social order continue if religious superstition declines? with the prohibitions of Christianity is sex better or worse than it was in the pagan world?) Freud does not have a *historical* perspective.

Nor really does Lacan. And yet because of his insistence on culture rather than nature, the symbolic order rather than the biologically determined real, Lacan moves a lot further towards a historical analysis than Freud, though his historical views surface mainly in scattered remarks and isolated sentences. It is a worthwhile achievement of Teresa Brennan's *History After Lacan* to have collated these, pretty well for the first time, exhibiting a consistency in their point of view. Most leftist readers of Lacan will have been struck by such anti-capitalist asides as his observation that the modern subject lives 'in a world where his [*sic*] needs are reduced to exchange values' (252) and it is good to have all this made explicit.

Lacan's history

Lacan's historical thinking is shaped by his reading of Heidegger and particularly by the lectures of Alexander Kojève on Hegel given in Paris from 1933. Lacan refuses Freud's account of the ego as only the perception/consciousness system enabling the subject to deal with the real world, calling it a 'mirage of objectification' (22) and accusing Freud of misrecognizing the degree to which the ego's perceptions of the real are entangled with desire. Lacan ferociously rejects contemporary ego psychology and its belief in strengthening the ego, which he equates with the American way of life, instead deconstructing the 'I' by showing the mechanisms of identification and disavowal by which its temporary unity appears to be brought about. But as frequent references to Descartes and Pascal make clear, for Lacan this 'I' consists of 'the *moi*, the ego, of modern man' (70), which began to come into existence 'at the dawn of the historical era of the "ego" ' (71).

The almost intractable default in this post-Renaissance *belle âme* is that his (and probably it is 'his') very rationality and reflective self-consciousness constitutes a misrecognition, a self-deceiving 'mirage' through which he is 'sure of being himself even in his uncertainties about himself, and even in the mistrust he has learned to practise against the traps of self-love' (165). None so vulnerable as the one sure he is invulnerable. The modern ego (here is one Heideggerian input) aims to convert the processes of temporality (Being) into a spatial fixity; as part of this development (another debt to Heidegger) the modern 'I' objectifies itself in post-Renaissance science and technology, believing it masters its world, misrecognizing the way it is mastered by it.

Since, as Lacan argues in his essay 'Aggressivity in psychoanalysis', aggression against the other is correlative to the energies bound to hold the 'I' together, then the modern ego, trusting in its own fantasies of autonomy and mastery as intensified 'by the barbarism of the Darwinian century' (26), will 'in modern neurosis' (25) win through to new levels of competitiveness, aggression, and desire for 'the domination of space' (28). And in the masculine subject that domination will include and support the attempted mastery of an innovative category of The Woman as the object both to make good his lack and confirm his identity by reflecting it back to him. Altogether, in its egotism and self-deception, the modern 'I' is gripped by what Lacan terms a 'social psychosis' (216).

Partly because it is so fragmentary even if consistent, Lacan's historical perspective develops very easily from his discussion of subjectivity. He enters into no analysis of mechanisms bringing together subject and history because essentially he treats history as an expression of the subject.

No synthesis where none possible

In the *New Introductory Lectures* of 1933 Freud commented on Bolshevism and the new Soviet state in an informed and sympathetic tone but makes clear how his notion of the social formation differs from the classic Marxist model. Since the child's superego is modelled on that of his or her parents, each subject becomes, Freud says, 'the vehicle of tradition':

> It seems likely that what are known as materialist views of history sin in underestimating this factor. They brush it aside with the remark that human 'ideologies' are nothing other than the product and superstructure of their contemporary economic conditions. That is true, but very probably not the whole truth. Mankind never lives entirely in the present. The past, the tradition of the race and of the people, lives on in the ideologies of the superego, and yields only slowly to the influences of the present and to new changes; and so long as it operates through the superego it plays a powerful part in human life, independently of economic conditions.[4]

The past Freud calls up here is not the historical past. His implication, against historical materialism and other histories, is that to concentrate upon the usual historical temporality which privileges the 'moment' of external social event (together with associated political structures and historical institutions) leads to disregard for another temporality in which tradition 'lives on' in people. Such thinking leaves no space for the production and reproduction of subjectivity. Attempts either to reconcile psychoanalysis with historical materialism or dismiss one in favour of the other (by claiming, say, that one believes in unchanging human nature while the other thinks human culture is alterable) essentially miss the point – Freud and Marx are talking about different things, different histories, different temporalities.

The Darwinian argument is that in order to succeed a species must develop not only instincts for survival, which (as many people know) Darwin monumentalized in *The Origin of Species* (1859) but also instincts for reproduction, which (not so well known) he wrote up in *The Descent of Man and Selection in Relation to Sex* (1871). Corresponding to the two instincts for survival and reproduction Freud theorized narcissism and sexual desire as forms of drive, that is instinct which has become signified or represented. Marx, like a majority of historians, is concerned with the history of changing human society; Freud, like Darwin, is thinking about the human species and subjectivity, not something beyond or outside history but rather something operating in another history and another temporality. The two different kinds of temporality, opening differently on to the notions of ideology and desire, are simply not commensurate.[5]

Well, whatever made us think they were? The answer has to be that we assumed history and the unconscious conformed (somehow) to a totality characterized by a single, uniform idea of temporality. Once again, Althusser's writing, in this passage more than somewhat at odds with his well-known view of determination by the economic 'in the last instance', is worth recalling, for he rejects the view of a single, uniform and linear (Hegelian) time and argues that *'there are different times in history'*. Each of the 'levels' of human practice has a specific, autonomous and independent temporality with 'their own time and history' and he goes on to name the different histories of: 'the productive forces'; 'the relations of production'; 'the political superstructure'; 'philosophy'; 'aesthetic productions'; 'scientific formations, etc.'[6]

But if both the objective dimension of the social formation and the subjective process of the unconscious follow their own temporalities, this does not mean, as Althusser insists, that empirically they *occur* independently and outside knowable relations. Following and illustrating this logic in an essay which, regrettably, has not so far been reprinted, Stephen Heath both discriminates and puts in relationship two notions of the subject, the subject of ideology and the subject of the unconscious. 'There is', he argues, 'no subject outside of a social formation' and 'social processes' which 'specify ideological places'. Yet this definition and specification 'does not exhaust the subject' whose construction has a 'material history', precisely that described by psychoanalysis.

> There is a material history of the construction of the individual as subject and that history is also the social construction of the subject; it is not, in other words, that there is first of all the construction of a subject for social/ideological formations and then the placing of that constructed subject-support in those formations, it is that the two processes are one, in a kind of necessary simultaneity – like the recto and verso of a piece of paper.[7]

So: the subject in ideology and the subject of the unconscious are distinct and cannot be theorized with a single totalizing conception yet are always empirically related so that (to follow Saussure's metaphor which Heath borrows) a change in one cannot happen without a change in the other (you cannot cut the front of the paper without cutting the back).[8]

It would be pointless to argue it is only the case either that external social structures become internalized subjectively or that human society is an expression of the needs and desires of the human subject. Both effects occur reciprocally and without a point of origin in a simultaneity which is not that of identity. On this showing, serious analysis must think the 'objective' world of historical events and the 'subjective' domain of culture together and alongside each other.

If no totalizing synthesis is available but one must write of both history and the unconscious, is it preferable to begin from history or the subject? Studies which take history as their foundation and point of departure, when they do co-opt ideas of the unconscious, never fail to transpose them into a reductive form simply by making them subordinate to the larger explanation in terms of the usual economic and social forces. On the other hand, as the example of Lacan suggests, you sound much more persuasive if you *start* from a psychoanalytic basis and then as appropriate move into an understanding of the historically changing forms of human subjectivity. Although in principle the conceptions of the human subject proposed by psychoanalysis is finite and fixed, in practice the mechanisms of subjectivity are so fluid, contradictory and permutable that they seem able to inhabit no matter what particular and devious recesses of historical specificity. Of this procedure – treating the social formation as itself a form of subjectivity – the work of Zizek is a stunningly successful instance, demonstrating how psychoanalysis can fill out understanding of such phenomena as the function of ideology, the figure of the Jew, the meaning of the creature in *Alien*.

Now to two examples, each of which may extend and confirm my previous argument in different ways.

Bowie

Suave, elegantly written, scholarly and well informed, Malcolm Bowie's *Psychoanalysis and the Future of Theory* promises in its title rather more than it delivers in its text. Its argument is that the future of literary theory may be safely entrusted to psychoanalysis because as a model of artistic textuality it (1) attends to the incompleteness of the text and its discrepancies; (2) appropriately implicates together the text and the critic's desire; (3) encourages the right effect of playfulness and risk in the critic's engagement with the text as against any heavy-handed tendentiousness claiming to reveal the text as it does not know itself.

This is not a new position but it is one to which I can respond with 'Fine, no problems, as far as that goes.' It's in the gaps, the omissions, that doubts encroach. Bowie writes:

> What interests me particularly is the way in which the work of art both maintains and blurs its own hierarchical distinctions, by seeking self-consistency for each of its separate modes or levels and then puncturing this consistency by allowing other modes or levels to interfere. This of course happens so often in those artifacts that we call 'works of art', and so conspicuously, that it has seemed to many commentators to provide art with one of its defining characteristics.
>
> (91)

He is at his happiest and best deploying psychoanalysis to explore the delights of the high culture text, writing memorably on Tiepolo, Mahler, Schoenberg. But at a certain point a decorous reticence about being too glibly explicit becomes evasion. While it may well be that blurring its own hierarchical distinctions does characterize many 'artifacts we call "works of art" ' (*if* the reader approaches them with this interest in mind) it might well characterize others we don't. It would mitigate the suspicion that *Psychoanalysis and the Future of Theory* is committed to a good old-fashioned high art formalism if it had tested for the blurring of hierarchical distinctions in *Terminator 2* or a Hitchcock movie. For there is a world outside that of Mozart and Proust, and psychoanalysis has much to say about that also.

Malcolm Bowie says he wants 'to create a fully engaged and theoretically self-aware playfulness of response to literature' (144), rejecting the view that the purpose of theory is to introduce 'a sense of civic responsibility or theoretical rectitude' into textual study (143). That's a tough option, and I have a nasty feeling a tone of rectitude is going to creep into my comments from now on (though I'll go on struggling against it). Isn't this kind of playfulness peculiarly individual, and, in a word dusty from the portmanteau of civic responsibility, liberal? That Bowie is turning psychoanalysis to this (political) end comes out, I think, in several ways (besides, that is, the imposed opposition of play *or* responsibility).

One occurs in the course of a fascinating and suggestive comparison of the sense of time and 'futurality' in Freud and Lacan with that theorized by Heidegger. *Psychoanalysis and the Future of Theory* offers the option of either 'chronometrical' time (linear, uniform, modelled on space) or 'modal' time (past/present/future in a changing, dynamic relationship to each other) (13). It is argued that for Heidegger time is modal, as it is for psychoanalysis, and indeed the critic of high art. Modal versus chronometric is another bad option, I think, because the alternative that counts here is singular versus multiple temporality (such as that Althusser proposes). Heidegger does not have just one time, 'primordial' time, the time of the subject in its being towards death, but *also* 'ordinary' time, the inescapable time of being with others. Silently ditching ordinary time, which is social time, Bowie privileges 'the modal time of the critic's desire' (48) as a kind of Bergsonian temporality of the self.

With the public sphere of the social thus attenuated, hardly any interval is left between text and context, art and its reading (even though it's affirmed that psychoanalysis poses the relation between text and reader as 'transactional and transferential', 97). Hence the way the examples are treated – less as readings produced in a context and more as how the texts are in themselves (proving themselves to be works of art by blurring hierarchies). *Psychoanalysis and the Future of Theory* discovers 'that psychoanalysis is of particular use in analysing works of art that originate in the same broad cultural context as itself' (110–11) but is not interested in asking why. The last chapter, on 'Freud and the European unconscious', certainly threatens some historical engagement; in fact it begins by joking that the term 'European unconscious', like 'Christian horsemanship', is a category mistake (117), retracts this so far as to say that the idea of the unconscious is profoundly European, rewrites that issue as 'How original is Freud?', gives six witty answers leading to the remark that 'Freud's "unconscious" is European, alas' (119), then glossing European as Viennese. So Freud's position in relation to Modernism (and European history) is reduced to tastes he shares with fellow-

Austrian, Robert Musil. All great fun and very playful but what this steps aside from is civic responsibility, not to mention theoretical rectitude.

Working with aesthetic texts and psychoanalysis doesn't have to be like this, but can, and I think must, be drawn out in conjunction (no totalities where none possible) with a sense of the social and historical. Despite denegations, *Psychoanalysis and the Future of Theory* does have a political intention: as part of the old quest for liberal self-fulfilment it aims to try out psychoanalysis as a new board for surfing the crests of high art.

Brennan

If *Psychoanalysis and the Future of Theory* can be criticized for lack in social vision, Brennan's *History After Lacan*, offering a total account of the modern psyche, contemporary commodity production, patriarchal domination and men's self-destructive exploitation of the natural world, definitely cannot. For my general line of argument about the articulation of history and the unconscious, the juxtaposition of the two texts is instructive, even exemplary, the one deficient in what totalization is possible, the other suffering from it in an impossible excess.

Claiming authorization in Lacan's historical perspective (which it describes) Brennan proposes that 'the ego's era' is characterized by a 'foundational fantasy'. As follows:

> *Thesis I: The subject is founded by a hallucinatory fantasy in which it conceives itself as the locus of active agency and the environment as passive; its subjectivity is secured by a projection onto the environment, apparently beginning with the mother, which makes her into an object which the subject in fantasy controls.*

(11)

Brought about in a process which represents temporality as space, the ego is founded in this hallucinatory split between (active) subject and (passive) object, and in the fantasy of objectifying the other as passive – whether this other is the commodity, Woman or the natural world: 'energy is bound in commodities and the technology that produces them, in a manner that parallels its bondage in hallucination' (13).

This is a very drastic abridgement of an argument whose ambition I found at once stimulating and infuriating, written up in a style both engagingly self-reflective and irritatingly insouciant. Some more detail will be given via my criticisms, which will concern, first, Brennan's theoretical strategy for dealing with the relation between the unconscious and history, and, second, issues raised by her (and Lacan's) attack on the Enlightenment and modernity.

In her methodological preamble (4–8) Brennan is, I think, right to make the historicist point that the very discourses of our time partake in 'the ego's era' and that contemporary distrust of concepts of totality may itself be symptomatic, but her dismissal of objections to totalizing as merely 'prejudice' (7) fails to take on board the very serious reasons, among them those advanced by Althusser and cited earlier, why we cannot treat the social and the psychic as any kind of seamless unity. For Brennan, in Thesis V, *'the means by which time is compressed for space is identical to the process of producing profit'* (17); and, again, 'the construction of a commodity binds energy in the same way that it is bound in the repression of a hallucination' (118). Identical? The same? Such formulations would efface all those uneven differences, levels and temporalities between and across the social formation and subjectivity.

Because it doesn't really recognize their existence, *History After Lacan* doesn't attempt to discuss or describe any mechanisms intervening between the social and the psychic. Whatever these are they are specific, and a body of writing potentially in tune with Brennan's project has analysed one such major structuring in its specificity, though Brennan makes no mention of it.

I'm thinking of the work by Laura Mulvey, Stephen Heath and others associated with the film journal, *Screen*, on the tradition of visual representation and the gendering of the gaze. From a basis in Lacan's theory of the look Brennan rightly notes that 'the spatial perceptions of people in given historical periods will vary' (49) and points to the way vision is promoted in consumer culture. From the same Lacanian basis, work on film moved on (particularly in Heath's 1976 essay on 'Narrative space')[9] to analyse the process of the (would-be unified and unconstructed) subject inscribed by Quattrocento space. Such work is successful precisely because, admonished by *Reading Capital*, it resists the lure of facile and unthinkable totalizations and concentrates on the specific signifying effects and effectivity of the high art tradition of the still image and then the other, different, specific effects of 'moving pictures'.

It is pertinent to wonder what energizes a desire for totality in which such specificities and differences are so easily set aside. It is, presumably, a desire for the One and the mother's body, which will show itself also in a thirst for presence and the real. So it does here.

Not recognizing how unstable is Marx's binary opposition between use value and exchange value,[10] Brennan is committed to the view that there is some 'process of natural exchange' (148) outside and opposed to the circulation of commodities. With the same consequence, her account of the founding of the subject via hallucination (which 'splits the subject', 12) seems to rely on its alternative, the real, in a way the full Lacanian concept of misrecognition does not. Whatever else is unsure in Lacan, it is surely clear – from his account of *objet a*, from the essay on the mirror stage, from his discussion of *La Chose* – that neither lack nor plenitude is originary since they emerge *together*, in a simultaneous process. How can it be then, at least within a Lacanian framework, that 'the mother's body', prerequisite for Brennan's foundational fantasy, is declared 'an origin before the foundation' (97)? Except, of course, that this is always the content of the fantasy of the mother's body.

Brennan, Lacan, modernity

Of its own project *History After Lacan* reflects, 'This is a one-sided theory of history, one-sided in that it analyses the dynamics of a totalizing trend, but neglects that trend's intersection with specific historical contexts' (82). This I think is an admission that Brennan's project has founded itself in one temporality – that of the unconscious – and not reached out towards another temporality, that of history. As a result, even though she says there's no going back to pre-modernity (74), it becomes fatally easy for her to present only one side of modernity, the worst.

Essentially, Brennan's critique concerns: the ego; science; aggression. Although she knows perfectly well that 'without a fixed point, there is nothing that marks the subject out as separate, with an individual history and personal memory' (109) she writes of the ego as structured by a hallucinatory fantasy in which an active subject becomes opposed to a passive object. Starting from the side of history several questions arise here. Has there ever been a speaking subject not able to mark out his or her individual identity (and to that extent, ego) in distinction from everyone else? When was there a speaking subject not constituted by his or her ability to mark itself off as subject from the rest of the world as object? And do such egos only belong to 'men (active in mastering the Woman as object) or can women have them too?

The need here, surely, is to historicize the ego in a well-known fashion by distinguishing between, say, the relative ego and the Cartesian or transcendental ego which misrecognizes itself as uncreated. And that ego – as Brennan hints more than once – 'gathers steam' (41) from the Renaissance.

Brennan's monocular view of modernity is especially conspicuous in her account of science. Its proclaimed non-emotionality and objective attitude (she cites Fox Keller, 1985) is, she says, imbued with feelings that are 'aggressive, sadistic and narcissistic' (72). In response you could argue that science is not motivated by aggression, sadism and narcissism (the discovery of penicillin, for instance?). It's better to concede that, like every other human activity, the practice of science is indeed libidinally charged but that the psychoanalytic account of this charge has very little to say about the social and historical effects of different scientific practices. Even if the discovery of penicillin was motivated by treating nature as an object (sadism) and feelings of competitive ambition (get there first), I'd say we are much better with penicillin than without.

Aggression Brennan locates in the ego, and in this adheres closely to Lacan's position in the essay of 1948. World historical records for the amount and nature of aggression around at any given time are notoriously subjective and unreliable. How do we assess Attila the Hun against Vlad the Impaler and Heinrich Himmler? Five thousand followers of Spartacus crucified along the road to Rome against twenty million Russian civilians shot between 1941 and 1945?

There could be a point to be made here from the history of English sport. Until around 1800 a common pastime was to tie a cockerel to a stick and throw stones at it until it was dead. This was called 'Throwing at Cocks'. In the period 1780–1850 the sport faded away, not least because of the activity of such organizations as the Association for Promoting Rational Humanity Towards the Animal Creation, founded in 1830.[11] I would say that this Association was strongly motivated by both a wish to sublimate desire into rational activity and by an abreaction from aggression. Against the view that aggression grew with 'the ego's era' has to be balanced all kinds of historical activities – from the anti-slavery movement to Amnesty International (neither independent of unconscious motivation) – whose historical tendency worked against aggression. It might be that as egoistic aggression increased, so did a corresponding abreaction.

A worthy demystification of Victorian positivism ('Look, they thought they were good and rational but they were just as much driven by power and lust as everyone else') should not encourage a false either/or – either only rational or only unconsciously charged activity. Similarly, the assessment of modernity should not be undertaken largely on psychoanalytic grounds ignoring historical contexts which demand a more balanced judgement. Modernity is a process of loss and gain we are still too deep inside to be able to compute adequately. But while modernity brought us children in coal mines, monads in the streets of Manchester and gas ovens in Auschwitz, in virtue of the same historical process it also imported democratic parliaments, suffragettes, condoms and cheaply available paperbacks from Routledge such as *History After Lacan*.

Lacan's savagely aggressive attack on the ego and its aggressivity remains to be accounted for. In the context of a writer who calls Freud to task for misrecognizing the desires of the ego, it becomes impossible not to think of the man of unspeakable egotism recorded in Elizabeth Roudinesco's recent biography of Jacques Lacan, a subject therefore reacting in his writing against his own egotism. And of course Lacan's historical vision needs itself to be historicized a little.

In a passage Brennan alludes to but, curiously, does not cite in full, Lacan writes:

> What we are faced with, to employ the jargon that corresponds to our approaches to man's subjective needs, is the increasing absence of all those saturations of the superego and ego ideal that are realised in all kinds of organic forms in traditional societies, forms that extend from the rituals of everyday intimacy to the periodical festivals in which the community manifests itself. We no longer know them except in their most obviously degraded aspects. Furthermore, in abolishing the cosmic polarity of the male and female principles, our society undergoes all the psychological effects proper to the modern phenomenon known as the 'battle between the sexes' – a vast community of such effects, at the limit between 'democratic' anarchy of the passions and their desperate levelling down by the 'great winged hornet' of narcissistic tyranny. It is clear that the promotion of the ego today culminates, in conformity with the utilitarian conception of man that reinforces it, in an ever more advanced realisation of man as individual, that is to say, in an isolation of the soul ever more akin to its original dereliction.
>
> (26–7)

Even without a sustained exposition (I have failed to locate the 'great winged hornet') it is clear how this stakes out a position against the Enlightenment and against modernity. Born in 1901, Lacan's attitude is far from uncommon among members of his generation – besides Heidegger himself, these are the views of people like Yeats, Eliot, Lawrence, Leavis and R. H. Tawney. In fact it's not easy to recall many writers of the Modernist period who don't believe it's all gone down the chute (Brecht? Hugh MacDiarmid?).

For us, fear of the great winged hornet notwithstanding, there's no going back to the 'organic forms in traditional societies' (and for the vast majority of people these were pretty awful). In the time of postmodernity that sense of shock and contemptuous rejection of modernity which Lacan feels is no longer possible. Modernity now does not present itself as a sudden, radical intrusion but as a familiar condition, as the necessary terrain which is to be contested and to which there is no thinkable alternative. Postmodernity would read the stand Lacan takes against modernity as typically Modernist.

Manchester Metropolitan University

Notes

1 Raymond Williams, *Politics and Letters* (London: New Left Books, 1979), p. 184.
2 Jonathan Dollimore, *Sexual Dissidence* (Oxford: Clarendon Press, 1991), p. 170.
3 Sigmund Freud, 'A difficulty in the path of psycho-analysis', *Standard Edition* (London: Hogarth Press, 1953–74), vol. 17, p. 141. The paper is not in the Penguin Freud Library.
4 Sigmund Freud, *New Introductory Lectures*, Penguin Freud Library 2 (Harmondsworth: Penguin Books, 1973), p. 99.
5 This argument is finely set out by Paul Q. Hirst and Penny Woolley in *Social Relations and Human Attributes* (London: Macmillan, 1982), especially in Chapter 8, 'Psychoanalysis and social relations'.
6 Louis Althusser and René Balibar, *Reading Capital* (London: New Left Books,1975), p. 99.
7 Stephen Heath, '*Anata mo*', *Screen*, vol. 17, no. 4 (Winter 1976), p. 61.
8 There is a question here which will have been noted already by readers of Lyotard's account of how differences between two conceptual schemes can only be assessed as differences from a point sharing some commonality with both. The 'simultaneity' Heath writes of refers to the simultaneity of historical and subjective processes in the life of a single subject. A third temporality, then, is required to construe 'events' in the other two different temporalities precisely *as* simultaneous.
9 See Stephen Heath, *Questions of Cinema* (London: Macmillan, 1982).
10 See the wonderfully veiled deconstruction of the opposition by Jacques Derrida in *Given Time I. Counterfeit Money* (Chicago: University of Chicago Press, 1992), pp. 157–62.
11 See Robert Malcolmson, 'Popular recreations under attack', in Bernard Waites *et al.* (eds), *Popular Culture: Past and Present* (London: Croom Helm, 1982), pp. 20–46.

Reviews

Josephine McDonagh

Ernst Behler, *German Romantic Literary Theory* (Cambridge: Cambridge University Press, 1993), xxiv + 344 pp., £45.00 (hardback)

Frances Ferguson, *Solitude and the Sublime: Romanticism and the Aesthetics of Individuation* (New York and London: Routledge, 1992), xi + 177 pp., £12.99 (paperback)

These books, both dealing with topics in Romantic critical theory, differ markedly in style. The differences are evident throughout – in the vocabulary, the chapter headings, down to the way that the sentences turn. They begin and end differently, have a different sense of a project, and a different notion of a proper scholarly apparatus – what you should and shouldn't do, for instance, with a footnote (and in Ferguson's case, to whom you might dedicate your footnotes). The differences in style are in some way comparable with a variance that Ernst Behler draws out between Schleiermacher and Friedrich Schlegel in their views on the proper modes of knowledge acquisition. While Schleiermacher is content to work from a position of puzzlement, to reach up by slow and steady progress towards a higher understanding attained through the accumulation of facts and insights, the latter believed that higher understanding came first. Behler cites Schlegel: 'It is not sufficient to understand the real meaning of a confused work better than the author understood it himself. You must also comprehend the confusion, including its principles, and be able to characterize and even reconstruct it' (279). In this comparison Ferguson is like Schlegel, and Behler like the steady Schleiermacher. If Behler hints at the difficulties that Schlegel and Schleiermacher may have had conversing with each other, we may legitimately ask how a conversation between Behler and Ferguson might sound – two critics who may seem to have more in common than not: both academics in North American universities, both scholars of European Romanticism; but who, when we listen in, are speaking in styles that are as distinct as different languages.

Learning a language requires us to be alert to context, but the constituency of a context is, in itself, highly debatable. These two books display strikingly different apprehensions of the limits of context. For Behler, who is writing about a coterie of writers within a relatively short time span, the early German Romantics (the Schlegels, Novalis, Wackenroder and Tieck) in the period 1795 to 1801, the context of his writers is brought to the fore. He includes a wealth of details of meetings, friendships, marriages, educations, collaborations, homes and dinner parties, weaving an intricate fabric of liaisons to form a backdrop to this extraordinary time of intellectual and creative production. Paradoxically we have little sense of Behler's own intellectual context: he adopts the role of the highly informed observer, watching anonymously as the pageant of Romanticism proceeds before him. Ferguson, on the other hand, gives us a vibrant sense of *her* intellectual context, while, purposefully, having little to say about the context of Romanticism. Her book is proposed as an intervention in the debates in critical theory that have been provoked – in the main – by the work of Paul de Man, and at her best, she is deft and compelling. Read together, however, the two books raise some interesting questions about contexts for contemporary academic work, about academic audiences, and about the place of history – our own and others' – in critical investigation.

Behler's book is a clear and scholarly work of synthesis and explication that guides us carefully through the work of these notoriously obscure writers. The proposition is the usual one – that these fragmentary and mystical works are nevertheless supported by a rigorous theoretical infrastructure, which can be abstracted, and then applied, in our interpretation of their work. Thus each of the six chapters ends with an 'example', in which the findings of the first part of the chapter are used in a reading of one particular work: for instance, the chapter on mysticism ends with a reading of Novalis's *Heinrich von Ofterdingen*. Behler's book is exemplary in its clarity, and will be invaluable to students of German Romanticism – a book to read, perhaps, *before* attempting Lacoue-Labarthe and Nancy's *The Literary Absolute*.

Early in the book Behler notes in passing the continuing significance of the early German Romantics' work, in that they foreshadowed the concerns of contemporary critical theory (signalling in particular the work of Adorno, Heidegger, Derrida and de Man), and have become a target of the 'fundamentalist critique of modernity and postmodernity' (8). While this is indisputable, Behler, in this book at least, seems surprisingly untouched by the concerns of modernity. There are virtually no further references to these writers, or discussion of the issues that would figure on a modernist (or postmodern) critical agenda. The status of knowledge is never in dispute nor is its relation to the context of its production and dissemination. The French Revolution, for instance, was an 'influence', but small in relation to the Germans' 'revolution in ideas'. Events and relationships have the odd status of being at once determining and determined: Hölderlin, for instance, '[did] not play a major role ... because his visit to Jena was accidental' (17). Despite its avowed interest in material detail, the stance of the book is idealist, mirroring his estimation of the work of the Romantics themselves, existing 'independent of historical relationships' (5).

Were Friedrich Schlegel to publish a book today, one imagines that his acknowledgements would be fulsome: 'Thanks to my brother, August, and to my friends, Johann Fichte, Rahel Levin, Novalis. . . . And to Dorothea, without whom ...' Behler imparts a strong sense of the cliquishness of Schlegel's circle – or at least an impression of a small group of writers in constant intellectual exchange. A similar sense is apparent in Ferguson's book: as the same names crop up in the acknowledgements, throughout the references, and even in the blurb on the cover, one has a feeling that this is a Small World. While the academic terrain of the late twentieth century may be more expansive than that of two centuries ago, in this book's representation, it is not necessarily more populous.

Nevertheless, Ferguson undertakes a big project that negotiates areas that Behler only hints at. On the one hand she attempts an historical argument about the rise of a concern with individuation, as exemplified within the aesthetic of the sublime, as the primary philosophical problem at the end of the eighteenth century. As she puts it, 'an anxiety about the relationship between the individual and the type ... [was] ... the characteristically aesthetic epistemological problem' (31). At the same time, she presents an argument about the significance of the aesthetic of the sublime for poststructuralism, by linking her readings of the familiar repertoire of the sublime – Weiskel, Hertz, de Bolla – with a critique of deconstructive materialism. In her account, deconstruction is another empiricism, and the sublime in particular is important because it 'resolved into' two intellectual positions – formal idealism and empiricism – that have remained in conflict ever since, a struggle which empiricism always wins. Ferguson's book goes against this current by holding out for Kant's idealism, which, she claims, used the sublime 'as the occasion for imagining that an empirical infinite... can be connected with the artificial systems of representing infinity that have no empirical correlates' (2). Deconstruction's attention to the technologies of meaning that always exceed meanings themselves and effect an inevitable loss of agency, not only repeats the sublime experience, but does so by endorsing an 'empirical infinite that makes language and society ... the infinite that humans can identify with only at their peril' (21).

The argument is extremely complex, and difficult not only for its boldness, the independence of its arguments, but also because its different parts, unfortunately, are not particularly well integrated. The book is divided into three unequal sections: the first three chapters deal with philosophical issues that emerge from Burke's and Kant's sublime as dealt with by recent theorists; the second three chapters have a more historical focus, in that they examine related debates of the Romantic period; the third section – just one chapter – is a critique of McGann's and de Man's claims to materialism. A number of the essays have been previously published, including Ferguson's influential essay, 'The sublime of Edmund Burke, or the bathos of experience', which appeared first in *Glyph* in 1981. One has a sense that this is an assemblage of essays produced over a long time span rather than a sustained performance. (The book was previously announced, under a slightly different title, as forthcoming in 1988.)

The essays in the short middle section come closest to making an historical argument, and provide the most stimulating and sugges-tive part of the book – although the relationship between the method here, and, most significantly, the critique of arguments about material-ism presented in the final chapter, is not explicitly worked through. These essays discuss some other Romantic discourses – the gothic, the population debates, and travel writing – which, Ferguson argues, share a common preoccupation with the 'individual and type' anxiety that, she holds, dominates the period. Thus she provides a compelling reading of Malthus's 1798 *Essay on Population* as expressive of a worry, *not* that there are or ever will be too many bodies, but that there are too many consciousnesses. In this way, Malthus becomes like a Romantic poet, sharing a desire for solitude, an escape from the encroaching demands of others. Ferguson suggests an explanation for the massive imaginative impact of an essay which was neither particularly original in its claims nor scientific in its methods; the vastly expanded second edition, published first in 1803, made a more serious contribution to political economy, social policy, and indeed, family planning, but it is the first edition that is endlessly cited in the works of this period. As Ferguson demonstrates, in the inflam-matory first edition Malthus traces the borders between barbarity and modernity, delineating the tragic destiny of the individuated, free, modern subject.

Ferguson provides two different contexts for her analysis of Malthus. One is with Wordsworth, who, she argues through a reading of 'Tintern Abbey', unlike Malthus, insists on the socialization of consciousness – that there must always be room for at least two (including Dorothy). The other context – surprisingly in a book that is otherwise unconcerned with the category of gender – is the feminist debate about reproduction. Ferguson takes up Germaine Greer's *Sex and Destiny* (1984): while Greer presents a feminist critique of the (still dominant) Malthusian battle between sex and resources, she does not, according to Ferguson, make any claims on behalf of women for consciousness; in that respect, Greer complies with Malthus, whose major anxiety, according to Ferguson, is that women will have consciousnesses too. The point is a rich one, in that it suggests the interrelationships between the histories of gender, reproduction, consciousness and aesthetics. But it is a peculiar one in another sense, because it rests on what seems to me to be a fairly wilful misreading of a passage in Malthus's essay. The passage in question expresses the concern that, when resources increase, women will be forced to marry beneath them, to men who are unable to keep them in the style to which they are accustomed. This, he writes, will be considered 'a real and essential evil' by 'the generality of people'. For Ferguson, the passage is 'the only account in his brief history of world civilization which attributes a consciousness to a woman, the only one, that is, that recognizes it might matter how a woman might feel about her lot in life' (123). But in this passage and elsewhere, Malthus is concerned less (if at all) for the unhappiness of women, than with the social chaos that will be brought about by the class miscegenation that is the inevitable consequence of progress. The term that is notable for its absence in Ferguson's critique is 'class'. This is not to imply that in the struggle of the grand narratives, class should necessarily win out. But it is to suggest that it is, to say the least, unlikely that in 1798 gender would have been on the political agenda and class not.

This returns us to the question of context. While Ferguson's intention to 'proceed on two fronts' – the theoretical and the historical – is to be welcomed, in this book we are left with the strange sense, not that we are in two places at one time (or perhaps two times in one place), but rather that the two begin to look too much like each other. That is to say, Romanticism's intellectual and social concerns start to coincide rather too neatly with those of Ferguson's very particular late twentieth-century agenda. In this case, the contexts of past intellectual labour have been assimilated into those of the present. The decision as to whether we read this tendency as a virtue, a symptom, or a misreading depends on our own intellectual contexts, and our own academic styles.

Exeter University

Lawrence Driscoll

James Miller, *The Passion of Michel Foucault* (New York: Simon & Schuster, 1993), 491 pp., $27.50 (hardback)

Louis Althusser, *The Future Lasts Forever: A Memoir* (New York: The New Press, 1993), 365 pp., $25.00 (hardback)

Along with the recent publication of D. A. Miller's *Bringing Out Roland Barthes*, Barthes's *Incidents*, and Hervé Guibert's fictionalized account of the last days of Foucault's life, *To the Friend Who Did Not Save My Life*, the appearance of Miller's work alongside Althusser's controversial 'confession', adds to the growing interest in excavating the private lives of various poststructuralist philosophers. While both publications created a series of debates in scholarly and popular journals, in France the news of Althusser's crime allowed the enemies of Marxism to assert how his actions simply reinforced their beliefs that 'communism = crime [and] philosophy = madness' (256). In his own way Miller is asking us to accept the same conclusions about Foucault insofar as his analysis suggests that poststructuralism = sickness.

By extracting a posthumous 'confession' from Foucault, Miller's conservative stance allows critics of poststructuralism to be reassured that Foucault was not so much a philosopher as a drug-taking pervert. However, what the works reveal is that both Foucault and Althusser are denied a chance to defend themselves against the charges that are made against them. In the case of Althusser he is silenced by the courts, and in the case of Foucault, Miller decides that the subject of his inquiry is also 'unfit to plead'. The result is that in both works the lives of the philosophers are laid out before us, allowing us to peruse the micropolitics of their private lives and pass judgement on their actions. While Foucault is unable to defend himself against the conclusions that Miller draws, Althusser is replying to the charges that were made against him, but only from the safety and confinement of the grave. As Althusser points out 'Any individual who is declared unfit to plead is destined to be placed beneath a tombstone of silence' (19). In both instances the lives of these two men are reduced to 'cases' which are always already closed and decided upon by the discursive formation in which their actions are presented.

Unlike Didier Eribon's biography, which kept a knowing distance from Foucault's private activity, Miller takes the 'hidden' life as his focus, a decision which generated a marked degree of controversy. *Salmagundi* devoted most of their Winter 1993 edition to a symposium on Miller's work, while Alan Ryan in *The New York Review of Books* finds Foucault's politics 'no more plausible than before'.[1] Paul Rabinow complains that the work is 'cheap and obvious and easy', while David Halperin and Judith Butler are equally angry with Miller's project, leading the latter to comment that Miller's presentation of Foucault's 'excesses', 'dovetails nicely with [a] culturally reactionary position'.[2]

What is most troubling about Miller's book is the catalyst from which it sprang. Miller tells us that the idea of the book occurred to him after hearing a piece of 'gossip' which suggested that Foucault had 'deliberately' gone into the gay culture of San Francisco knowing that he was HIV positive. Miller wanted to follow this 'trail of gossip' so as to settle his mind, because, as he anxiously asks, 'what if the story were true?' (376). Yet Foucault has already stated, 'Do not ask me who I am, and do not ask me to remain the same. . . . More than one person, doubtless like me, writes in order to have no face' (19). One of the difficulties of the book is that rather than deconstructing the binary of the surface 'mask' and the 'hidden' Self, Miller's text appears to be driven by an anxious need to see and know the 'real' story behind the name 'Michel Foucault'.

In a lecture given at the College de France, Michel Foucault suggested that 'it would be interesting to write a history . . . starting from the problem of the philosophical life' (Miller 379). Taking up this lead, Miller declares that his book 'is not a biography' (5), but, in the spirit of an anti-biography, is 'a narrative account of one man's lifelong struggle to honour Nietzsche's gnomic injunction, "to become what one is" ' (5). To live one's philosophy is thus to answer Nietzsche's call, and, in approaching the limits of Being, one begins to perceive, in Foucault's words, 'the many images that have never turned into poetry' (107). Olivier Corpet and Yann Moulier Boutang in their foreword to the Althusser text (which contains an appendix entitled 'The Facts') also feel that this work should not be read as a biography but as poetry. Insofar as the subject matter of Althusser's text is madness they suggest that '[we are therefore] in the realm of fiction' (8). If Miller's text is often held together by an anxiety to follow Foucault into the deepest recesses of his behaviour, then reading Althusser is also an exercise in authorial anxiety as we watch him grapple with the truth of himself in the face of a society which judged him guilty. The pleasure, albeit slight, comes when Althusser breaks through his haze of paranoia and psychoactive drugs and appears to be at peace with himself and his past.

To 'understand' Foucault's life or Althusser's actions (to make them safe, to explain them) a certain distancing often arises. In Miller's case he frames Foucault through Bataille's theories of transgression, in which an individual's behaviour, by taking thought to its breaking point, renews 'the project for a general critique of reason' (143), opening a space in which the Self can uncover its 'reality' and become 'free'. Casting his light towards Foucault, Miller quotes Deleuze's remark that 'an individual acquires a real proper name only through the most severe exercise in depersonalization' (195). Given this framework Miller takes us through Foucault's 'philosophical life', focusing on those moments and activities which can be seen as 'limit experiences' in which the philosopher comes into focus as a 'real' subject, at precisely those moments when he dissolves at the limit, metamorphosing into Blanchot's 'thought from the Outside'. For Althusser however, becoming 'the thought from the Outside' is impossible, seeing as how his madness places him on the Outside of discourse, positioning him at the furthest distance possible from the truth, or at least from the chance to speak his truth and be heard. For Althusser 'becoming Other' involves not a liberation but a process of depersonalization at the hands of the Ideological and Repressive State Apparatus which he had so clearly outlined earlier in his career. He clarifies this alienation in his discussion of what he calls 'the fortress'. He describes himself as being 'in a fortress, confined to solitude by the walls of my impenetrable anguish' (270). While this fortress kept him entrapped it also allowed him protection from the outside world: for Althusser *qua* madman, the Ideological State Apparatuses are now indistinguishable from the Repressive State Apparatuses. On a couple of occasions Derrida and Macherey paid a visit to 'the fortress' and talked at length with Althusser, while Foucault, after visiting, 'went away convinced [that Althusser] was getting better' (271).

If Althusser's text disturbs us by the fact that a philosopher murdered his wife, then what disturbs Miller is the possibility that Foucault willingly, not to say wilfully, adopted a sexual lifestyle which for Miller was also tantamount to suicide and murder. For Althusser the questions of suicide and murder are again the focus. He states how he wrote *The Future Lasts Forever* so as to resist a desire to destroy himself, and tells us that he had been intent on destroying everything in his life, including his wife, and that '[he] wanted at all costs to destroy [*himself*] because [he] had never existed'

(277). It was thus the remark of a woman friend who told him that she did not like his 'will to self destruction' (277) which 'practically inspired me to write this little book' (277).

Drawing upon Foucault's early fascination with death and suicide, Miller, while enjoying a kind of voyeuristic disgust, transforms these desires into manifestations of Foucault's wish, following Seneca, 'to rejoin ourselves' (20). Miller suggests that Foucault's early suicide attempts and fascination with death were related to unease about his own homosexuality, while the spectre of drugs is raised by citing Foucault's companion, Daniel Defert, who tells us 'I don't know if he injected . . . but the drugs Foucault used at that time were . . . certainly stronger than mere alcohol or hashish' (56). Questions of homosexuality, suicide and drugs thus set the stage for a work in which Miller plans to reveal the place of these three leitmotifs as 'limit experiences' that lie at the heart of the Foucauldian *œuvre*. At some level Althusser's 'limit experiences' (drugs, suicide and murder) take on a more sombre tone, and leave us not with someone who finally became what he was but someone crushed by the institutions which kept him under their supervision. Only towards the end of the book, when Althusser's sanity appears somewhat tangible, do we sense that this Artaudian figure has possibly come close to rejoining himself, and perhaps for the very first time.

As an example of Miller's strategy to link the private life and the work, he frames *Discipline and Punish* not only within the events of May 1968 in Paris and Foucault's work with prison reform, but also takes up the question of Foucault's sexuality in relation to this text. Miller thus suggests reframing the opening scene of the book (the torture and execution of Damiens), as a limit experience parallel to the theatrical 'whips, chains, lancets . . . cells, operating tables, [and] dungeons' (265) of the gay S/M scene. Foucault's interest in S/ M is thus seen in the light of his suggestions towards exploring 'an erotics of truth' in which the theatricality and depersonalization of S/M practices, like the brothel in Genet's *The Balcony* becomes a space where one can destroy and re-invent the self, engaging in a Nietzschean game of truth: 'a game played with the body itself' (269). Foucault's experiments with S/M thus free the Self from Reason by giving birth to the Body Without Organs that Artaud hoped would emerge from his own Theatre of Cruelty. While we cannot wish to see Althusser's murder of Hélène as part of an 'erotics of truth' what may be liberatory is the act of writing this memoir, as he says, an act which represented 'a process of my (re)taking in hand my own existence' (278). Foucault's existence, on the other hand, remains firmly in the grasp of Miller.

Miller goes into detail concerning Foucault's visits to California's gay subculture, as well as informing us of his experience with LSD in Death Valley. Miller seems intent on making a meal out of every detail that he has uncovered but is often unable to follow through convincingly. For example, he outlines the impact of this one drug experience on Foucault's work, describing how, because of the 'insights' regarding sexuality that the drug provided, Foucault gave up 'his original plan for a monumental seven-volume work' (252) on the history of sexuality and shifted the focus away from masturbation towards 'the incest taboo' (439). While this relies on assuming that the unconscious is a cage which can be unlocked with the key of drugs, the event seems unable to support the grand effects that it was supposed to have caused. During the same passage Miller then gestures in footnotes towards Foucault's alleged involvement with his sister. Was LSD supposed to have somehow reminded Foucault of a long forgotten sexual encounter with his sister?

Although he goes to great lengths to take into account what one critic described as his own possible 'pathological homophobia' (384), Miller desires to preserve in his work 'an overriding commitment to telling the truth' (383) while simultaneously claiming not to offer 'a summary verdict' on Foucault's behaviour. This sense that unveiling 'reveals' the Self beneath the mask, rather than actually creating the subjectivity that we perceive, also emerges in Miller's metaphors surrounding Foucault and AIDS. While LSD is discussed in terms of a 'key' that unlocked his unconscious, so S/M and AIDS are also seen as keys that can help us to 'unlock' the secret of Foucault, casting a 'revealing light' (378) on the Subject. The rhetoric of the closet, as Eve Sedgwick has recently pointed out, plays a large role in our structures of knowledge, and Miller suggests that the 'truth' of homosexuality is somehow always locked away and unable to speak its name, until the revealing light of the doctor, detective or biographer is cast into the darkness where pathologies lurk. In this respect David Halperin rightly directs us towards what he sees as Miller's deployment of an 'illusory knowingness'.[3]

At one point, Miller draws our attention to Foucault's comments on Roussel's apparent suicide in which he said that the ' "impossibility, here, of determining" what the dead man had in mind means that "every discourse" about his work runs the risk of "being deceived less by a secret than by the awareness that there is a secret" ' (382). In part then, the 'appeal' of this text, as well as the 'freak show' aspects of Althusser's text, emerges from the belief that there is a secret which can be uncovered, and so make visible and audible (and hence knowable and safe), the love (or the murder) that dare not speak its name. By treating drugs, S/M and homosexuality as 'limit experiences' Miller returns them to the place of the Uncanny and the pathological, at the same time that they are made 'familiar' by 'uncovering' them. In spite of his own intentions, Miller focuses on what Foucault refers to as the Unthought, and by making difference thinkable and familiar, essentially robs it of its ability to unsettle power. What we see in Althusser however is that power is only slightly disturbed by madness and has developed a keen set of instruments and medicines for containing it: madness would appear to be able to unsettle power momentarily but is unable to move beyond it. Althusser, as we have seen, is not liberated by madness, but becomes imprisoned in his own fortress.

In 'The discourse of language' Foucault warned us that 'taboos are not always to be found where we imagine them to be.'[4] However, tucked away in Miller's acknowledgements we read that Leo Bersani had suggested to Miller that perhaps he was 'too fixated, but from the outside, on the "extreme" elements in Foucault's sexuality'. Bersani said that Miller's prose style, although it evokes 'some *very* sympathetic dad-scholar-doctor', nevertheless tended to make the subject of Foucault's sexuality 'even more impenetrable than it might be', needlessly complicating 'something which, finally, may not be that difficult to understand, may not be as mysterious as "*expérience-limite*" tends to suggest' (468).

Foucault suggested that in the traditional history of ideas the point was to look for the 'unity of a work' and its 'hidden meanings'.[5] In this sense Miller is not as true to the spirit of Foucault as he would wish, for if the limit experience is an explosion, a 'caesurae breaking the instant and dispersing the subject',[6] then Miller's approach reassembles the scattered fragments which constitute the Self, recontaining the ruptures that could unmake the bourgeois subject. For Althusser however, he needs to locate the fragments to shore against his ruin, and *The Future Lasts Forever* is a record of his attempt to make sense of a life which he felt he had nearly destroyed. Althusser is thus quite happy to be able to rebuild his life in the days following his release from Soisy in 1983. What these two works could be said to highlight is the mechanisms of power that Foucault and Althusser outlined theoretically and confronted in their lives. Both works unfold the intertwined discourses of the police and the policed, and direct our concern to the ways in which the discourses which we would employ to produce the 'truth' of ourselves, are intricately bound up with the discourses that trap and imprison us.

University of Southern California

Notes

1 See *The New York Review of Books* (18 April 1993), p. 14.
2 ibid.
3 See Eve Kosofsky Sedgwick, *Epistemology of the Closet* (Berkeley: University of California Press, 1990). For Halperin's article see *Salmagundi*, 97 (Winter 1993), pp. 69–93.
4 See *The Archeology of Knowledge* trans. A. M. Sheridan Smith (New York: Pantheon Books, 1972), p. 232.
5 ibid., p. 230.
6 ibid., p. 231.

Shiva Srinivasan

Daniel Gunn, *Psychoanalysis and Fiction: An Exploration of Literary and Psychoanalytic Borders* (Cambridge: Cambridge University Press, 1990), 251 pp., £27.50 (hardback), £10.95 (paperback)

Robert Samuels, *Between Philosophy and Psychoanalysis: Lacan's Reconstruction of Freud* (New York and London: Routledge, 1993), 165 pp., £35.00 (hardback), £12.99 (paperback)

Gunn's text is that rare creature: practical criticism that is characterized by a rigorous consciousness of method. His subtitle is a true indication of what he has accomplished. The text is filled with metaphors of borders, journeys, frontiers, explorations, and adventures. The model for such a discursive space comes from Freud himself. Gunn seems to identify with Freud the Conquistador: an identification that is not without structural consequences for this text.[1] The metaphor of borders helps Gunn to avoid all the obvious mistakes. Psychoanalysis is not appealed to as an authority: it functions instead as a theoretical partner. Gunn also shies away from teleological accounts of psychoanalysis which would insist that there is a straight line from Freud to Lacan. (This perhaps is the main difference between the two books reviewed here.) Gunn's textual strategy is deliberate: he seeks to circumnavigate the lure of Lacan's 'absolute mastery' without a direct confrontation with the Master himself. This makes possible appropriations that are not unduly respectful of the Lacanian Legacy. Gunn invokes instead Lacanians like Serge Leclaire and Maud Mannoni, whose work has just started to make an impact on literary criticism.

Lacan also appears a lot less intimidating when read through disciples and dissidents.

The work of Leclaire and Maud Mannoni helps to . . . show how

Lacan's theories ... can be of vital use when the analyst is confronted by intense need or desperate deprivation – in autistic or
psychotic children, for example. They show the radical importance
of language and utterance in what Freud's patient 'Anna O.'
appropriately called the 'talking cure'.

(4)

Gunn is careful in his invocation of both authors and analysts and
attempts to provide a rationale for almost all his theoretical choices.
This text is designed to appeal to students of comparative literature
and critical theory. Gunn attempts again and again to map the
analogical possibilities inherent in psychoanalysis and literature. Here
is an example. The text begins with a consideration of the similarities
between the act of writing and the act of free association in the
analytic situation. Both are fraught with anxieties, resistances, and a
sense of futility. They both demand a willingness to 'work through'
this resistance in the hope that something will emerge in the end to
justify the effort involved. Gunn writes that:

> [t]he idea of giving up one's precious time to go to someone's
> office and sit, or lie, talking, once or several times a week, whether
> one feels the inclination or not; not just talking, but talking about
> difficulty, about the unresolved bits of one's self and past; and
> this to a largely silent listener, whom one has to pay for the
> privilege! It might be hard to imagine anyone doing this volun-
> tarily.

(1)

Bizarre as such an attempt might seem, it bears a curious resemblance
to the act of writing. As autobiographies testify, there are very few
authors indeed who look forward to the act of writing.

Analogies lean heavily on the conjunction 'and'. Gunn thinks
aloud on this problem in a manner that is reminiscent of Shoshana
Felman's influential intervention on the methodological problems of
psychoanalytic literary criticism.[2]

> In the title of the present book, the stressed word is perhaps the
> 'and'. In the course of my explorations, I shall encounter a broad
> range of apparent dualities, alternatives, or antinomies which will
> often turn out to be necessary paradoxes or complements. Psycho-
> analysis *and* fiction, as I wish my title to read; and as both may
> be – engrossed in negativity *and yet* dynamically enabling.

(2)

The success of this book lies in Gunn's ability to realize the potential of this 'and'. He distances himself from any overweening theoretical ambition. This is not primarily a work of theory, but one of practical criticism. Gunn's set of concerns is life, literature, and psychoanalysis. He does not prioritize any of these in particular, but seeks instead moments that represent the intersection of these sets. Gunn begins typically with an experiential statement about life, this is then followed by how literature and psychoanalysis have handled the same problem. He ends not with a dogmatic statement, a piece of pure knowledge that the reader can take away from the text, but instead with a gentle probing of the new pattern that emerges as a result of his reading.

The text is in two parts with three chapters each. Both the parts have haunting titles. The first is called 'A family affair'. The second is titled 'Play it again'. The first part offers readings of Kafka, Leclaire, and Mannoni. The second focuses on Proust and Beckett. Though both are extremely well written, the first may prove more interesting as it offers rare glimpses into the Lacanian clinic. Gunn's paradigm of *l'écriture psychanalyse* is a text by Leclaire called *On tue un enfant* (1975). This text offers an understanding of how psychoanalytic texts work and by implication, 'psychoanalysis itself' (39). Leclaire is also of interest because his text enacts the desire of the analyst thereby calling into question the model of analytic neutrality that is privileged in classical psychoanalysis. Leclaire's work seeks to emphasize that '[a]nalysis is no neutral activity, but a passion. As Kafka lets his reader feel that no reading is innocent, so Leclaire makes it clear that no analyst or analytic session is innocent either' (39). Gunn seeks to highlight the element of ambivalence in such a passion. Even the title of Leclaire's text with its pun on Freud's title, 'On bat un enfant', demonstrates the ubiquity of ambivalence. 'The title . . . provokes both by the unspecific "on" ("one"), by which "I" may be implicated, and by the present tense of the "tue" ("is killing"), suggesting as it does that the process is a habitual, hence a familiar one' (40). Here ambiguity becomes a signifier of ambivalence.

Gunn close-reads the text, including the significance of its cover in the 'Points' edition, which depicts Duccio's painting of 'The Massacre of the Innocents'. Duccio's representation is littered with the corpses of dead infants. In the foreground of the painting is the image of a man 'plunging a sword deep into a baby's side' (40). Gunn's object in invoking this image is to understand why an infant's death should inspire such horror. This is perhaps not such an irrelevant question in the light of 'Operation Irma' and the daily diet of such images that have become commonplace in television newscasts. Can psychoanalysis throw any light on the ability of such images to 'move' us? In the context of Duccio's painting, and of infanticide as such, Leclaire suggests that if such a situation is intolerable, it is precisely because it concerns 'a realisation of our most secret and profound wish' (Leclaire quoted in Gunn, 42). Leclaire's contention then is that if parents are deaf to the suffering of their children, it is because, in Gunn's words, 'the deepest wish of adults may be the death of children' (42). Gunn's concern with Leclaire's problematic is not so much with infanticide in its literal sense, but in how a certain mode of parental love can take on the form of murder. Leclaire distinguishes between the 'fantasy-child' and the 'biological-child'. The failure to kill the former leads to the real-life suffering of the latter. Freud calls attention to the lure of the 'fantasy-child' – the child without faults who is all that the parents were not but wanted to be – in his paper 'On narcissism: an introduction' (1914). Leclaire details the varying modes of infanticide through the case history of an analysand he calls 'Pierre-Marie'. This Pierre had to bear the burden of replacing a brother who died in infancy. His mother's inability to mourn sufficiently the death of her first born results in an invasion of Pierre's desire.

> He is in search of his dead brother whom he must kill again, once and for all. In order to find his own place and his own desire Pierre-Marie has to kill the child of his mother's unconscious need, and so stop being another's 'child-king', pre-empted in his own desire by the force of his mother's primary narcissism.
>
> (44)

This is a familial plot that we are only too familiar with since the publication of D. H. Lawrence's *Sons and Lovers* (1913). Leclaire's importance, however, lies in his ability to emphasize not so much the desire *for* the mother but the desire *of* the mother. For Leclaire, the inability to kill the fantasy-child will result in the fantasy of killing the real child, albeit unconsciously. Leclaire's argument does not restrict itself to the pathological consequences of a particular turn in the family plot, but poses the question of killing fantasy-children as an ethical imperative. What the fantasy-child signifies is the lure of being as plenitude. The imperative that Leclaire speaks of is logically necessary but not sufficient. The 'marvellous child' cannot be killed once and for all:

> Whoever does not mourn and mourn repeatedly the marvellous child that he would have been, remains in limbo, in a milky light shed by a hopeless state of waiting which casts no shadow. But whoever believes he has settled his account once and for all with

the figure of the tyrant, is exiling himself from the sources of his genius, and is taking himself to be strong-minded in the face of the reign of ecstasy.

(Leclaire quoted in Gunn, 45)

Mannoni's concerns are not unlike those of Leclaire. She too seeks to chronicle the devastating consequences of parental desire on an infant. Mannoni is particularly concerned with the ways in which the body *suffers from the signifier*. Mannoni's encounter with Lacan's work is motivated at least in part by the desire to understand the ways in which children can be taught to name their own desire. The child's problem is understood through the child's relation to the Symbolic Order from which it seems to be excluded at least in part. In Gunn's summation of the predicament that Mannoni constantly grapples with in her clinic: 'The underlying factor linking Maud Mannoni's child-patients is that they are all suffering from a degree of exclusion, which runs from partial to total, from what Lacan calls the realm of the Symbolic' (78). Gunn goes on to remind the reader that 'where the Symbolic is deficient, the Real whose prime site is the body, calls on the Imaginary . . . to make up the deficit' (78). This lack in the Symbolic translates into an inability on the part of the subject to realize its own desire. By being subject to an alien desire that comes from elsewhere, the subject is threatened with a loss of its own body. Lacan has argued that it is not enough to *be* a body, it is as important to *have* a body. The symbolization of the body becomes possible only with the successful deployment of the 'shifter' – the pronominal 'I'. Crucial though this transition is from *being* to *having*, it is a precarious achievement. The notion that one owns the body by virtue of being 'in' it, is, according to Lacan, a common fantasy. The proof of this assertion lies in the fact that 'the body one "has" is ever ready to be overtaken by the body one "is" (as the experience of illness and the threat of death remind one)' (80).

Gunn also uses French poststructuralists like Roland Barthes, Gilles Deleuze, and Jacques Derrida in his attempt to understand the structural oppositions of metaphysics, especially their embodiment in psychoanalysis and literature. Gunn steers away from the deconstructive world-view of the Deleuzean 'simulacrum' and Derridean '*différance*' after a conscientious summary of their attempts to address the problems of identity, difference, the nostalgia for presence, etc. Though Gunn concedes that the authors who preoccupy him – Proust, Beckett, and Kafka – deploy narrative modes that would endorse the deconstructive project, he believes that a purely differential model of cognition is blind to the needs of the subject. Gunn believes that such a model can at best embody only a half-truth. In this context Gunn invokes Mannoni's analysand who suffered his mother's headaches. To tell such a child who suffers, for whom the pain is Real, that the pain is a 'realistic illusion' that results from the deployment of the shifter is 'deeply irrelevant in the face of overriding *need*' (181). Gunn imagines an imaginary exchange between a patient in analysis and Derrida. Whereas for the former it would be necessary to arrive at some notion of identity, for the latter the deconstruction of presence and identity is a theoretical imperative. Gunn plays off Derrida against another Jacques – a patient of Mannoni for whom it was impossible to grow out of a sense of unity with his mother. Jacques's nostalgia for presence, for 'a stage before repetition and ambivalence' is to be located in infancy. For Gunn, and one may add psychoanalysis, this nostalgia does not go away. 'As we become adults we do not cease to be children. Childhood is waiting as a model of an original presence, and it pounces whenever we pick up a pen and start to write. It may pounce, equally, whenever we turn to psychoanalysis, or pick up the work of Beckett or Proust' (182). Gunn gladly accepts the Derridean assertion that psychoanalysis is metaphysical by virtue of buying into the 'metaphysics of presence'. He argues that by turning the clock back on Oedipus, *vis-à-vis* Melanie Klein, Lacan's notion of a postlapsarian desire implies an Edenic past by logical implication. Furthermore, psychoanalysis cannot do without a moment, albeit a hypothetical or mythical one, before repetition. To answer Derrida's charge then:

> If psychoanalysis does partake of a 'metaphysic' of presence, as Derrida suggests, it does so not for narrowly epistemological reasons. It does so for reasons that can be better described as ontological. For as I have shown, psychoanalysis seeks in some measure to correspond to the implausibility – the impossibility even – of any *meta-physic* which its chosen subjects or patients experience.
>
> (189–90)

What unifies Gunn's project is his concern with how psychoanalysis and literature handle this problem of origins. Both literature and psychoanalysis cannot but seek origins whether or not such a quest can be successful. As Gunn puts it: '[w]e fantasise our origin by virtue of the fact that we originate in fantasy. We desire to rediscover it because we are desiring beings' (191). The attempt at rediscovery is, however, beset with paradox. But psychoanalysis cannot resolve this paradox, it can only extend it through the tropes of ambivalence and repetition. Gunn's analogies may be said to meet their conclusion within the space of transference-love. It is in love that ambivalence and repetition manifest themselves as tropes of identity. Gunn returns to his contention that 'working-through' in the transference is akin to the literary process and hence the endless fascination of psychoanalysis for literature:

> It is not that love abolishes repetition, but that . . . it absorbs it and transforms it. It does so in just the way that the act of reading cuts into and across the paradoxes of presence and absence, self and other, allowing a new, less hostile, more playful space to emerge, such as that which can exist between lovers.
>
> (196)

Robert Samuels too is interested in transference and repetition, but it is the way that Lacan repeats Freud that concerns him. Lacan's transference to Freud, his celebrated 'return to Freud', forms the main theme of Samuels' text. Repetition is always marked by difference but Samuels' notion of repetition appears more teleological than Gunn's. Samuels' book is an attempt to uncover 'the inner logic of Freud's thought as it relates to psychoanalytic practice and theory' (1). In order to articulate the inner logic of this discourse he turns to the ternary structure of Lacan's conceptual schema that is marked by the registers of the Real, the Imaginary, and the Symbolic. These registers open up psychoanalysis to philosophy: psychoanalysis becomes an attempt to address the questions and paradoxes of contemporary philosophy. To drive this point home, Samuels identifies the registers of the Real, the Imaginary, and the Symbolic with the philosophies of existentialism, phenomenology, and structuralism respectively. And again, these registers are also identified as analogues of the Sartrean modes of existence where the subject can be differentiated in relation to its mode of existence as a Being-in-Itself (Real), Being-for-Itself (Imaginary), and Being-for-Others (Symbolic). Samuels attempts to show that these registers have always served the role of a structural matrix in Lacan's thought from as early as the latter's doctoral dissertation on paranoia in the 1930s.

This conceptual matrix is then identified with the history of philosophy, psychoanalysis, and the temporal logic of the subject in Lacan. Samuels even draws a parallel between the temporal logic of a set of categories and the order of its discovery in the history of psychoanalysis. He invokes Lacan's authority for this move, but it is not very clear if a rhetorical strategy in the Lacanian text (a metaphor) is being interpreted literally (as a model) here. In his introduction Samuels writes:

One of Lacan's central, underlying arguments is the division of the psychoanalytic movement into three periods. The first is the initial discovery of psychoanalysis by Freud, the second is what Lacan describes as the forgetting (or repression) of Freud by the school of 'ego psychology,' and the third is Lacan's own 'return to Freud'. This return is an attempt to read Freud in a structured and logical way that makes manifest certain latent patterns of Freud's thought.

(1)

Though Samuels' schematism is not without its pedagogical advantages, he does not pause to consider at length what sort of an epistemology this would imply. The term 'ternary' is invoked again and again as though it were synonymous with the term 'logical'. This is all the more important in that Lacan himself expressed dissatisfaction with the so-called ternary schema of the Real, the Imaginary, and the Symbolic and added the Symptom (*le sinthome*) in the 1970s as that which marks the intersection of these orders. Samuels' use of the American semiotican Charles Sanders Peirce's ternary schema of Firstness, Secondness, and Thirdness is a case in point. Though there is nothing wrong in the identification of the Peircean schema as an analogue of the Lacanian schema, the over-enthusiastic mapping of these schemas only dilutes the logical rigour that Samuels seeks to establish. The Peircean schema runs the risk of being elevated into a loosely constructed metaphor where anything that connotes Firstness, Secondness, or Thirdness is game for mapping. Samuels notes that '[n]ot only can Peirce's categories be used to articulate the logical movement of Lacan's conceptions of the Real, the Imaginary, and the Symbolic, but also to articulate the logic of Freud's two topographical structures: unconscious/conscious/preconscious and id/ego/superego' (9).

The best part of Samuels' book is his exposition of Lacan's work on 'logical time' and its relation to Freud's pioneering *Project for a Scientific Psychology*. Here, unlike the loose invocation of the Peircean categories, Samuels' exposition and claims on behalf of the Lacanian notion of logical temporality are worked out with admirable lucidity. Samuels' account is based on a paper by Lacan that is not available in the Alan Sheridan translation of the *Écrits*. This paper, which is entitled 'Logical time and the assertion of anticipated certainty', is used as a logical paradigm in Samuels' exposition of how the Lacanian registers operate in relation to the subject. This account of logical time is also of interest because of its structural similarity to Lacan's use of Edgar Allan Poe's 'The Purloined Letter', where a matrix of subject positions is articulated in relation to the instant of the look (Real), the time of understanding (Imaginary), and the moment of the act (Symbolic). Again, this very ternary structure helps us to understand the function of perception, consciousness, and memory in Freud's *Project*. Perception is structured as a Real event: it is linked to the physical law of inertia and the discharge of excitation. The model for this process is the reflex arc. The tendency to keep excitation to a minimum can only function in relation to an external stimulus. In the case of internal needs the law of constancy or homeostasis replaces the model of the reflex arc. Samuels: 'This secondary function thus delimits a dual relation (Secondness) between a primary form of stimulation (Real) and a secondary form of resistance and inhibition (Imaginary). Later in Freud's work, this pseudo-psychological process of resistance and inhibition becomes translated into the psychological defenses of the ego' (15). Memory is neither perception nor consciousness: it is instead a network of differential elements like Saussurean signifiers. If the *Project* is read through the grid of the Real, the Imaginary, and the Symbolic, it becomes a lot easier to understand the Lacanian claim that the unconscious is structured like a language.

Samuels also translates the ternary structure of the Real, the Imaginary, and the Symbolic into the axes of Schema L. This schema serves as the conceptual metaphor of Samuels' book to such an extent that it could very well be subtitled 'The semiotics of Schema L'. Again, it is important to note that Lacan moves away from this schema to others, like Schema R, the so-called 'graph of desire', topological objects like the Borromean knot, the inner eight, the torus, the cross cap, etc. The significance of this shift is never explored. In fact, Samuels barely mentions these developments in his account of Lacan's work. The Schema L is invoked with such a measure of satisfaction that it begins to function as the text's Imaginary. Though the analogues that Samuels deploys in relation to the schemas are a useful point of entry into these different models, Lacan elsewhere explicitly dissociates his ternary schema from Freud's. Alexander Leupin calls attention to this problem in his introduction to a recent anthology of Lacanian approaches to the so-called 'sciences of Man'. Leupin focuses explicitly on the Schema L.:

> In light of Lacan's subsequent elaboration, it is possible for us to understand the deficiencies of the schema L. One of them is its bidimensionality, which prevents any conception of the void essential to the fields of both truth and exactitude. . . . The void, in the 1954 schema, is present only in the circles marking the ego

and the Other, not between the exigencies [Real, Symbolic, Imaginary]; therefore, at this point their relationship has to be conceived as full. But more important, the schema L and, afterward, the schema R . . . are analogical: they cover the subject's real structure by an intuitive geometrical perception. In other words, being non topological, they participate in the imaginary order. Hence the necessity of a transformation or evolution from an intuitive geometry to a topology that can overcome the imaginary aspects of the schemas to ground them in the logic of the Symbolic order.[3]

Leupin quotes Lacan on this: 'Here it is: my *three* . . . are not Freud's. My *three* are the Real, the Symbolic, and the Imaginary. I have come to position and base these three upon a topology of the Borromean knot' (Lacan quoted in Leupin, 42). Samuels does not focus adequately on the epistemological differences between the Freudian and Lacanian schemas. Furthermore, in his account of the Schema L, he doesn't mention its relation to the void at all. Samuels also doesn't explain the theoretical significance of the schema's diagrammatic representation. Leupin notes that the dashed lines represent 'whatever is unconscious' (12) – another point that Samuels doesn't take up. This cannot but leave the reader wondering why the pattern of lines varies from one use of the schema to another. However, apart from these avoidable blemishes, the reader will find a lot that is useful in this book.

Samuels also improves upon Gunn's attempt to distinguish between Derridean *différance* and the Lacanian *objet a*. It is the emergence of the analyst as the *objet a* at the end of analysis that will help us to distinguish between a poststructuralist notion of psychoanalysis, where interpretation can go on and on forever, predicated as it is on the differential function of the signifier, and the Lacanian conception of the end of analysis. For Lacan, analysis is not interminable. What terminates the analysis is the emergence of the *objet a* as the desire of the analyst. Samuels notes that 'in his silence, the analyst represents that which cannot be said and it is because of the introduction of this limit of language that the subject gains the possibility of determining the difference between the sayable and the unsayable' (144). This is a more felicitous formula than the one available in Gunn's book where, despite a suspicion that analysis has more than one axis, the author is forced on the defensive with the humanist argument of the patient's 'suffering'. So though Gunn is right when he announces that in its search for origins and the question of identity psychoanalysis functions ontologically rather than epistemologically, he never gets around to elaborating the role of the *objet a* in this ontology. It is Samuels' ability to press the questions that Gunn does not have the space to elaborate at length that makes it profitable to read these texts in tandem.

University of Wales College of Cardiff

Notes

1 On Freud's different theoretical personas, esp. Freud the Conquistador, see Malcolm Bowie, 'Freud's dreams of knowledge', in *Freud, Proust and Lacan: Theory as Fiction* (Cambridge: Cambridge University Press, 1987), pp. 13–44.
2 See Shoshana Felman's introduction to *Literature and Psychoanalysis* (Baltimore: Johns Hopkins University Press, 1977), pp. 5–10.
3 See the introduction to *Lacan and the Human Sciences*, edited by Alexander Leupin (Lincoln: Nebraska and London: University of Nebraska Press, 1991), pp. 11–12.

Balz Engler

Constance Classen, *Worlds of Sense: Exploring the Senses in History and Across Cultures* (London and New York: Routledge, 1993), 172 pp., £11.99 (paperback)

The ecology of the senses has not been a popular subject in theory since Marshall McLuhan; it was discredited partly for the political positions he stood for, partly for the way he made it possible for a scholarly tradition to be exploited as a fad; Walter J. Ong's *Orality and Literacy* (1982), published in the 'New Accents' series, was not able to change this. It has not been helpful either that the oral has been associated with Presence, and as such has been rejected in deconstructivist thinking (e.g. in Derrida's *Of Grammatology*). The visual has continued to reign supreme. But even where the ecology of the senses has been taken seriously, its study has usually been restricted to the ear and the eye, the senses addressed by the modern media; these so-called new or distance senses also allow us to place ourselves in perspective to the world surrounding us. Other senses recognized as such by Western culture, like smell and taste (the old, chemical ones) have largely been neglected, or their gradual loss has been lamented.[1] Moreover, because we tend to view (language is revealing) the senses in terms of biology, they have not been subjected to the kind of scrutiny that, in other areas, has shown (caught again) things seeming perfectly natural to be socially constructed.

In recent years, smell and its role in culture, however, have experienced a revival of interest, marked, among others, by studies like Dan Sperber's *Rethinking Symbolism* (especially Chapter 5), Annik Le Guérer's historical account *Les Pouvoirs de l'odeur* (not mentioned by Classen), Michel Onfray's *L'art de jouir*, which has a chapter on philosophers' noses (Kant's contempt for the nose!), or, most recently, Hans J. Rindisbacher's impressive *The Smell of Books*.[2]

Increasingly, the nose (or 'olfaction') is also replacing the ear in defining the Other in questioning the dominance of the eye in the sense hierarchy of Western culture. Constance Classen's book, *Worlds of Sense: Exploring the Senses in History and Across Cultures* belongs in this context, even though its ambitions are of a more general kind, to study 'the interaction between culture and perception' (1). It offers a stimulating, and occasionally confusing survey over a vast field; it touches on many topics that invite further exploration and raises many questions without offering satisfying answers.

The book consists of two parts, the first dealing with the senses in history, the second with the senses across cultures. In a brilliant first chapter, 'The odour of the rose: floral symbolism and the ol-factory decline of the West', the history of rose-growing (mainly in England) is used to sketch a history of the senses, ascribing the shift from the olfactory to the visual to the rise and spread of rationalist and empiricist thinking. Starting with the claim that a modern version of Shakespeare's 'A rose by any other name would smell as sweet' would have to read, 'would look as beautiful' (7–8), she gives an account of how visual appearance increasingly took over from smell in rose-growing, also how the walls built around gardens to contain the intensive scents were removed in the eighteenth century to offer perspectives (the building of prisons in the eighteenth century as described by Foucault offers less pleasant examples). She juxtaposes the situation in the pre-modern period, which to her spans the time from Homeric Greece to the sixteenth century, to the modern period after that, not only setting up an (all too neat) opposition between smell and sight, but extending it to religion and science, essence and surface, community and individualism, domestic manufacture and industry, and also women and men. This simple outline runs into difficulties when the revival of interest in olfaction since the nine-teenth century has to be accounted for; Classen cannot take it seriously as a renewed sensory shift but has to play it down as mere fashion (36). Obviously the history of the senses, for which much intriguing anecdotal material is presented here, is more complex and more interesting than this.

The next two chapters deal with problems of nature versus culture. Three cases of feral children (the Wild Boy of Aveyron, the 'wolf children' of India, and Kaspar Hauser) are used to show how their senses changed when they were socialized. Classen's assumption seems to be (her argument is vague, but suggestive on this) that these children had lived in a natural state before they were introduced into society, a problematic assumption, even a bizarre one in the case of Kaspar Hauser. Similar problems appear in the chapter on 'Words of sense' which discusses items in the vocabulary that have shifted their meanings from one sense to another; Classen assumes that there was once a time when words were 'less divorced from their original meanings' (59–60). But again her observations are stimulating, although it is not always easy to say of what. Touch, for example, seems to lend itself most easily to such transfers, smell least.

The second part of the book begins with a chapter showing how, even in a culture dominated by sight like ours, olfactory symbolism continues to play an important if unapparent role, especially in marking social differences. There is, for example, a three-fold distinction between women: sluts and prostitutes are identified with stench, maidens, wives and mothers with pleasant, non-threatening odours, seductresses with heavily sweet and spicy fragrances. Inodorateness, on the other hand, is used to some extent to classify men as 'clean' and 'no nonsense'. This is interesting, but Classen, returning to history, then begins to speculate: 'the use of perfume by men, once widespread in the West, declined with the rise of the machine at the time of the Industrial Revolution.' Possibly men, in order

> to enter into the new world of the mechanical other, ... had to renounce the fragrances which are metaphorically antithetical to the symbolic inodorateness of the barren, insensible machine. This metaphorical opposition between fragrance and machinery may also explain in part why our modern media (such as television and computers) are so tellingly devoid of odours.
>
> (93–4)

Here, the author's urge to make generalizations leads her from an interesting observation to wrong-headed conclusions in a manner typical of the book. The rise of the bourgeoisie, the role of religion and the attitudes to the body associated with it, are neglected, and her argument is unrelated to the one informing her book as a whole, the increasing dominance of the eye in Western culture.

The last two chapters illustrate the role of the senses in cultures alien to the Western one. The chapter on 'Literacy and anti-culture: The Andean experience of the written word' shows how literacy, so highly prized in our culture, has been considered something negative by Andean peoples, a technique associated with colonialist exploitation; here Classen is close to accepting the McLuhan/Ong model of orality and literacy. The last chapter then contrasts three sensory models that are difficult to classify in Western terms, that of the Tzotzil in Mexico (based on heat), of the Ongee on Little Andaman Island (based on smell), and that of the Desana in Colombia (based on colour). This account impressively dislodges McLuhan's and Ong's opposition of oral and literate cultures. The dominant sensory medium, according to Classen, can only be understood 'within the context of a particular culture and not through generalized external sensory paradigms' – comparisons are odourous, to speak with Dogberry. Western sensory paradigms impose 'one kind of visuality – that of the West – and one kind of aurality – that of the generic non-literate "tribal" culture' (135) on all cultures. The 'imprecision' that our visual culture may find disturbing can be normative for an olfactory culture, and where a visual culture, due to perspective, 'may emphasize location, an olfactory culture will emphasize movement' (136). There are curious parallels between such an observation and recent discussions of signifying practice in our culture.

This is an important book because of the questions it raises and the work it suggests, rather than the answers it gives. It reminds students of culture of the role of the old senses, and of how the ecology of the senses may change in history. In particular it suggests new interpretations of pre-modern artifacts (e.g. of the senses in Shakespeare's works) and a reconsideration of modern visualist notions of the text. In more general terms it challenges the Enlightenment traditions of academic practice and the kind of knowledge it produces.

Basel University

Notes

1 Dietmar Kamper and Christoph Wulf (eds), *Das Schwinden der Sinne* (Frankfurt: Suhrkamp, 1984).
2 Dan Sperber, *Rethinking Symbolism* (Cambridge: Cambridge University Press, 1975); Annick Le Guérer, *Les Pouvoirs de l'odeur* (Paris: Bourin, 1988); Michel Onfray, *L'art de jouir: Pour un matérialisme hédoniste* (Paris: Grasset, 1991); Hans J. Rindisbacher, *The Smell of Books: A Cultural-Historical Study of Olfactory Perception in Literature* (Ann Arbor:

University of Michigan Press, 1992). Smell has even made it to the best-seller lists, with Patrick Süskind's novel *The Perfume*.

Gene Fendt

Roger Poole, *Kierkegaard: The Indirect Communication* (Charlottesville: The University Press of Virginia, 1993), 318 pp., £35.50 (hardback)

Roger Poole's book, *Kierkegaard: The Indirect Communication*, is, of course, a direct communication. Its thesis may be seen in the colon which marks the connection between Kierkegaard and the indirect communication, for his argument is not about the pseudonymous authorship, which by itself is but one half of the first form of indirect communication, nor yet about the two-streamed authorship concluded with that oversized *Postscript*, nor yet about the entire authorship, but extends to the man himself – the one whose spine may have been bent as a question-mark to his age: which is ours. 'What seems a mere problem of methodology is in fact a statement about the lived body in ethical space' (1). According to Poole 'indirect communication' has multiple significances. First, it refers to the communication made up of 'the aesthetic and the edifying stream of texts' (9). While this was Kierkegaard's *modus communicandi* his body was his own – he could deploy it as a 'part in that chain of doubly reflected communications' (18). This body is largely unproblematic, 'largely uncommmented upon, and was certainly not sketched' (17).

Within this first version of indirect communication there is a further split, within the aesthetic works, 'between what the text appears to be about and what . . . the text is really about' (9). In those aesthetic works, the authors – under the cover of serious philosophical, theological or psychological inquiries – practise Hegelian Lego with the aim of showing that the Emperor (the Danish academy, or Heiberg, or Martensen) has no clothes. Poole reads *The Concept of Irony, Repetition, The Concept of Anxiety* and the *Postscript*, in some places line by line, to show precisely how the authors deconstruct the categories of the emperor at issue. This deconstruction, Poole says, is the primary intent and effect of the texts, which are 'not only not meant to deliver a clear univocal communicatum, but are positively meant to refuse instruction and to disseminate doubt' (9). Among other things, what follows is that 'there is no Kierkegaardian doctrine of repetition' (82). This is the kind of claim which, if taken seriously, would end careers, for it demonstrates that a large number of present professors have been going naked; therefore it will not be taken seriously. Nonetheless, it may be true. In this regard we should remember that Martensen did not show up for the defence of the master's thesis, and that Heiberg did not review the *Concept of Anxiety*. Perhaps these books are cut from cloth so indistinguishable from their own clothes that . . . .

When the little harbour town became ironic en masse with the *Corsair* cartoons, irony, and so the first form of indirect communication, became impossible for Kierkegaard. He was, thereby, forced to create 'a new embodiment' (267) and a new form of communication. What *The Corsair* achieved, according to Poole – whose historical and even psychological reconstructions are well-evidenced, insightful, and almost always convincing – was the subtraction of Kierkegaard's body from his own possession and use: 'The body could no longer be used as he wanted: it had to be regarded as the great Copenhagen public wanted' (18) – its significance was a press significance, its value an unvoicable vowel. This public inflection upon the text of his body forces Kierkegaard to reconsider his signifying activity, a reconsideration which Poole uses as a figure of the shift from 'the medieval world of cohesive signs' to the world of the popular press.

> But the incursion of the popular press into that [medieval] world spells its quick demise. Once a popular press has the power to disturb and modify the relations of similitude and signature for its reading public, the divinely coherent order of signs is displaced by the day-to-day indexicality of Vico's 'Age of Men'. The individual is left virtually helpless before the communicative task. Anything he or she says will be instantly assimilated to the publicly received view of it.
>
> (200)

At this point (Chapter 7), Poole enters a long excursus on Husserl's theory of signs, the presuppositions of which he thinks (again using the ratio of apophrades) Kierkegaard 'in many respects shared'. But if 'Husserl's theory of signs still inhabits that "medieval" world of "correspondences" and "signatures" that Foucault describes' (201), it is hard to believe that Kierkegaard – post-Romantic Magister Irony that he was – would significantly share them. It may well be that Johannes Climacus, himself an early medieval saint born of a Cartesian meditation, would accept the Husserlian thesis that 'meaning in the full sense is a function of subjective intentionality, and with every movement towards externality, that fullness is dissipated or corrupted' (204), but as Poole has already argued against taking the concluding *Postscript* (among others) as Kierkegaard's own it is at least questionable that a theory of signs so tied to Cartesian meditations is shared by that indirect communicator who precedes Derrida as a conscious practitioner of disseminative discontinuities and aporias of supplementarity.

What needs to be called into question here is whether that ego from which both Descartes and Husserl begin, and which Derrida, among others, is at pains to deconstruct, ever existed or could exist, and so whether its 'meanings' have any sense apart from language (or more generally, signs). To stick to the texts at hand, the question should be raised whether Kierkegaard himself believed such a view, or whether, in fact, his problem with constructive systematic philosophy and theology (à la Hegel, Heiberg, Martensen) is precisely due to its unreality, an unreality from which his most famous (and most philosophical) pseudonym takes his life: the separate ego which means. In such an imaginary world language is indeed the snake in the Edeny grass as Vigilius Haufniensis suggests. But such a view is science fiction, and when translated into German *Wissenschaft* merely becomes fictional science – precisely what Poole has shown all the pseudonyms are showing.

In short, if such a view – the ego born apart from language, which, given language, seeks to express its original non-linguistic meanings in the procrustean forms of indexical signage – is philosophically untenable, as it seems to Wittgenstein, among others, to be, we should consider long and hard before we saddle Kierkegaard with it. This is especially so since none of his work seems to depend on his holding it, and in fact much of it seems to work wonderfully as a deconstruction of philosophical problems arising within that view.

But this is an excursus. And if the excursus fails, or operates from a false premise, the point Poole wishes to make still rings true. For as the Corsair subtracted from Kierkegaard his own body's use as a signifier, just so the mass media – a set of structures which enact the diabolical principle of levelling and make distinction unrecognizable as such (231) – reduces communication to sound bite and cliché. These being the new conditions, indirect communication needs a new form to combat it; communication itself must take on new form.

The second kind of indirect communication replaces irony and doubled reflection with reduplication and 'stepping out in character'. Kierkegaard, after 1846, turns from 'aesthetic indirection' to 'the indirection of an embodied sign' (254f) and the stakes are thereby raised – to blasphemy or salvation, to offence or faith. Though Poole never states things quite that strongly, his analysis shows it (cf. 258); for in those last *Instants* and in the *Training in Christianity* the line begins to blur – though Anti-Climacus takes pains to keep it clear –

between anyone who suffers for the truth and the suffering truth: an embodied sign is an embodied sign and the difference between Christus and Imitatio Christi is not something we can see. And so the man with the crooked back, who began by raising questions to the Danish academy, ended by himself becoming a question to the world. And such a question is an indirect communication.

University of Nebraska, Kearney

John Hill

Mark Jancovitch, *The Cultural Politics of the New Criticism* (Cambridge: Cambridge University Press, 1993), 215pp., £30.00 (hardback)

Tobin Siebers, *Cold War Criticism and the Politics of Skepticism* (Oxford and New York: Oxford University Press, 1993), 163 pp., £11.95 (paperback)

At its simplest the ongoing conflict in English Studies in America can be seen as an effect of the difference in approach between the New Critics and the so-called New New critics, or poststructuralists. Both these books are concerned with addressing the difference which generates this conflict. In *The Cultural Politics of the New Criticism* Mark Jancovitch sets out to reassess the nature of that difference with particular regard to the current perception that New Criticism represents an aesthetic retreat from the social: he tells us that his starting point was finding himself 'impressed by the similarities between the positions of the pre-war New Critics (Warren, Ransom, Tate) and those of the post-structuralists themselves' (ix), and that his primary goal is to present a reappraisal of New Criticism, particularly with regard to its *political* inspiration. In *Cold War Criticism and the Politics of Skepticism* Tobin Siebers demotes the importance of the difference between these two critical modes by recontextualizing them in a wider, and homogenizing, historical field. He suggests that contemporary conflict in criticism derives from an inherently conflictual mindset which actually unites all post-war 'sceptical' criticism, including the second generation of New Critics (Wimsatt and Beardsley), as well as his other examples: Geoffrey Hartman, Stephen Greenblatt and Paul de Man. Siebers argues that this critical mindset is generated by the fundamental, all-informing, oppositional political environment of the cold war.

Siebers starts from an interesting position: that a relationship can be established between the kind of criticism popular in the academy and the international political climate of the post-war world. The connection he identifies operates on two levels. First, all these 'modern' critical modes share the label 'Sceptical', having 'made a virtue of cold war paranoia' (34). Just as the cold war state lives in a perpetual condition of mistrust and doubt, so the cold war critic institutionalizes interpretative suspicion with regard to truth claims, valuing instead ambiguity, irony, indeterminacy. Second, within the overall sceptical unity of these positions, the particular status of cold war relations at any one time may be seen reflected in a particular current form of sceptical criticism, so that Siebers claims to be able to map the changes in the dominant criticism to the circumstances of the cold war then obtaining.

The nature of the relationship of that scepticism with cold war politics is hard to establish. Sometimes the argument suggests a simple case of mirroring between criticism and wider politics, in that the suspicious nature of modern critics simply reflects the suspicious climate of the times. Siebers seems to indicate this when he writes,

> We are afraid that the cold war will never end, and so the history of the cold war is the story of our skepticism about endings, intentions, and calculations concerning numbers, troop movements, weapons, negotiations, and claims to truth and falsehood. We are forever watchful and on our guard. Our fear contributes an essential part to the cold war mentality.
>
> (29)

Siebers implies that in such an environment critics of the cold war era became sceptical critics 'naturally'. However, there is another kind of relationship suggested, one in which sceptical criticism represents a turning-away from the cold war world, a reaction against it rather than a mirroring of it: for Siebers it can be seen in the interest and energy expended on the process of canon formation. He writes that the New Critics 'quickly established a canon of poetry to found the new republic in which a purer democracy would defeat totalitarianism and bring an end to the cold war' (31). Here literature stands as an ideal other world, where conflict over the canon replaces real conflict. Thus, for Siebers, a strange kind of non-political politics replaces real politics, and all the apparent 'political' or 'ethical' content of the continuing interpretative debate actually represents a rejection of the fear and difficulty of politics in the cold war, and, he argues, 'we come to prefer the purity of our skepticism to the chaos of the real world' (33).

This is the accusation at the heart of this book: literary criticism has become isolated to the point where even when it is most apparently political it is not political at all. The second half of Siebers's book forms an interesting commentary on the political and ethical content of recent debate. It deals with the question of ethics as formulated by writers such as J. Hillis Miller, and with the political implications of de Man's association with Nazism. Siebers contrasts de Man's critical refusal to fall into the error of taking a position with what Siebers sees as Jane Tompkins's laudable political engagement in her criticism, noting that she 'does not stop interpreting once she discovers that interpretation is not an internally coherent activity but a political one' (120) – a point worth making. There is also a discussion of Hannah Arendt's writing on the Eichmann trial and on the unavoidability of story-telling for human understanding and hence the inescabability of story-telling and story-reading in human political affairs. But seeing such stories as stories does not lessen the power of the individual truths they tell: Siebers' message is that the nettle Arendt grasped by telling Eichmann's story, and not letting him be devoured into a formulaic account of an abstract or stereotyped Nazism, is one we must all grasp.

It may be wondered, with all this discussion of Eichmann, de Man (and Heidegger's Nazism is in there too), what happened to the cold war: the potentially interesting metaphor of the cold war with its rigid ideological binarism gets submerged into a rather nebulous perception of a generally negative political world, of which Nazism and the Holocaust are as much a part as the cold war itself. Thus the book's original idea, that sceptical criticism has come about as a response to the particular circumstance of the cold war, actually becomes merely a reworking of the notion that the predilection towards such thought (called, say, postmodernity) is in part a reaction to the terrible events of the twentieth century.

The first half of the book is nevertheless overtly concerned with the cold war, with finding a correspondence between particular critics and the historical events of the post-war East–West stand-off, though even here the first pair of critics with which Siebers is concerned – Wimsatt and Beardsley – seem in their demand for objectivity and careful reading to be reacting as much to the events of the Second World War as the cold war itself, identified here only as a 'chaotic and dangerous time' (45). Thus, in the insecurity of those times, the New Critics' unemotional close reading becomes the means to restore some semblance of confidence in interpretation. Siebers' second critical index of the post-war period is Geoffrey Hartman's deconstruction, identified here with the Carter years, the key period of détente in the history of the cold war having been passed over with no apparent correspondence in contemporary criticism. Hartman is seen as a critic informed by a suspicion of charisma, even of any notion of a unified self. Siebers writes that deconstructive critics 'arm themselves against the dictator within by refusing to dictate anything' (49). Close reading is no longer a protection against error, the only protection lies in a turn inward: in such critical navel-gazing or 'hermeneutics of indeterminancy' Siebers finds an explicit correspondence with the 'stuttering diplomacy' of the Carter presidency (50). Siebers confidently states that this critical engagement with the self

> certainly reflects the dominant political advice of the late 1970s that Americans should monitor more closely their political process, their dependence on oil and their commitment to human rights and the poor.
>
> (51)

However, this assertion is not the only way to read these events. America did go through a period of navel-gazing after Vietnam and Watergate, but the Carter administration that followed could be seen as an attempt to restore a moral foundation to American foreign policy with its linkage of such policy with human rights. It did continue to assert American interests abroad, as Siebers notes with regard to the Ethiopian/Somalian conflict and the Carter Doctrine's statement of America's right to intervene in the Gulf. I am not saying that such a reading of America at this time as outward-looking, or certain of itself, is any more useful or accurate, just that the attempt to map the broad strokes of American foreign policy on to particular critical approaches seems fraught with difficulty. It should also be noted that Watergate – as a kind of seminal American loss of political faith – was not a cold war event, and that the seventies malaise was as much down to such internal events as to the external conflict with the Communist bloc. Even Vietnam, while clearly a cold war event, impacted on the United States as much as a military failure as it did as an example of the failure of cold war politics. To some extent it could even be said that it was the perceived loss for Americans of the cold war relevance of the Vietnam conflict that resulted in the domestic political pressure to withdraw: Americans went in to hold back the domino progress of Communism and ended up killing peasants in My Lai. Vietnam could thus be seen as a distraction from the certainties of the cold war which Carter's ending of détente, and the so-called 'second cold war' under Reagan, actually sought to restore.

The critic Siebers uses to illustrate the Reagan period is Stephen Greenblatt. But again, although this was a period of cold war intensification, with an escalation of both anti-Soviet rhetoric and of the arms race, what Siebers focuses on is less the external situation than the internal 1980s remodelling of American ideology in terms of a heightened individualism and a substitution of market forces for social policy. Greenblatt's view of the cultural exchange in Shakespearean theatre is described in the following terms:

> The theatre is the realm of social energy as such, which Greenblatt defines in terms that strikingly recall the market economy as conceived by Reaganomics.
>
> (60)

It may be that there is a link between the dominant mode of criticism and the political situation in which the critic is working, but Siebers fails to demonstrate convincingly that it is the particular circumstance of the cold war which generates this linkage as his thesis overall sets out to demonstrate.

Jancovitch's study of New Criticism includes a similar attempt to map a particular criticism on to a particular historical/political environment. Essentially he seeks to show that there was an implicit anti-capitalist bias in the Agrarianism from which New Criticism sprang, and could thus be seen as 'a cultural criticism of bourgeois society' (13). In this respect critics (like Siebers) who find that critique manifested only in a withdrawal from society into the idealized aesthetic world of art are mistaken. Jancovitch goes on to suggest, in terms which are nevertheless reminiscent of Siebers's cold war theory, that 'While it is certainly true that the New Criticism was appropriated by bourgeois intellectuals in the 1940s and 1950s this was not because it was a bourgeois form' (18). Indeed, as he points out, due to the peculiar position of economic dependence which the cultural sphere is subject to, bourgeois intellectuals often hold anti-bourgeois political positions. However, he suggests that in the fevered political climate of the 1940s and 1950s in America it was 'difficult' for intellectuals to openly adopt a left-wing position, and 'as a result' many were attracted to the New Criticism. It offered them an anti-bourgeois ideology which had no taint of Soviet sympathies' (18). Thus, like Siebers, Jancovitch also sees a linkage between New Criticism and the cold war, though he does argue that linkage in a more convincing manner, describing it less as an unconscious causal connection than as a rational response to the repressive political climate then operating. If the radical conservative southern agenda of the New Critics themselves sits uneasily with a left critique of capitalism Jancovitch at least provides an explanation of how and why it might nevertheless absorb a wider oppositional constituency.

The detailed discussion Jancovitch presents of Ransom, Tate, and Warren seems chiefly aimed at refuting the widely held contemporary perception that the New Criticism represented a formalist retreat from social reality. Instead, all three are shown to be overtly concerned with a social critique in their literary analysis. Jancovitch writes that 'for Warren, even those literary forms associated with a social formalism were a response to the specific problems of modern society' and that he defines literature as 'a form of social engagement' (62). But the key point for New Critics is that unlike Marxists they maintain the specificity of literary critique by holding that it is 'the way in which texts use their sources which was important, not their sources or their positions' (68).

Thus Jancovitch has suggested that New Criticism does have an implicit social-critical position, one which, due to the particular political climate, actually included a wider range of critical thought than might be imagined from its Agrarian origins, and that this critical stance is carried over in a specific fashion into the New Critics' work on literature. Jancovitch finds parallels between this and poststructuralist criticism. He cites Gerald Graff's work on the conflict in the university to show that literary studies has since its inception been riven by differences over its definition, and that this primary difference is essentially between a scientific, philological tendency, and a tendency toward cultural criticism – tainted as an academic pursuit by the perception of its 'subjective impressionism'. New Criticism, Jancovitch suggests, has to be read as anti-positivist in these terms, defining itself as such through its focus on the signifying process. He writes:

> Ransom claims that while 'science abhors the figurative, the tropical', art can resist positivism by making these forms its own 'object of knowledge...'. Rather than suppressing the productivity of these forms, literature could resist modern society by identifying the limitations and contradictions of positivist discourse through an investigation of the properties of language and meaning.
>
> (143)

It is this emphasis which Jancovitch sees as providing common ground between New Criticism and poststructuralism. Indeed, the deconstructive foregrounding of the irredeemably figurative nature of language chimes with the approach which he describes in the work of the New Critics. It is this joint perception which allows Siebers to collect both groups under the heading of 'sceptical' criticism. The difference which Jancovitch nevertheless maintains between the two lies in the critical attitude toward this endless figuration. Where the New Critics wrestled with the production of meaning in society from such tropological play, deconstruction stops at the point of indicating the figurative limits of language and meaning, and therefore refuses to proceed in authoritarian 'error' to interpret texts. This is the same point Siebers made when praising Tompkins's acceptance of the necessity to make interpretations, however compromised in positivist terms. Thus both these books are symptomatic of the common perception that postmodern criticism, in its ethical rejection of ascriptions of meaning to human cultural activity, actually results in a political enfeeblement: the refusal to interpret easily translates into an incapacity to act socially for fear of transgressing individual difference; and so while appearing a radical alternative to conservative values, postmodernism, as Siebers suggests, can be seen as the cohort of the tendency which produced the Reaganite/Thatcherite individualistic 1980s. Jancovitch's point then is that in the basic positivist/critical divide which Graff identifies in English Studies over the last century or so, the postmodernists (such as exponents of deconstruction) actually embrace the debate in positivist terms by presenting a crudely realist conception of knowledge – and then rejecting it as impossible to achieve. The New Critics, however (whom Jancovitch sees as modernist), are able to take a position in the absence of positivist foundations. The question which he does not address in any detail is whether this perception of the political incapacity of postmodernist thought is a fair one. Derrida, for one, is clear on the ethical requirement to take a position. Hillis Miller's work on ethics, as dismissed by Siebers, defines ethical behaviour as the demand to take a position in the absence of the absolute grounds that would justify it – in literary terms, the demand to make a reading, an interpretation, in the always-already compromised field of textuality. Amongst critics informed by postmodern theory, Jane Tompkins is not a voice crying out in a wilderness barren of interpretations, nor are the New Critics different from their successors in deriving their mode of engagement with literary works from a politically charged vision.

Foreign Affairs College, Beijing

Printed in the United States
by Baker & Taylor Publisher Services